ADOBE® PHOTOSHOP® CS3 HOW-TOs

100 ESSENTIAL TECHNIQUES

CHRIS ORWIG

Adobe

Adobe Photoshop CS3 How-Tos

100 Essential Techniques

Chris Orwig

This Adobe Press book is published by Peachpit.

Peachpit
1249 Eighth Street
Berkeley, CA 94710
510/524-2178
510/524-2221 (fax)

Peachpit is a division of Pearson Education.

For the latest on Adobe Press books, go to www.adobepress.com.
To report errors, please send a note to errata@peachpit.com.

Project Editor: Victor Gavenda
Editor: Jill Marts Lodwig
Proofreader: Jill Marts Lodwig
Production Editor: Connie Jeung-Mills
Compositor: ICC MacMillan Inc.
Indexer: Rebecca Plunkett
Cover and Interior Design: Mimi Heft

ISBN-13: 978-0-321-50904-8
ISBN-10: 0-321-50904-8

9 8 7 6 5 4 3 2 1

Printed and bound in the United States of America

Dedication

To my favorite three girls - Kelly, Annika and Sophia!

Contents

CHAPTER ONE

Getting Started

Adobe Photoshop CS3 is an essential and incredibly fun tool for perfecting images. If you are an amateur or seasoned pro who is interested in learning how to create more communicative, compelling, and breathtaking images, this book is for you!

Adobe Photoshop CS3 How-Tos approaches Photoshop from a professional photographic perspective. In pro photography, the quality of an image is defined by how it affects the viewer. Thus, all the techniques in this book are designed to help you create images with impact. My hope is that the 100 clear and concise tips that are presented in this book will catapult you to new creative heights.

This book is designed to help you quickly and easily acquire the technical skills that enable you to be more creative. As you become more familiar with it, you'll find it is packed with valuable techniques. If you're like me, you may be tempted to skip ahead to read about the techniques that are most pertinent to your own workflow. That approach works with this book, but be sure to read this chapter thoroughly, since it aims to provide a solid footing in Photoshop that can help increase your overall creativity. In particular, it discusses specifying color, settings, and preferences; customizing the interface; and more.

Let's get started!

#1 Managing Color

Have you ever edited an image in which the color looked good on your monitor, but not as good in the final print? Color management is the critical step in Photoshop workflow that clarifies the communication between a monitor and printer.

The goal of color management is to minimize the difference between color created via light (monitor) and color created via ink (printer), so that in the end, the color is accurate. Of course, nothing is more gratifying than seeing a printed image in which the color is spot on!

You can specify color management settings in Photoshop using the Color Settings dialog box. The default Color Settings preset is North America General Purpose 2 (**Figure 1a**).

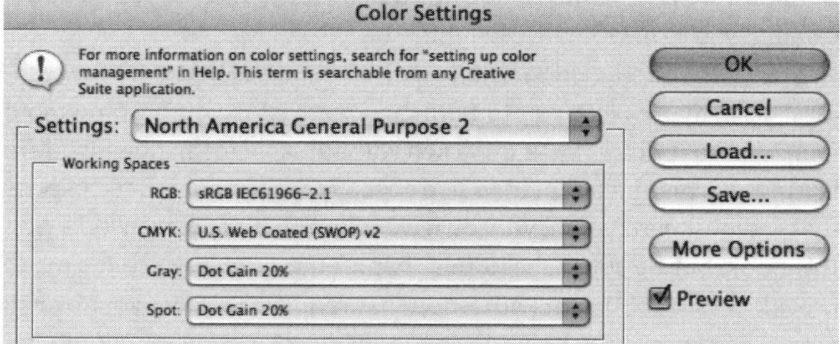

Figure 1a The default Color Settings preset, North American General Purpose 2, uses the sRGB color space.

For us photographers, this setting is less desirable because it uses the sRGB color space. To make a long story short, this color space has a limited number of colors. While the number of colors is adequate for viewing images onscreen, it's inadequate for high-quality printing.

Choose the North American Prepress 2 preset instead. It uses the Adobe RGB color space, which accurately handles a much wider range of color (**Figure 1b**).

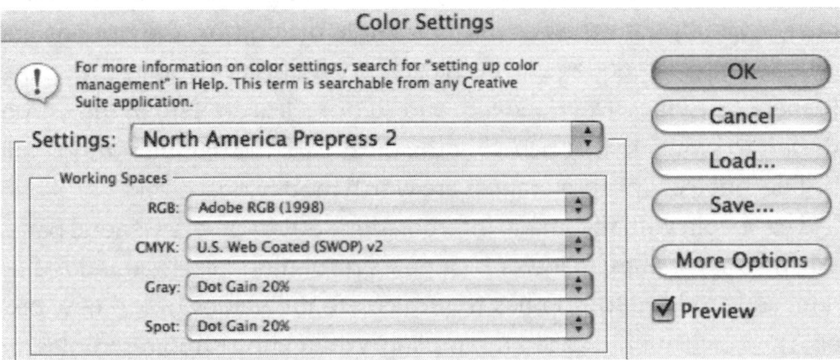

Figure 1b Switching to the North American Prepress 2 preset changes the working color space to Adobe RGB.

Tip

To help you create high-quality, color-managed prints, be sure to read Chapter 14. It covers the specifics for accurate color printing.

For the Color-Curious

If you are interested in digging deeper into the topic of color management, take a look at *Real World Color Management, 2nd edition* (from Peachpit Press) by Bruce Fraser, Fred Bunting, and Chris Murphy.

#2 Modifying Preferences

You can customize Photoshop to suit your own way of working by changing various program options.

Choose Photoshop > Preferences (Mac) or Edit > Preferences (Windows) to open the Preferences dialog box. Because Photoshop provides many more options than can fit in a single dialog box, the options are grouped into categories, and each category is displayed on its own pane (General, Interface, File Handling, and so on). Click an item in the list on the left to switch to that pane. For the most part, the default settings will be fine, but a couple preferences are worth modifying.

Let's begin with the Image Interpolation setting on the General pane. When you resize an image or change its resolution, pixels are added or removed, and Photoshop has to recalculate the values of the new pixels. This calculation is called resampling. When Photoshop resamples an image, it has to calculate, or *interpolate,* the pixel values in the image. Photoshop can perform this calculation using one of several interpolation methods—which one it uses is up to you.

To designate which one you'd like to use, select General on the left of the Preferences dialog box, and then choose a setting from the Image Interpolation menu. In my case, because I tend to start with large Camera Raw files that I resize downward, I designate Bicubic Sharper as my default interpolation method. This setting applies to any operation that uses a tool that resizes the image, such as Crop, Free Transform, and so on (**Figure 2a**).

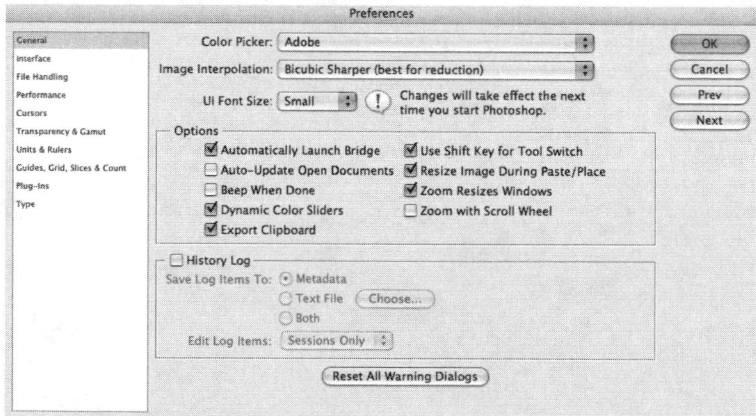

Figure 2a Choose Bicubic Sharper when sizing your images to a smaller dimension.

Note

If you find that you typically begin with smaller images and then enlarge them, be sure to choose the Bicubic Smoother setting as your interpolation method.

The Options area of the General pane contains another preference you definitely want to turn on. If you select the Automatically Launch Bridge check box, every time you open Photoshop, Adobe Bridge will launch simultaneously. As you'll discover in Chapter 3, Bridge is an important component of Photoshop. By turning on this preference, you'll be able to jump to Bridge whenever you want. Even if you're not using Bridge now, by the time you've finished reading Chapter 3, you will be!

Another preference you'll want to pay some attention to is located in the File Handling pane. In the File Compatibility area of that pane, deselect Ask Before Saving Layered TIFF Files. Why turn this preference off? Because when you save your work in Photoshop, most of the time you likely will save it as a TIFF file, so you don't need the hassle of having Photoshop ask you about saving the layers every time you save the document (unless of course you are a glutton for pain) (**Figure 2b**).

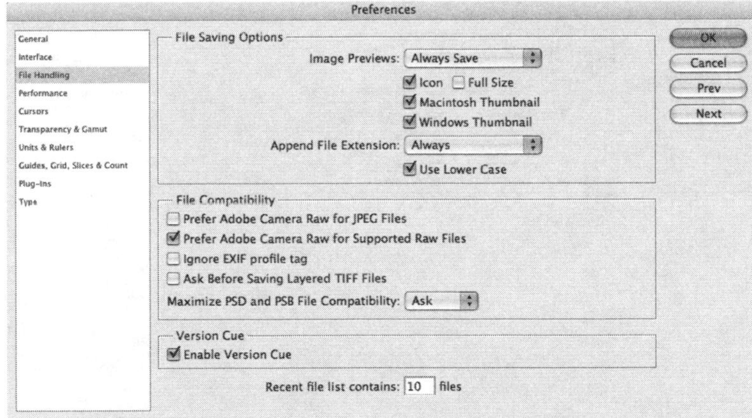

Figure 2b Deselect the Ask Before Saving Layered TIFF Files option to save time.

If the files you are working on will need to be opened in an older version of Photoshop or Adobe Photoshop Lightroom, you may want to select Always from the menu beside Maximize PSD and PSB File Compatibility. With this setting enabled, every time you save a layered

Image Interpolation

Photoshop gives you opportunities to override the default image interpolation method on a case-by-case basis. For example, in the Image Size dialog box, you can use the Resample Image menu to choose the image interpolation method to be used for only that one operation.

file, a composite version of the image will be added to the file so that it can be opened by applications that don't support Photoshop layers.

The Performance pane provides access to controls that let you tailor Photoshop to the particulars of your hardware. Photoshop is a glutton for memory—the more you can give it, the happier it is and the more smoothly it runs. By default, Photoshop uses your computer's RAM—the fast, chip-based memory on the logic board. But if you have many images open at once, or several large images with many layers, you may fill RAM to overflowing. In this case, Photoshop begins using empty space on your hard drive as memory, and as a result, your computer's performance takes a nosedive, since accessing a hard drive is much slower than accessing memory chips.

One way to avoid this problem is to make sure Photoshop has access to as much RAM as it needs. In the Memory Usage area of the Performance pane, drag the slider to the right to assign more RAM to Photoshop. If you run other programs at the same time as Photoshop (for example, if you listen to iTunes as you work), don't move the slider to 100%. Leave some RAM for those other applications (**Figure 2c**).

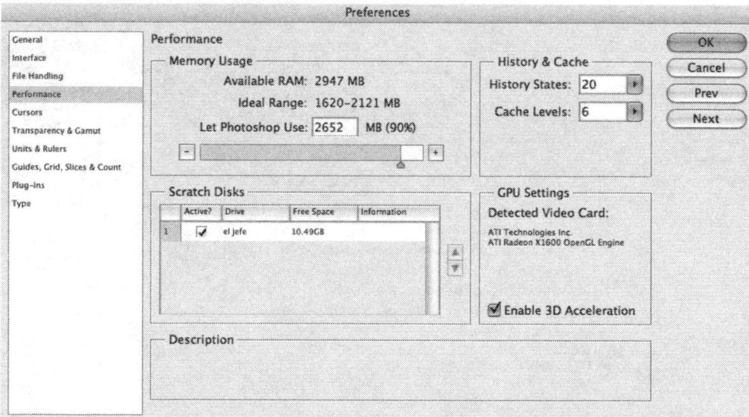

Figure 2c Improve performance by increasing the amount of RAM available to Photoshop.

The Type category also contains some useful preferences. Select Type, and in the Type pane look at the Font Preview area. To the untrained eye, it looks as if these preferences haven't changed very much in CS3. But if you click on the Font Preview Size menu, you'll discover the Adobe development team has a great sense of humor. New to CS3 are larger font previews: Extra Large and Huge (**Figure 2d**).

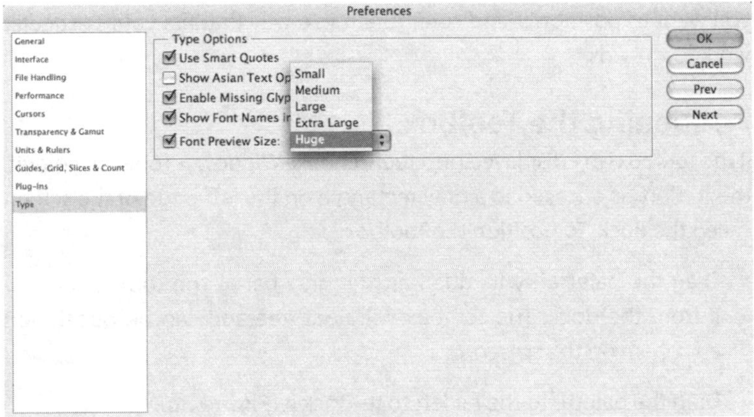

Figure 2d Change the Font Preview size to meet your own workflow needs.

How big is huge? And where can you find this font preview? Select the Type Tool (or press the T key) and open one of the Font menus in the options bar (**Figure 2e**).

Figure 2e The Font Preview size displays sample text at various sizes. In this case, the size selected is Huge.

Reset Preferences

If you want to reset your preferences to their default settings, when you next launch Photoshop, press and hold Alt + Control + Shift (Windows) or Option + Command + Shift (Mac). You will be prompted to delete the current settings.

#3 Introducing the Toolbox

When you're working in Photoshop, you want to have the Toolbox open so that you can easily make selections, type, paint, draw, retouch, and more. Because you will reach for the Toolbox frequently to switch tools, you want to position it and configure it in a way that fits your particular workflow needs.

Positioning the Toolbox

If the Toolbox isn't displayed onscreen, choose Window > Tools. By default, the Toolbox is encased in a gray rectangle on the left edge of the screen called the dock. To position the Toolbox:

- Drag the palette by its title bar (the gray bar at the top) to remove it from the dock. The Toolbox will float free and can be positioned anywhere on the screen.
- Drag the palette to the far left to re-dock it (**Figure 3a**).

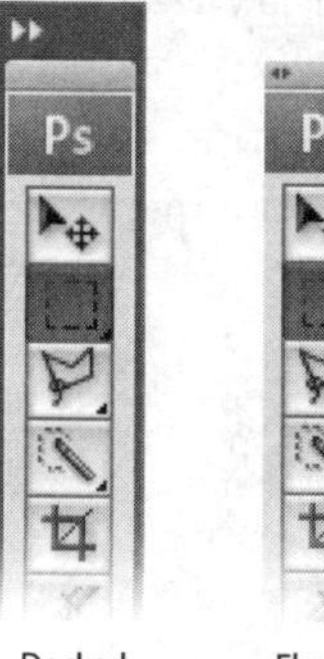

Figure 3a The Toolbox may be positioned either in the palette well or floating anywhere on screen.

To configure the Toolbox:

- Click the double arrows at the top of the Tools palette to switch between single-column and double-column format (**Figure 3b**).

Figure 3b Click the double arrows to display the tools in one or two columns.

Identifying tools

The Toolbox groups related tools together. When viewing the Toolbox in a single column, notice that the first group of tools is used for selections, cropping, and slices. The next group of tools is great for drawing, retouching, burning and dodging, and more. If you move the cursor over a tool, a tool tip displays the name of the tool and its keyboard shortcut (**Figure 3c**).

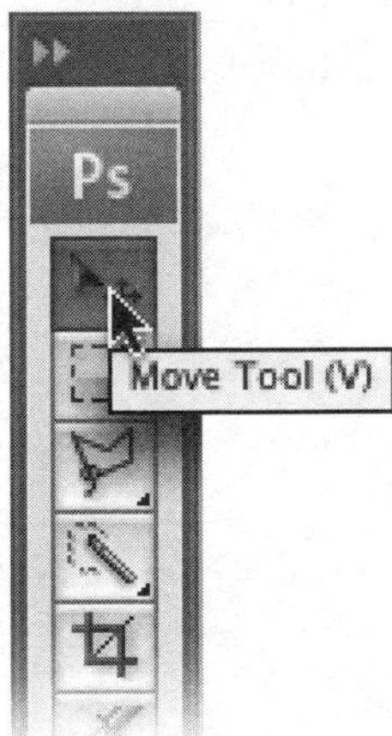

Figure 3c Point at each tool with the mouse pointer to display a tool tip.

Selecting tools

To select a tool, click it. To use a tool that's hidden in a pop-out menu (indicated by a small triangle), click and hold on the tool. When the pop-out menu displays, select another tool (**Figure 3d**).

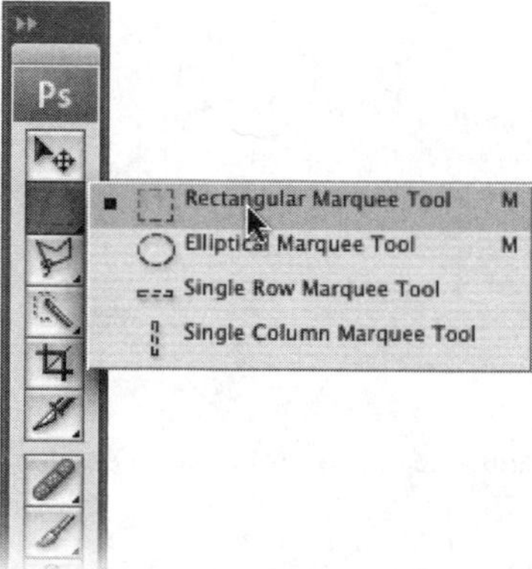

Figure 3d To display and select hidden tools, press and hold on a tool's icon.

The hidden tool replaces the original tool in the Tools palette.

To quickly switch tools, you can press the keyboard shortcut shown in each tool's tool tip. For example, you can press the V key to select the Move tool or press the T key to select the Type tool. (If the text input cursor is flashing, you cannot use the single-letter shortcuts. Finish typing and exit the text field, and then try the single-letter shortcuts.)

#4 Using the Options Bar

The options bar appears below the menu bar at the top of the workspace. Because the options bar is so useful, you will want to keep it visible.

- When you first launch Photoshop, the options bar is docked at the top of the window.
- You can move the options bar in the workspace by using the gripper bar (the gray bar on far left), and you can dock it at the top or bottom of the screen.
- To open and close the options bar, choose Window > Options.

The options bar is context-sensitive—it changes as you select different tools or different items in your document. Some settings in the options bar (such as painting modes and opacity) are common to several tools, and some are specific to one tool. Click on any tool in the Toolbox to view the options. For example, when the Type tool is selected, the Type tool options are visible in the options bar (**Figure 4**).

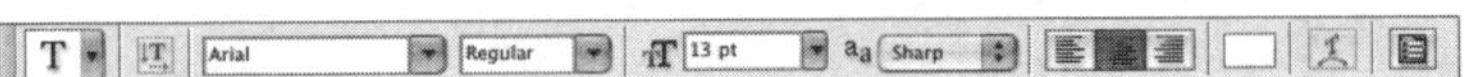

Figure 4 When the Type tool is selected, the options bar lets you choose text-related parameters, such as font family, style, size, anti-aliasing, color, alignment, and more.

Tips

To reset a tool's options to their default settings, right-click (Windows) or Control-click (Mac) on the tool's icon in the options bar and choose Reset Tool. Choose Reset All to do the same for all tools at once.

When you want to focus only on the Toolbox and options bar, press Shift + Tab to hide the rest of the palettes while keeping the Toolbox and options bar visible.

#5 Customizing the Interface

One of the most anticipated and celebrated new features in Photoshop CS3 is the updated user interface. It is streamlined and customizable in ways that were previously unimaginable. (An added bonus is that Adobe has revamped the user interfaces of all the programs in Creative Suite 3 so that they're consistent in look and operation.) The intent of these new features is to provide the user the ability to dedicate more screen real estate to the image without having to lose quick access to the tools and palettes. At the same time, you can customize the interface to fit your particular needs.

By default the Photoshop palettes are gathered into groups and stacks and stored in a dock on the right edge of the screen. Palettes can be collapsed into icons to save space, and these icons can also be grouped, stacked, or docked. Drag any palette by its title bar (or palette icon) out of the dock to a new location. In this manner, you can either have the palettes "float" as they did in previous versions of Photoshop, or you can group them or stack them with other palettes to suit your working needs.

Palette docking

A dock is a vertical collection of palettes or palette groups, attached to the left or right edge of the screen. Each dock is surrounded by a dark-gray rectangle. When dragging a palette or palette group into a dock, a blue horizontal or vertical line appears when the palette is hovering over a *drop zone*. This line tells you that if you release the mouse, your palette will be added to the dock.

- To dock a palette, drag it by its tab into the dock, or to the top, bottom, or in between other palettes. When the blue drop zone appears, release the mouse button (**Figure 5a**).

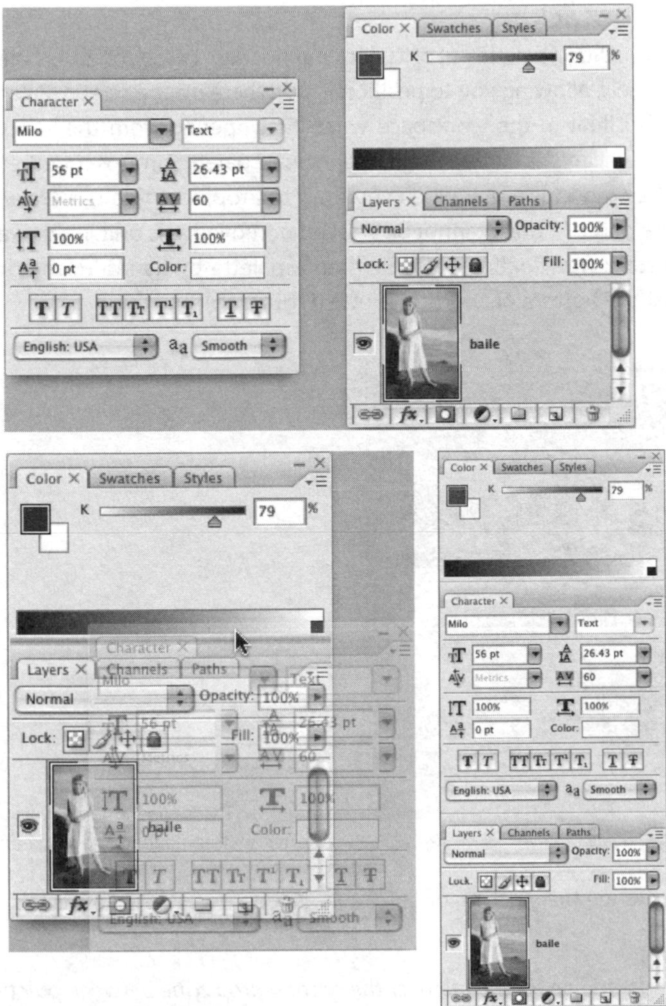

Figure 5a A palette can be docked with other palette groups. At the top, the Character palette is floating and separate from the other palette groups. On the lower left, the Character palette is docked in between the Color/Swatches/Styles and Layers/Channels/Paths palette groups. On the lower right is the final result.

- To dock a palette group, drag it by its title bar (the solid empty bar above the tabs) into the dock's drop zone and release.
- To remove a palette or palette group, drag it out of the dock by its tab or title bar. You can drag it into another dock or make it free-floating.

Palette stacking

When you drag a palette out of its dock but not into a drop zone, the palette floats freely, allowing you to position it anywhere on the screen. Palettes may also float in the workspace when first opened from the Window menu. You can stack free-floating palettes or palette groups together so that they move as a unit when you drag the topmost title bar. (Palettes that are part of a dock cannot be stacked or moved as a unit in this way.)

To stack free-floating palettes, drag a palette by its tab to the drop zone at the bottom of another palette (**Figure 5b**).

Figure 5b The Navigator and Layers palettes are free-floating and stacked.

To change the stacking order, drag a palette up or down by its tab.

Note

Be sure to release the tab over the narrow drop zone between palettes, rather than the broad drop zone in a title bar.

To remove a palette or palette group from the stack so that it floats by itself, drag it out by its tab or title bar.

Palette icons

Docked palettes are displayed full-size by default. Click the double-arrow icon at the top of the dock to expand or collapse the palettes that are in the dock into a set of icons. (**Figure 5c**).

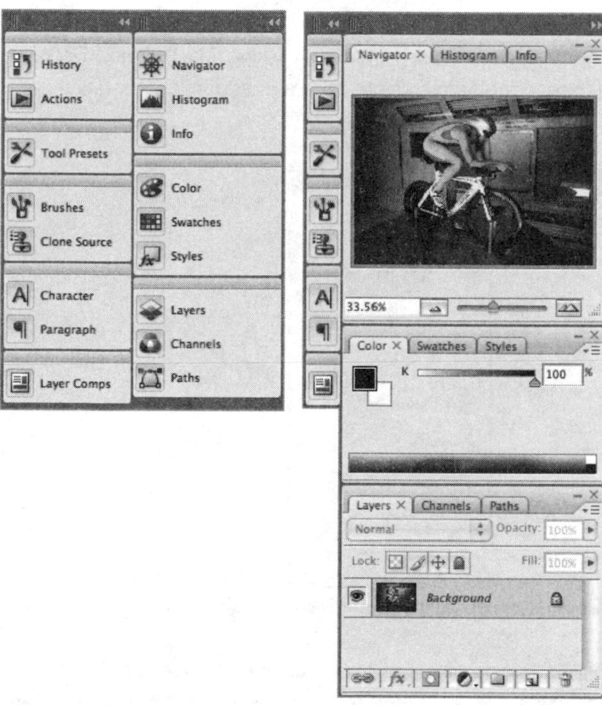

Figure 5c On the left are two docks in which the palettes have been collapsed into icons with labels. At right, the same docks are shown in different configurations: the dock on the left has been resized to hide the icon labels, and the dock on the right has been expanded.

By viewing the palettes as icons, you can dedicate more screen space to the image. To use a collapsed palette, click its icon to expand it. Click the double-arrow icon to expand or collapse all of the palettes in the dock.

Tip

To better see the labels of iconized palettes, drag the edge of the dock to widen it.

Palette Controls

To minimize a palette, palette group, or stack of palettes, click the Minimize button in its title bar.

Most palettes have more options than can fit on the palette itself. You'll find these extra options and commands listed on the palette menu, which you open by clicking the icon on the upper right of the palette.

Palette Preferences

By default, once you expand a palette that has been turned into an icon, it stays expanded until you close it. If you'd rather that it collapse automatically as soon as you click somewhere else, choose Preferences > Interface and select the Auto-Collapse Icon Palettes check box. You can also change the preference setting by right-clicking (Windows) or Control-clicking (Mac) within an iconized palette and choosing Auto-Collapse Icon Palettes from the context menu (**Figure 5d**).

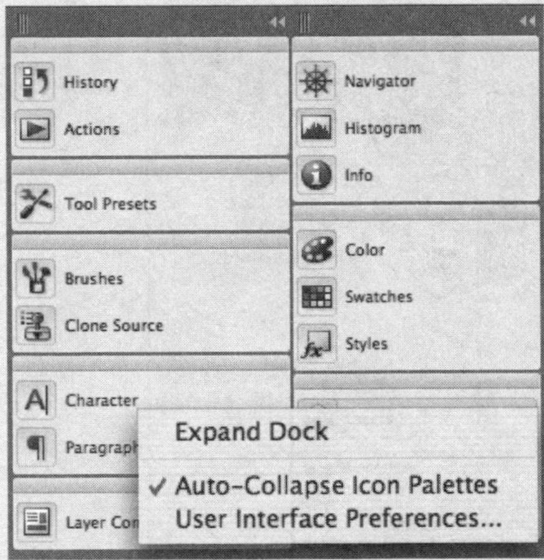

Figure 5d Use this context menu to enable or disable palette auto-collapse.

Also by default, Photoshop will respect your custom arrangement of palettes and keep them where you've put them from one session to the next. However, if you want to reset palettes to their default locations each time Photoshop launches, choose Preferences > Interface and deselect Remember Palette Locations.

Full Screen View mode

One of my photographic mentors (and heroes) is the acclaimed photographer Ralph Clevenger. When creating and working on photographs, Ralph is fond of repeating, "reduce and simplify." One way of following this mantra in regard to Photoshop is to reduce onscreen clutter by using different screen modes built into the program. The choices are:

- **Standard Screen mode.** The default mode, in which document windows, all palettes and the options bar are visible.
- **Maximized Screen mode.** The document window expands to fill the space between the docks.
- **Full Screen mode with Menu Bar.** The active document window fills the entire screen surrounded by 50% gray and no scroll bars.
- **Full Screen mode.** The active document is centered in a full-screen black background with no title bar, menu bar, or scroll bars.

You can cycle through these screen modes by clicking the Change Screen Mode button on the Toolbox or by pressing the F key (**Figure 5e**).

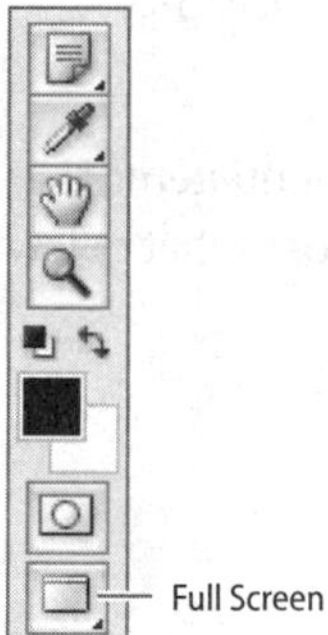

Figure 5e Pressing the Change Screen Mode button displays a menu of screen modes.

Tip

To further simplify your workspace, press Tab to hide everything except the document windows and menu bar (if it's showing). Press Tab again to make the palettes and the options bar reappear.

Less Is More

Be sure to simplify the interface at least once per image so that you can really focus in on the content itself. Are you wondering if it's really necessary to minimize or hide the entire Photoshop interface? I believe it is, and here's why:

This morning my three-year-old daughter was so focused on putting blueberries in her cereal that she knocked over her milk. Isn't this a familiar scenario, even for us adults? We're so focused on the task at hand that we don't notice the inadvertent mistakes we make in the meantime. I find that using Fullscreen mode and pressing Tab to hide the Toolbox and palettes helps me step back and really see what's going on.

Remember that being good at Photoshop is not simply about learning how to create; it's also about learning how to see.

#6 Choosing a Workspace

The new CS3 interface is clean, simple, refreshing, and customizable. However, if you are migrating to CS3 from a previous version of Photoshop, the new interface organization may throw you off. Not to worry. You can try out different layouts. From the Workspace menu on the options bar or from Window > Workspace, choose Workspace options. If you're looking to change the interface back to how it looked in previous versions, simply choose Legacy (**Figure 6a**).

Figure 6a Click the Workspace button in the options bar to view different workspace configurations.

If you want to highlight throughout Photoshop the menu items that are new or that have been added or modified in CS3, choose What's New in CS3. (**Figure 6b**).

Figure 6b As a result of choosing Window > Workspace > What's New in CS3, the Convert for Smart Filters and Vanishing Point commands on the Filter menu are highlighted.

#7 Help, How-Tos, and Training Videos

Photoshop is a profoundly deep application, and at times its depth can be overwhelming. At the same time, help is always just a short click away. One of the most valuable built-in help tools is the Adobe Help Viewer. To launch it, Select Help > Photoshop Help. You can browse by topic or enter a request in the Search field (**Figure 7a**).

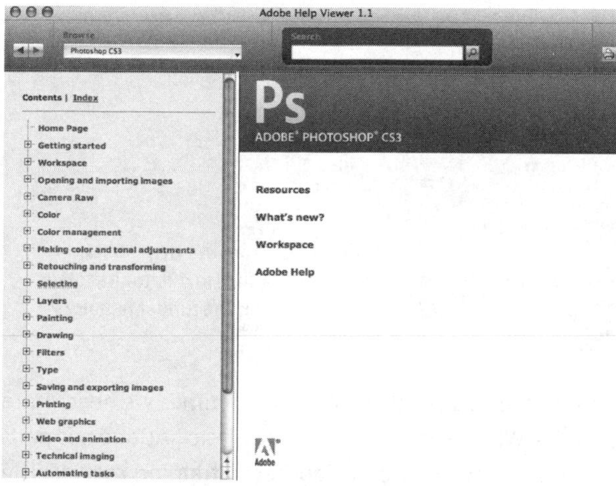

Figure 7a The main screen of the Adobe Help Viewer.

Another way to take advantage of the Adobe Help Viewer is by browsing the How To items on the Help menu. Each item has a submenu of specific tasks, and selecting any of them opens the appropriate topic in Adobe Help Viewer. If you're new to Photoshop, be sure to scroll through these How To items because they will help you get up to speed on many Photoshop fundamentals (**Figure 7b**).

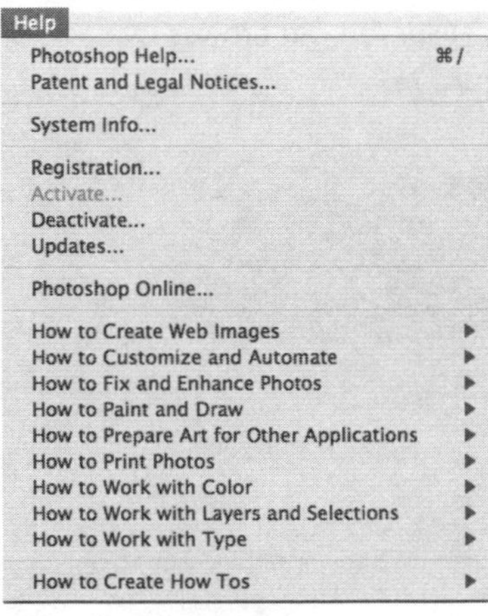

Figure 7b From the Help menu, select any of the How To topics to get up to speed on the fundamentals of Photoshop.

The Adobe Help Viewer is a good resource, yet at times we need more than text and graphics. Where can you go for more help? Adobe has partnered with Lynda.com to provide free video-based training movies. The series of video-based training movies that ships with the CS3 product line can be accessed for free online at: www.adobe.com/designcenter/video_workshop. As an aside, I created two Adobe Video Workshop training videos about printing and the Photomerge command—be sure to check out them out (**Figure 7c**)!

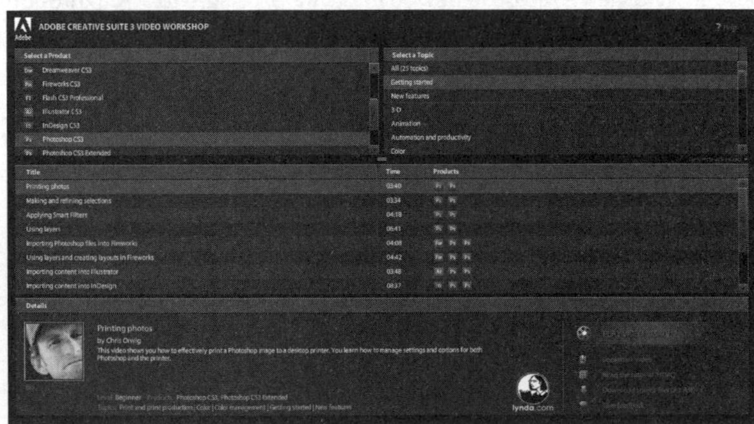

Figure 7c Get more help from the Adobe Video Workshop.

CHAPTER TWO

Working with Digital Image Files

It's never been a more exciting time for those of us who are interested in digital imaging. We are literally in the midst of a digital revolution, where new technological discoveries are spawning remarkable creativity, vitality, and growth. As a result, knowing how to work with digital files has never been more important.

This chapter is designed to function as a cornerstone to the rest of the work you do in Photoshop as you read through the book. It will hopefully get you up to speed on many of the fundamentals of digital imaging, and how to open, save, and resize them, among other things.

#8 Opening Documents

There are several methods of opening an image file into Photoshop. You can use Adobe Bridge, the powerful file browser application that ships with all of the Creative Suite products (and which I'll discuss in Chapter 3). If you'd rather stay within Photoshop, however, simply choose File > Open or press Ctrl + O (Windows) or Command + O (Mac) and navigate to the location where your image file is stored. By default, you'll use your operating system's Open dialog box (**Figure 8a**).

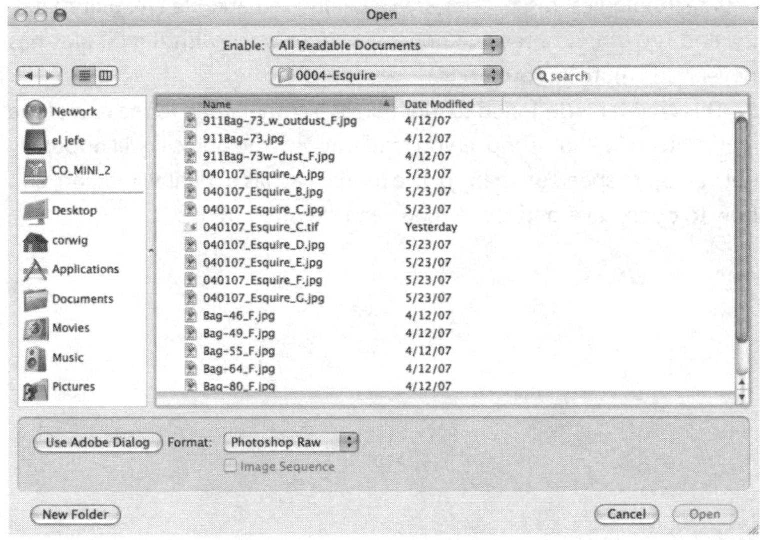

Figure 8a The Open dialog box in Mac OS X.

In most situations, this works fine, but Photoshop offers an alternative method of navigating to a specific file. To use this method, click the Use Adobe Dialog button in the bottom left corner of the Open dialog box. This replaces the standard dialog box with one customized to fit the needs of Photoshop users (**Figure 8b**).

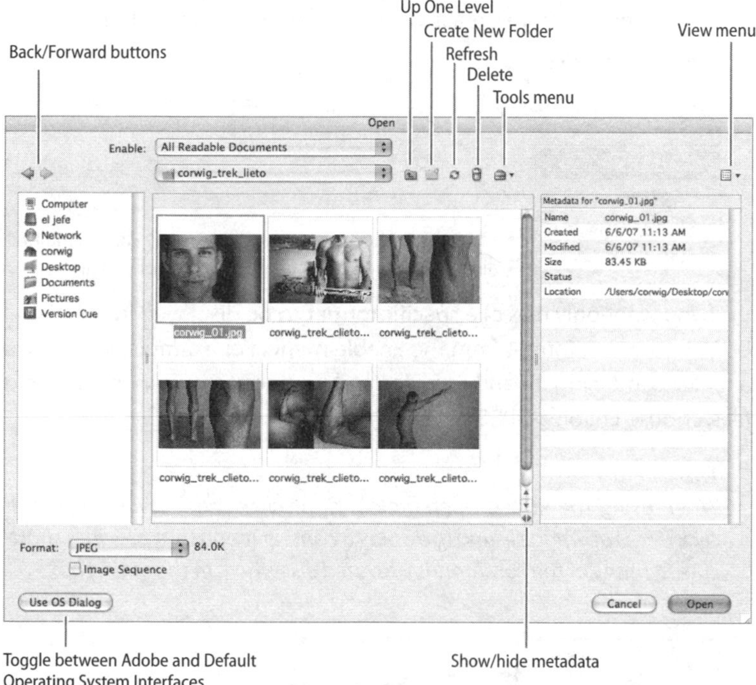

Figure 8b The Adobe Open dialog box, in Thumbnails view.

The Adobe Open dialog gives you several features that aren't available in the standard operating system Open dialog box:

- Buttons at the top of the dialog box let you refresh your view and delete files and folders.
- Commands on the Tools menu let you locate a file in Windows Explorer or the Mac OS Finder, display a file in Adobe Bridge, add the file to your list of Favorites, and more.
- You can toggle the display of metadata for a particular file by selecting the file and then clicking the double arrow on the lower right of the file.

(continued on next page)

Creating a Time-Lapse Movie in Photoshop CS3 Extended

If you are using Photoshop CS3 Extended, you can open a sequence of images to create a time-lapse movie:

1. Make sure the images are named sequentially, such as image_1.jpg, image_2.jpg, and so on.
2. Select File > Open, and make sure that you're using the Adobe Open dialog.
3. Select the Image Sequence option.
4. Select the first image in the sequence and click Open.
5. In the Frame Rate dialog box, choose a rate and click OK.

Finding Recent Files Quickly

Select File > Open Recent to view a list of recently opened files. To allow more files to be displayed in this submenu, select Edit (Windows) or Photoshop (Mac) > Preferences > File Handling and then increase the number in the Recent File List Contains field (up to a maximum of 30).

- You can use the View menu to choose among different ways of displaying your files. Icons and Thumbnails views are self-explanatory; Details is similar to list view in the standard Open dialog, and Tiles combines the information from Details view with smaller versions of the Thumbnails (**Figure 8c**).

Figure 8c Choose Thumbnails from the View menu to display shrunken but readable versions of your images.

If you want only files of a specific format to be displayed in the dialog box, choose that format from the Enable menu. For example, if you have a folder containing .tif and .jpg files and you want to view only the .jpg files, choose Enable > JPEG.

Tip

When using the Adobe Open dialog, right-click (Windows) or Control-click (Mac) an image listing to display a context menu that provides shortcuts to many of the commands provided elsewhere in the dialog box.

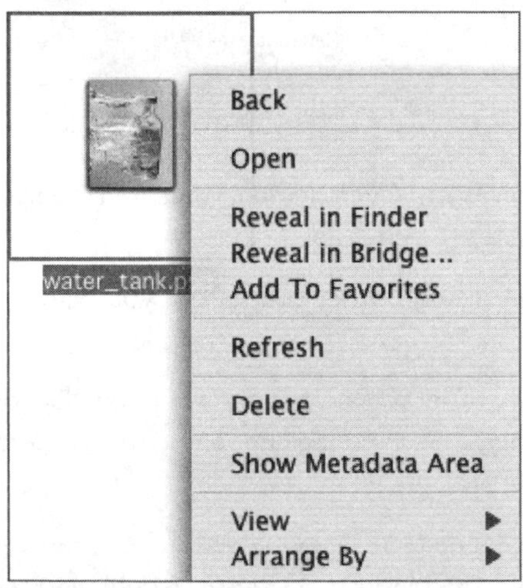

#9 Understanding the Document Window

In Photoshop, each open image is displayed in its own document window. Crucial information about the image is displayed within the top and bottom edges of the window (**Figure 9a**).

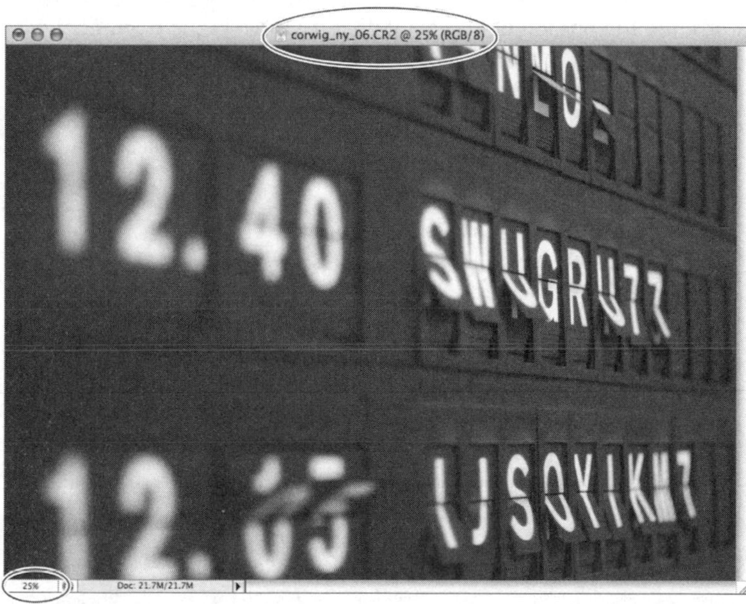

Figure 9a The frame of the document window contains valuable information about the file displayed within.

At the top of the window, the filename is listed first (in this case, corwig_ny_06.CR2). To the right of the filename is the zoom percentage, which is also displayed on the lower-left of the window. At a zoom of 100%, each individual pixel in your image is represented by a pixel in your display. This is useful if you're preparing images for Web pages, because it shows you how large the image will appear in a Web browser. If you're working with higher-resolution images that will be printed, you probably want to use a smaller zoom percentage.

One way to adjust your view of an image is to use the Navigator palette. Choose Window > Navigator, and then click the Zoom In or Zoom Out buttons or drag the Zoom slider to change your zoom percentage. You can also drag the red rectangular box in the image thumbnail to reposition the portion of the image that is visible in the document window (**Figure 9b**).

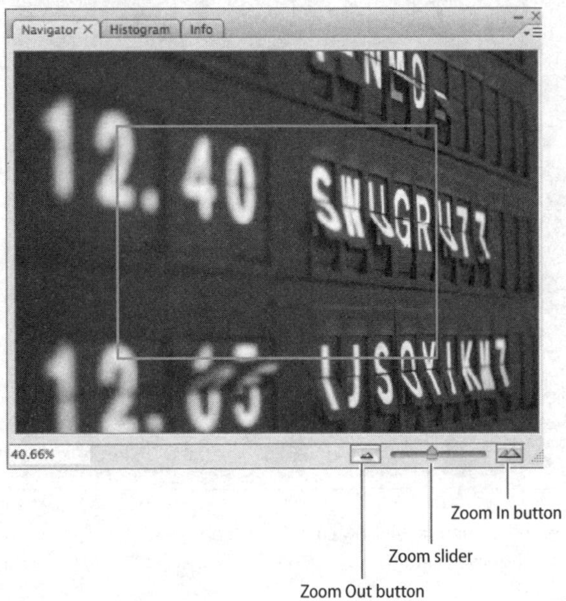

Figure 9b Use the Navigator palette to adjust zoom or to realign the image in the Document window.

Returning to the top of the document window, you'll find the color space and bit depth in parentheses, to the right of the zoom percentage. In this case, the color space is RGB and the bit depth is 8 bits per channel. To change the color space and/or bit depth, choose your options from the Image > Mode submenu (**Figure 9c**).

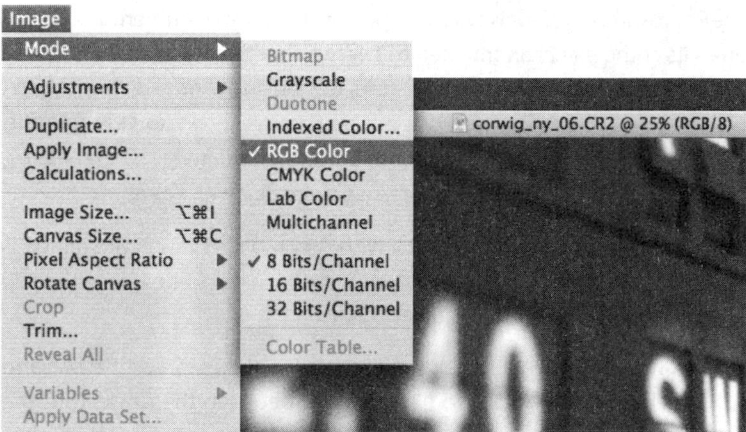

Figure 9c Choose Image > Mode to change the color space and/or bit depth of an image.

On the lower-left edge of the document window is the status bar. The status bar displays the current zoom percentage and information about the image file itself. Clicking the status bar directly produces a thumbnail showing how the image will print on the paper that is selected in the Page Setup dialog box. Click the arrow at the right end of the status bar to open a menu containing commands that let you see the image in Adobe Bridge or choose the information to be displayed in the status bar (**Figure 9d**).

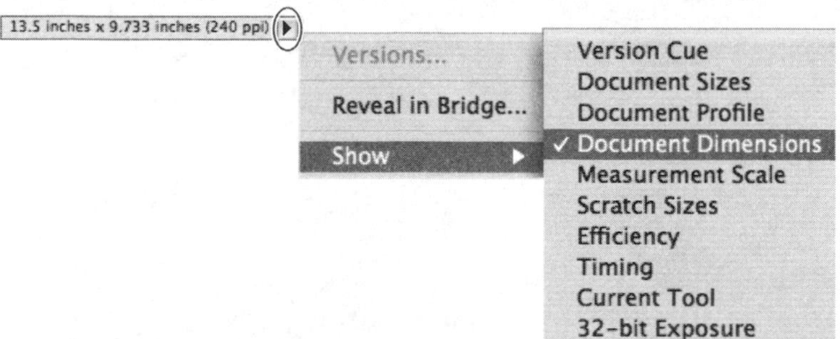

Figure 9d Click the arrow at the right end of the status bar to choose the information that will be displayed.

#10 Using Full-Screen Mode

Quick Mode Change

Press the F key to cycle through all four screen modes.

The Photoshop interface is a rich and powerful work environment, but sometimes its complexity can threaten to overwhelm the image you're working on. You'll find that sometimes it's helpful to strip away some of Photoshop's bells and whistles so that you can concentrate on the image itself. To this end, Photoshop allows you to choose among four different *screen modes,* which simplify the overall interface to a greater or lesser extent:

- **Standard,** the default interface with menu bar in which the image is displayed in a standard document window with a title bar at the top and scroll bars along the side and bottom.
- **Maximized,** in which the document window loses its title bar and scroll bars and expands to fill the space between the docks (but the menu bar is still present). Any space within the window that is not occupied by the image is filled with a light gray surround.
- **Full-Screen Mode with Menu Bar,** in which the document window (without title bar or scroll bars) fills the entire screen (except for the menu bar), again surrounded by light gray.
- **Full-Screen Mode,** in which the document window (free of title bar and scroll bars) fills the entire screen (surrounded by a black background), and the menu bar is absent.

Choose a mode from the Screen Mode menu, or cycle through all four modes by clicking the Screen Mode button (**Figure 10a**).

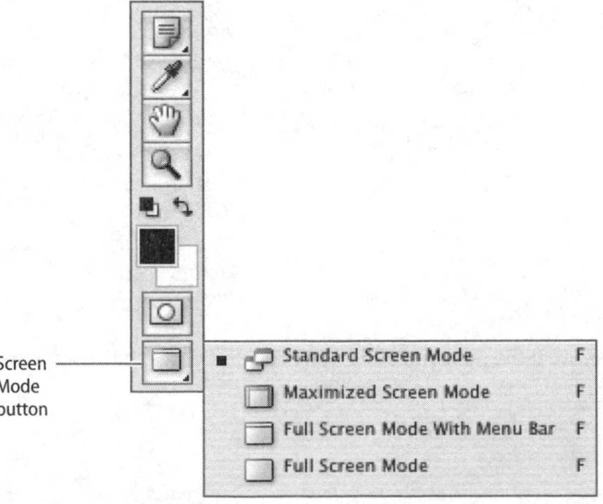

Figure 10a Choose a screen mode from the menu at the bottom of the Toolbox.

For photographic work, the ideal mode is Full-Screen Mode with Menu Bar. When viewing your images in any screen mode other than Standard, you have the option of changing the background color. Right-click (Windows) or Control-click (Mac) on the background and choose Gray, Black, or a Custom color from the context menu (**Figure 10b**).

Figure 10b Use this context menu to change the color of the background when using a nonstandard screen mode.

Tip

If you have chosen one of the two full-screen modes, it is best to position the image near the top of the monitor. Select the Hand tool from the Toolbox or press the spacebar to access the Hand tool, and move the image by dragging. Positioning the image near the top of the monitor will help you have better posture while working in Photoshop.

Simplifying the Interface Quickly

The full-screen modes provide a stripped-down environment for editing images. There are times when photographers need to simplify the interface even further so that they can focus on the image. To accomplish this, press Tab to hide the Toolbox and the other palettes. Try examining your work in this context, as it may help you discover both the weaknesses and the strengths that you might have otherwise overlooked.

#11 Understanding Digital Images

Because digital cameras are very much a part of our lives today, it's worth taking a few minutes to delve into the concept of digital images.

When a digital camera snaps a photo, light from the scene being photographed falls onto millions of microscopic electronic sensors. Equally tiny filters separate the light into its red, green, and blue components, just as the cells in the retina of the human eye do, and each sensor records the intensity of each of the three colors at that particular location. All of this information is converted into numbers, and is saved as a digital image file.

As you can probably imagine, the more data points (or *pixels,* for "picture elements") there are in the file, the more accurately the digital image will reproduce the original scene. Because every camera snags pixels in the millions, their data-capturing ability is measured in *megapixels.* Also, the more megapixels an image contains, the more you can enlarge it for printing without losing clarity.

When editing an image in Photoshop, often you often adjust its *tonality,* or distribution of light and dark areas. Photoshop has several tools to help you do this, and many of them include a histogram to give you an overview of the tonality of an image. A *histogram* is a simple bar chart that shows how many pixels an image contains at each brightness level. The Levels dialog box contains a histogram, with brightness levels starting at 0 (pure black) at the left, running to 255 (pure white) at the right (**Figure 11a**).

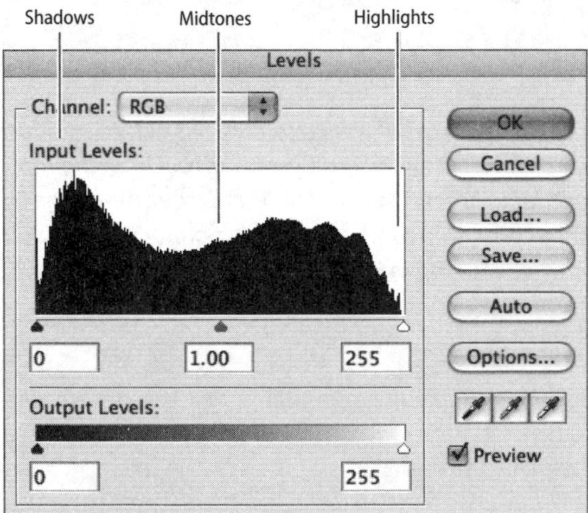

Figure 11a The histogram in the Levels dialog. Notice the black-to-white gradient in the Output Levels area—it graphically illustrates the range of brightness levels represented by the histogram.

Understanding how to read a histogram is incredibly helpful for analyzing images. Keep in mind, however, that Photoshop is about more than analysis and description—it is designed to help you to improve your images, too. In Chapter 9, I'll show you how to use the sliders under the shadows, midtones, and highlights regions of the histogram in the Levels dialog box to make adjustments to the range of tonal values in an image.

You don't have to keep a particular dialog box open to track the brightness values in an image. Choose Window > Histogram to open the Histogram palette, which contains nothing but a histogram (**Figure 11b**)! Keep it open while you work to monitor the changes to the distribution of tonalities in your picture.

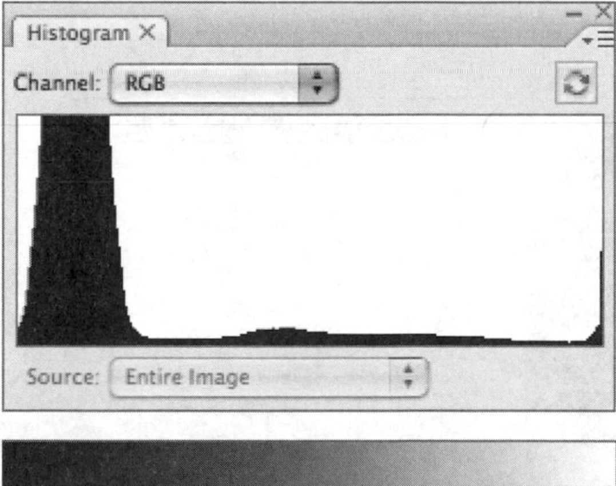

Figure 11b The Histogram palette (I've added a grayscale ramp of brightness values from 0 to 255 below the palette as a reference). Compare this to the histogram in Figure 11a; that image has a pretty good distribution of brightness values, but the tall peak at the left end of the graph shows that this image is very dark.

#12 Resizing Images

Almost every file that is opened in Photoshop will need to be resized. How you resize is important—if something goes wrong, the rest of your Photoshop work will be in vain. Not to worry, you'll master the process of accurate resizing in no time.

When a digital file is created with a digital camera or scanner, a specific amount of information is captured. (Or when you create a new file in Photoshop, you select a specific size containing a specific number of pixels). Once that amount of information is set, you must decide what changes need to be made before the image can be printed, published to the Web, and so on.

Use the Image Size dialog box to resize images. It contains settings for the pixel dimensions, document size, and resampling options, to name a few (**Figure 12a**).

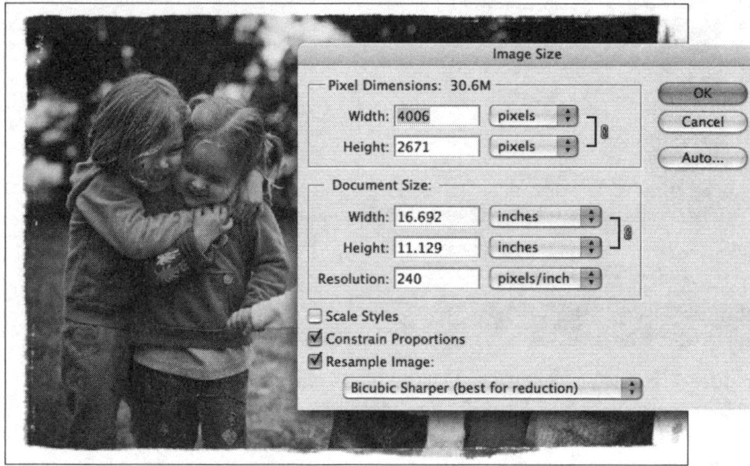

Figure 12a Use the Image Size dialog box to resize images.

The information in the Pixel Dimensions area shows you the amount of information currently in the image. The fields in the Document Size area allow you to set how those pixels will be distributed when you make a print of a certain size. The resampling options at the bottom of the window instruct Photoshop about what to do if it has to discard pixels (when sizing down) or create pixels (when sizing up). Here's how the resizing process works:

1. Choose Image > Image size to open the Image Size dialog box.
2. Select the Constrain Proportions check box to maintain the current ratio of pixel width to pixel height.
3. Deselect the Resample Image check box. We don't want to throw away pixels just yet.
4. In the Document Size area, change the resolution to your desired output (for example, 300 pixels/inch).
5. Now select the Resample Image check box.
6. Resize the image. The easiest way to do this is by changing the Height and Width fields in the Document size area to your desired output (for example, 8 x 10 inches).
7. In the Resample Image menu, choose the type of resampling that is recommended for the task at hand, and then click OK (**Figure 12b**).

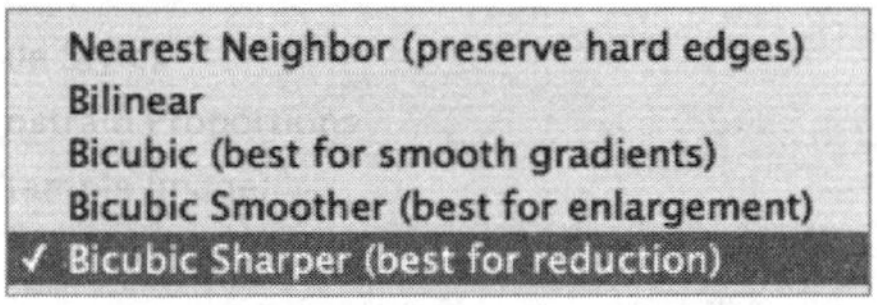

Nearest Neighbor (preserve hard edges)
Bilinear
Bicubic (best for smooth gradients)
Bicubic Smoother (best for enlargement)
✓ Bicubic Sharper (best for reduction)

Figure 12b Choose the resampling method that is appropriate to the task at hand.

Note

If the proportions of your desired output size are different from those of your image, you won't be able to use the Image Size dialog box to resize your image. In this case, use the method in the following How-To.

Image Size Dialog Shortcut

One of the most common adjustments you will make in Photoshop is to adjust the size of an image. To open the Image Size dialog box, press Ctrl + Option + I (Windows) or Command + Option + I (Mac).

#13 Cropping and Straightening Your Images

Check Your Settings Before Cropping

Before you actually crop an image, you should make sure that you've chosen the correct default Image Interpolation method. (See How-To #2 if you've forgotten how to do this.) Using the appropriate method ensures that the image will look as sharp as possible when resized.

It is usually best to crop and compose on camera, but there are times when cropping within Photoshop is essential for image resizing or for other creative reasons.

In addition to the resizing method described in the previous How-To, you can also use the Crop tool to resize your images.

To use the Crop tool, select it from the Toolbox and then enter the desired dimensions and resolution in the options bar. For example, enter 8 in (for inches) in the Width field, 10 in in the Height field, and 300 pixels/inch in the Resolution field (**Figure 13a**).

Figure 13a The options bar, when the Crop tool is active.

Next, drag on the image with the Crop tool to draw a marquee around the area you want to keep. You can drag the marquee to reposition it, or drag the marquee handles to resize it. To apply the crop, press Enter (Windows) or Return (Mac), double-click inside the marquee, or click the Commit Current Crop Operation button (labeled with a checkmark) in the options bar.

Straightening using the Ruler tool

Have you ever shot a photograph only to notice later that it was crooked? Here is an easy fix for crooked images:

1. Select the Ruler tool (**Figure 13b**).

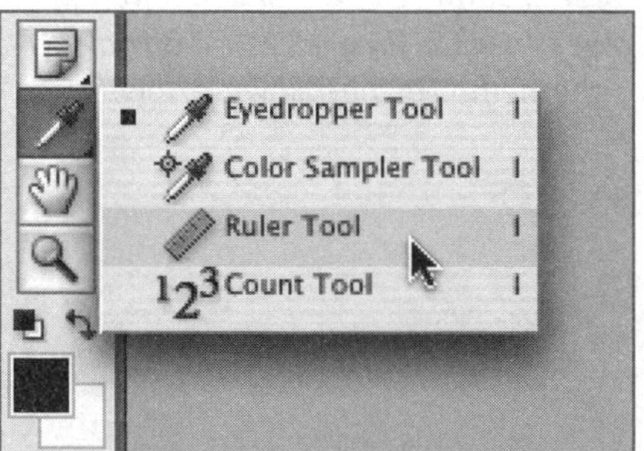

Figure 13b By default, the Ruler is hidden underneath the Eyedropper tool. Click and hold on the Eyedropper to access the Ruler.

2. Find an element(s) in the image that should be horizontal—a line of stonework on a building, for example—and drag the Ruler along that element. In **Figure 13c**, I dragged from the top of one spire to the other.

Figure 13c
Drag the Ruler tool along a line in your image that *should* be horizontal.

3. To open the Rotate Canvas dialog box, choose Image > Rotate Canvas > Arbitrary (**Figure 13d**).

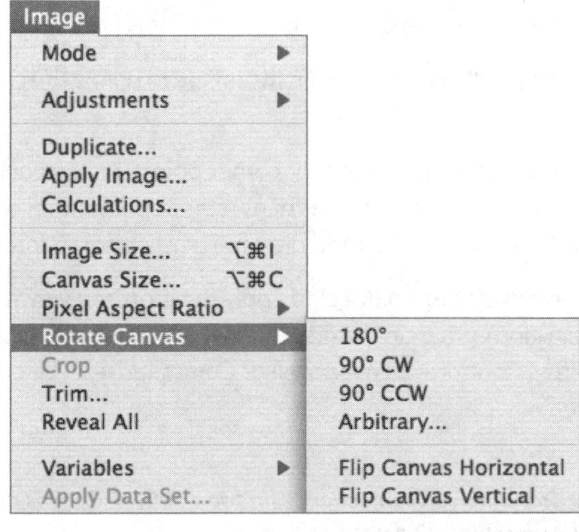

Figure 13d
After drawing a line with the Ruler tool, choose Image > Rotate Canvas > Arbitrary.

(continued on next page)

Making "Vertical" Lines Vertical

Even if your image has no clear horizontal elements to use as the basis for straightening, the Ruler tool trick also works with vertical elements. Drag the tool along a line that should run straight up and down (like a wall), choose Image > Rotate Canvas > Arbitrary, and then click OK. Photoshop is smart enough to realize that the line you drew is meant to be vertical, and rotates the picture accordingly.

Cropping Using the Marquee Tool

To apply a crop quickly, use the Marquee tool. Select the Rectangular Marquee tool (or press the M key). Make a marquee selection and select Image > Crop.

4. Click OK to rotate the image. The line you drew with the Ruler tool is now perfectly horizontal.

Composing using the Crop tool

In certain scenarios, it may be helpful to rotate an image when you want to make the composition more dynamic. Take for example this great photograph captured by my wife, Kelly (**Figure 13e**). The rotation in the image makes it dynamic and interesting.

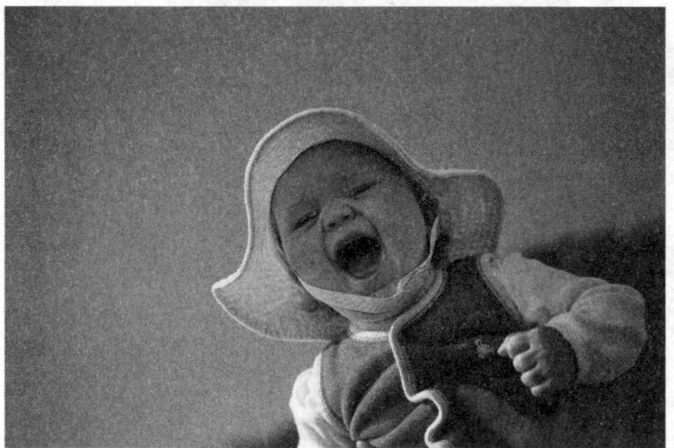

Figure 13e To apply a more standard rotation, choose Image > Rotate Canvas.

To recompose an image using the Crop tool:

1. Select the Crop tool, and then drag within the image to define the crop area.
2. Move your cursor toward one of the four corner points. As the cursor nears a corner point, it changes into a "bent" cursor pointing in two directions, signifying rotation. Click and drag the bent cursor to rotate.
3. Press Enter (Windows) or Return (Mac) to apply the crop and view the results. If it doesn't look good on the first try (as it often doesn't), don't be dismayed. Press Control + Z (Windows) or Command + Z (Mac) to undo and try again.

    Note

    To apply a more standard rotation, choose Image > Rotate Canvas and choose one of the preset rotation options.

#14 Saving Images

The last step in a Photoshop workflow is to save the image. The most straightforward way of doing this is to choose File > Save or press Ctrl + S (Windows) or Command + S (Mac). If you've already saved the file, you won't see anything—your file will be saved to disk, and you'll be free to continue working.

If this is the first time you've saved the image, the Save As dialog box appears (**Figure 14a**).

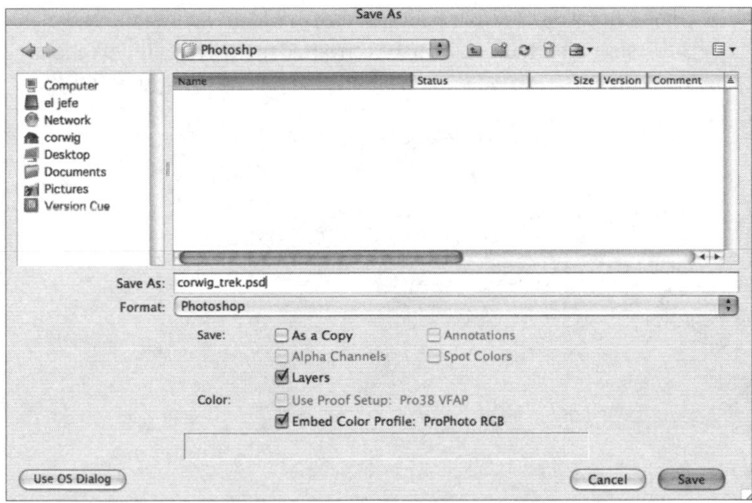

Figure 14a The Save As dialog box.

The Save As dialog box allows you to define several file parameters, chief among them the file's name and its format. In fact, if you ever want to change the name or format of a file that's already been saved, choose File > Save As or type Ctrl + Shift + S (Windows) or Command + Shift + S (Mac) to summon the Save As dialog box. If your image file includes layers and you want to preserve those layers in the new file, remember that you need to save your document in PSD, PSB (Large Document), PDF (Photoshop PDF), or TIFF format.

Another important step when saving files is to select the Embed Color Profile check box. This will "tag" your document with a specific color profile. By way of analogy, you can think of color profiles as similar to size tags on clothing (in essence, Small, Medium, Large). The size tags clarify the garment's dimensions and take the guesswork out of shopping. In the same way, Embed Color Profile takes the guesswork out of color and leads to more accurate color reproduction.

Changing the Format of Multiple Images Quickly

You can change the format of multiple images quickly using Photoshop's Image Processor script, rather than opening multiple images and saving them one at a time. Choose File > Scripts > Image Processor. In the Image Processor dialog box, select a folder of images to be converted to a specific file type and/or resized to dimensions of your choosing, and then click Run (**Figure 14b**).

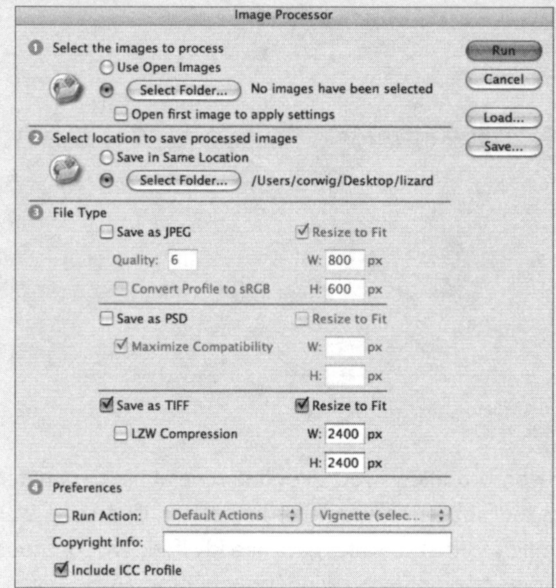

Figure 14b Use the Image Processor script to convert and process multiple files at one time.

CHAPTER THREE

Using Adobe Bridge

Ansel Adams grew up in Marin, California, just across the bay from San Francisco, before the Golden Gate Bridge was built. As an adult, the bridge played an important role in Ansel's photographic journey, as it gave him newfound, easy access to not only the great and scenic city of San Francisco, but also to the absolute architectural and scenic beauty of the Golden Gate itself.

In many ways, you can think of Adobe Bridge as not unlike Ansel Adams' Golden Gate: It provides unique access to your images and for many photographers has become an integral and enjoyable part of their creative workflow.

Adobe Bridge is an access-point application designed to help you browse, locate, and organize your images. It also can help you import, edit, process, and even order prints without ever launching Photoshop. While you may find you often use Bridge instead of Photoshop, keep in mind that the two applications make great teammates. One of the main reasons that Bridge is gaining prominence is because it allows you to open images directly into the Adobe Camera Raw plug-in, where you have access to a wealth of sophisticated image-editing tools. And Adobe Camera Raw isn't just for RAW images—you can also use it with images in JPG and TIFF format as well.

#15 Modifying Bridge Preferences

No Pane, No Gain

The Preferences dialog box in Bridge is organized just like its equivalent in Photoshop. If you need a quick refresher course in navigating the dialog box's options, see How-To #2, Modifying Preferences.

If you are going to make the leap to using Bridge, you'll want to get your preferences dialed in. Choose Edit > Preferences (Windows) or Bridge > Preferences (Mac) to launch the Preferences dialog box (**Figure 15a**).

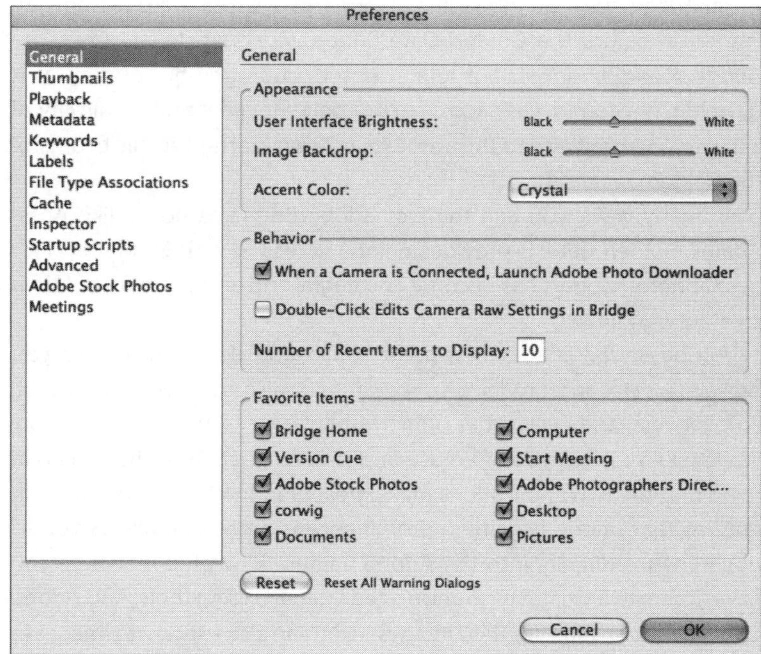

Figure 15a The Bridge Preferences dialog box, showing the General pane.

> ***Tip***
> *The keyboard shortcut for opening the Preferences dialog box is the same in Bridge as in Photoshop: Ctrl + K (Windows) or Command + K (Mac).*

Most of the default preference settings are fine, so we'll focus only on the ones that are most important to modify.

In the Appearance area of the General pane, verify that the settings for User Interface Brightness and Image Backdrop are what you want. Drag the Image Backdrop slider to the left or right to change the brightness of the Content and Preview panels. Drag the User Interface Brightness slider to change the brightness of the Favorites, Folders, Filter, and Metadata panels, as well as the borders of the interface. Keep in mind that the

Image Backdrop color will also be designated as the background color of any slide shows you generate using Bridge (learn more about slide shows in How-To #20).

Switch to the Thumbnails pane, and in the Performance and File Handling area, select the option Prefer Adobe Camera Raw for JPEG and TIFF files (**Figure 15b**).

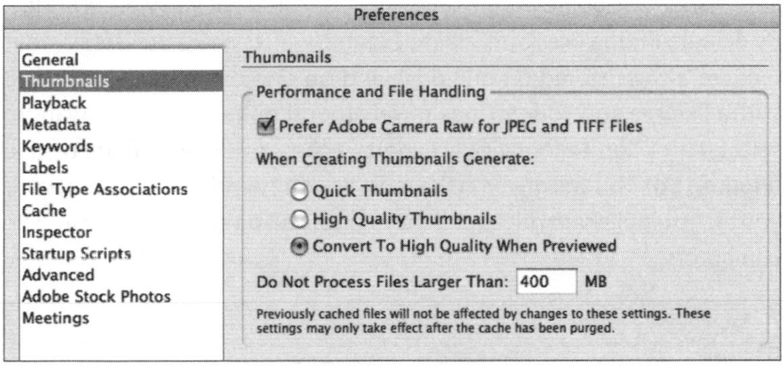

Figure 15b To take full advantage of Adobe Camera Raw, enable Prefer Adobe Camera Raw for JPEG and TIFF Files. (For more details on Camera Raw, see Chapter 4.)

Enabling this option makes it easy to use the powerful Adobe Camera Raw plug-in to process TIFFs and JPEGs.

Bridge allows you to assign colored labels to your images—very handy for organizing your files. Although the colors themselves are hard-wired into Bridge, you can choose your own names for the labels. Switch to the Labels pane, where you can enter custom text for each label (**Figure 15c**).

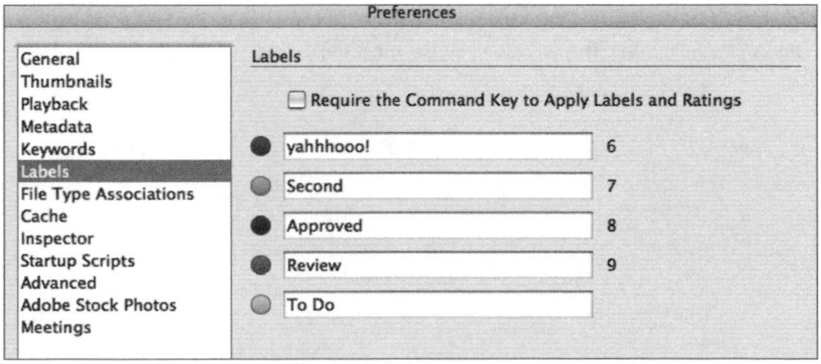

Figure 15c In the Labels preferences, you can apply custom names to labels.

Labels in Photoshop and Lightroom

Lightroom is becoming more and more popular with photographers. If you find yourself using Adobe Bridge and Adobe Photoshop Lightroom, be sure to use the same custom names for your labels in Bridge that you use for your labels in Lightroom. That way both programs will be able to recognize the same set of labels.

Photoshop Bridge Shortcut

The more you use Bridge, the more frequently you will navigate back and forth between Photoshop and Bridge. The shortcut for navigating between Photoshop and Bridge is Ctrl + Alt + O (Windows) or Command + Option + O (Mac). You can use this shortcut from either application. In Photoshop, use the shortcut to open Bridge. In Bridge, use the shortcut to open Photoshop.

I like to use a red label for my best images, so I've changed the name of the red label to "yahhhoooo!" Make sure the option Require the Command Key to Apply Labels and Ratings is deselected. This will speed your image rating and organizing.

Last but not least are the options in the Cache preference pane. *Cache* refers to the area on your hard disk that Bridge uses to store descriptive information (including thumbnails) about the files that you view in Bridge. By default, Bridge uses a centralized cache, which works well when your files are always stored on one drive and on one computer. However, if you're like me and your images travel around quite a bit, you'll want to select the option Automatically Export Caches to Folders When Possible (**Figure 15d**). This will give you the most flexibility and is the best option if you use multiple hard drives or if the images will be accessed on multiple computers.

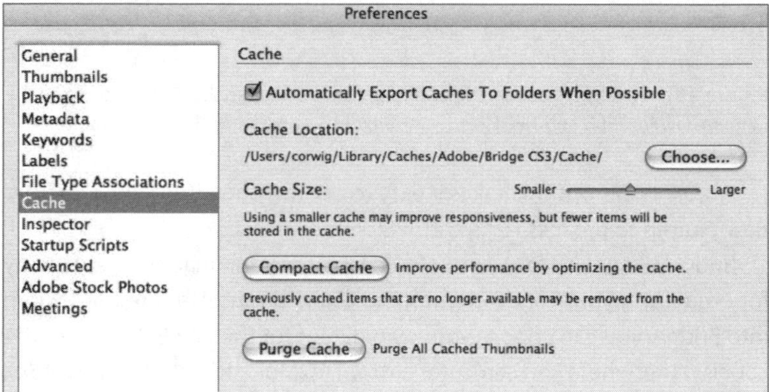

Figure 15d In the Cache Preferences pane, select Automatically Export Caches to Folders When Possible. This will give you the most flexibility.

#16 Working with the Bridge Interface

You can configure Bridge to fit your own workflow needs. You may at times want to use Bridge as if it were a big, functional tool like a sledgehammer—hammering through the organizing and processing of a large number of images. Other times you may want to use it as if it were a small detail tool like a wood carver's chisel—slowly and artistically chipping away at organizing and processing a small group of your best images.

At the top of the Bridge window you will find tools for navigating through folders, creating new folders, rotating or deleting images, and more. The main Bridge interface is made up of various panels (**Figure 16a**).

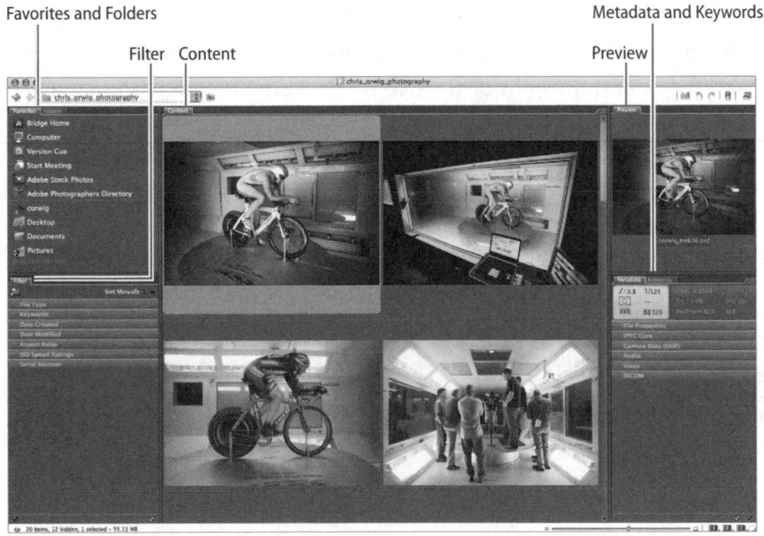

Figure 16a The default workspace in Bridge.

At the heart of the interface is the Content panel, which displays thumbnails of the images contained in the active folder. Accompanying the Content panel are a number of other panels, which maybe visible or hidden, depending on how you've configured your workspace:

- **Folders** allows you to navigate the folder hierarchy on your hard drive.
- **Favorites** offers you quick access to frequently used folders.
- **Filter** allows you to display a limited selection of files based on criteria you choose.

(continued on next page)

Useful Keyboard Shortcuts

- To simplify the interface, press the Tab key to hide the left and right side panels. Press Tab again to bring them back.
- At times you may want to view only the thumbnails and not the accompanying file names, labels, and so on. Press Ctrl + T (Windows) or Command + T (Mac) to toggle the display of the information.
- To quickly change the file name of an image, select the file and press F2 to highlight the file name. Now all you need to do is type away!

Bridge Speed Tips

- The quickest way to expand or collapse a specific panel is to double-click the panel's tab. You can also double-click either vertical divider bar to collapse the panels on that side of the Content panel.
- Choose a different workspace from each of the numbered menus in the lower right corner of the window. Then simply click a number to switch to the workspace you've chosen from that menu.
- Right-click (Windows) or Control-click (Mac) any thumbnail(s) to open a context menu containing many commands, including Open, Copy, Reveal in Finder, Batch Rename, Label, and more.

- **Content** displays the thumbnails previews.
- **Metadata** displays the metadata for the selected file (or files).
- **Keywords** lets you assign keywords to images.
- **Preview** displays a larger view of the selected image.

(There's also an Inspector panel, but it is used only with Version Cue, a feature which is beyond the scope of this book).

You can arrange the panels to create a workspace that suits your working style. Move a panel by dragging its tab, or resize panels by dragging the horizontal or vertical divider bar that separates them. Once you have the panels arranged the way you like them, you can save the arrangement as a custom workspace by choosing Window > Workspace > Save Workspace and give it a distinctive name. Your custom workspace will then appear on the Window > Workspace submenu, along with the six preconfigured workspaces that ship with Bridge.

You can also use any of the three menus (labeled 1, 2, or 3) in the lower right corner of the Bridge window to choose a workspace. To the left of these menus is a slider that controls the size of the thumbnails in the Content panel. Drag the slider to the left to make the thumbnails smaller, or to the right to enlarge them. Click the double-arrowhead icon in the lower left to collapse or expand all panels except the Content panel (**Figure 16b**).

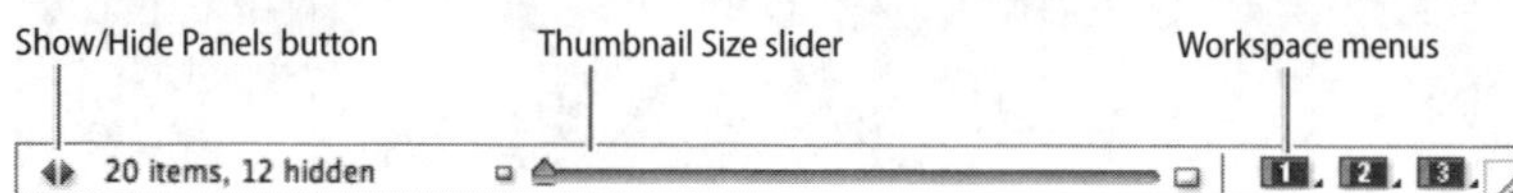

Figure 16b Use the controls along the bottom of the Bridge window to customize the workspace.

#17 Rating, Sorting, and Searching

Whether we're capturing an event with a digital camera or creating Web site design variations for a client, it seems that today we're creating more content than ever before. The upside of all this content creation is that it makes for an incredibly exciting time full of unprecedented discovery and creativity. The downside is that most of our thousands of digital files are completely unorganized and, as a result, seemingly inaccessible. Of course, this is one of the main functions of Bridge—to help you keep all your creative efforts within easy reach. Here's a good way to use Bridge to that effect:

Bridge Overview

To get up to speed on how to best use Bridge, be sure to watch the following free video: www.adobe.com/designcenter/video_workshop/?id=vid0090

Note

When you are ready to review and edit your images, plan on making multiple editing passes—in essence, be sure to go through your images more than once.

1. Click the first image of the set to display it in the Preview panel.
2. Press the arrow key to select and preview the next image.
3. Continue previewing your images and, as you do this, assign labels, star ratings, or a combination of both to the files. To do this, choose the appropriate label or rating from the Label menu. When an image has a label applied, it shows up as a strip of color beneath its thumbnail in the Content panel. Ratings appear as a row of stars within the colored label (**Figure 17a**).

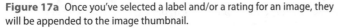

Figure 17a Once you've selected a label and/or a rating for an image, they will be appended to the image thumbnail.

Filtering Shortcuts

Here are some valuable shortcuts you won't find anywhere else!

- If you want to filter your images so that you see only those with a specific rating or label, hold Ctrl + Alt (Windows) or Command (Mac) and press any key from 1 through 9. This is a quicker alternative to clicking an item in the Ratings or Labels categories in the Filter panel.
- To display all files that have any label at all, press Ctrl + Alt + Shift + A (Windows) or Command + Option + Shift + A (Mac).

It's a good idea to employ a specific strategy for your rating system. For example, on my first passes, I tend to rate the keeper images as four or five stars by holding Ctrl (Windows) or Command (Mac) and pressing 4 (or 5). Then in the Filter panel, I click the criteria that correspond to the images I want to see (**Figure 17b**).

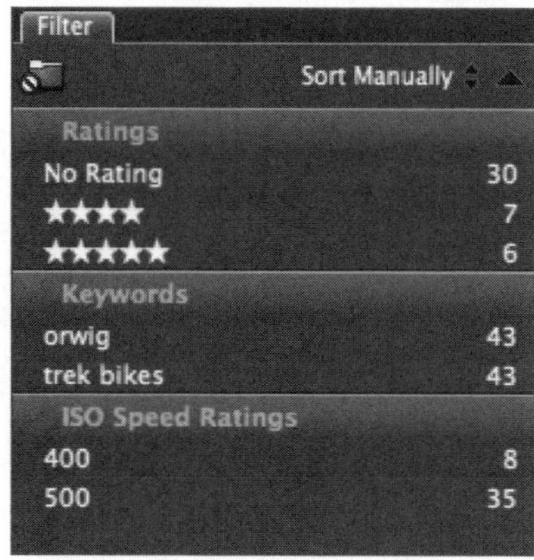

Figure 17b Choose criteria in the Filter panel to filter and display images that meet those criteria.

If you need to find a file by more specific parameters, such as by the date it was created or its dimensions, select Edit > Find or press Ctrl + F (Windows) or Command + F (Mac). This will launch the Find dialog box, where you can add specific details for your search. Choose an item from the first menu in the Criteria area to search by Filename, Date Created, File Size, Height, Width, Keyword, Label, ISO, and more (**Figure 17c**).

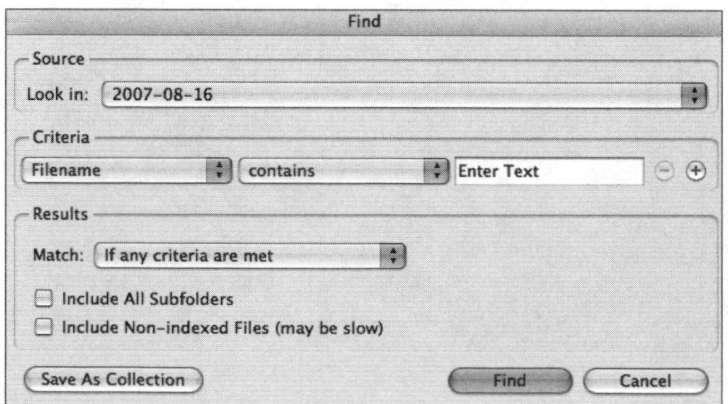

Figure 17c The Find dialog box offers many options for image searching.

#18 Modifying Metadata and Keywords

Many of the powerful Bridge features that allow you to organize, search, and keep track of your files and versions depend on the metadata in your files. Essentially, metadata is a set of standardized information about a file, such as the author name, copyright, keywords, the camera settings in force when the image was created, and so on. In other words, metadata is data about data. You can consider an image to be nothing more than data, and the metadata is the information that describes the image, such as the file type, the size, or the date it was captured.

Metadata is valuable because you can use it to streamline your workflow and organize your files. Bridge provides two ways of working with metadata: through the Metadata panel and through the File Info dialog box.

Let's begin with the File Info dialog box. Select an image, and then choose File > File Info (**Figure 18a**).

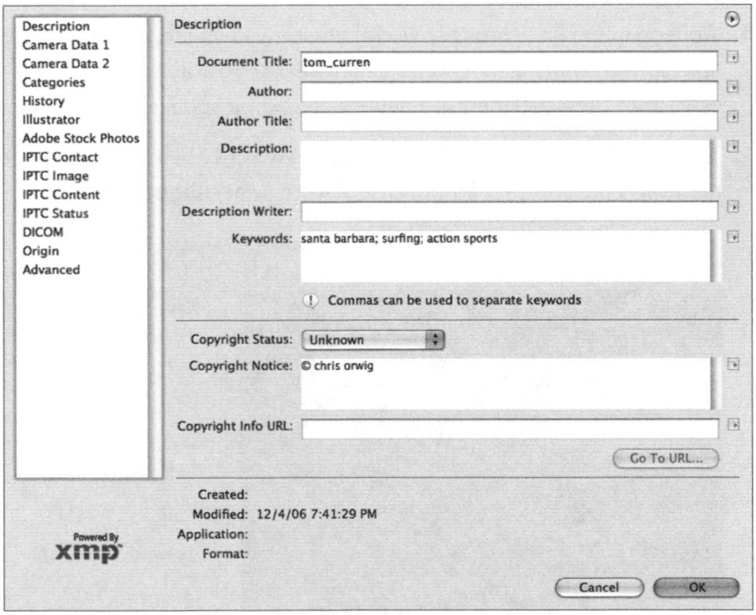

Figure 18a Use the File Info dialog box to view or edit an image's metadata.

This dialog box displays quite a bit of information. At first glance, it may look a little like overkill, but many of the settings in it are important. In particular, you may want to add keywords and copyright information.

If you want to save the metadata you have entered as a template for use with other images, click the arrow on the upper right and choose Save Metadata Template from the menu (**Figure 18b**). Once you've saved the template, you can apply it to other files.

Figure 18b Save templates containing commonly used metadata.

Editing metadata within Bridge is easier than ever. Choose Window > Workspace > Metadata Focus. Notice the Keywords and Metadata panels on the left. Adding keywords to your images is a critical step in digital asset management, so let's begin there:

1. Working in the Keywords panel, click the New Keyword button or New Sub Keyword button (or choose either New Keyword or New Sub Keyword from the panel menu). A new default name appears in the panel.
2. To create the new keyword or new sub keyword, type over the default name and press Enter (Windows) or Return (Mac) (**Figure 18c**).

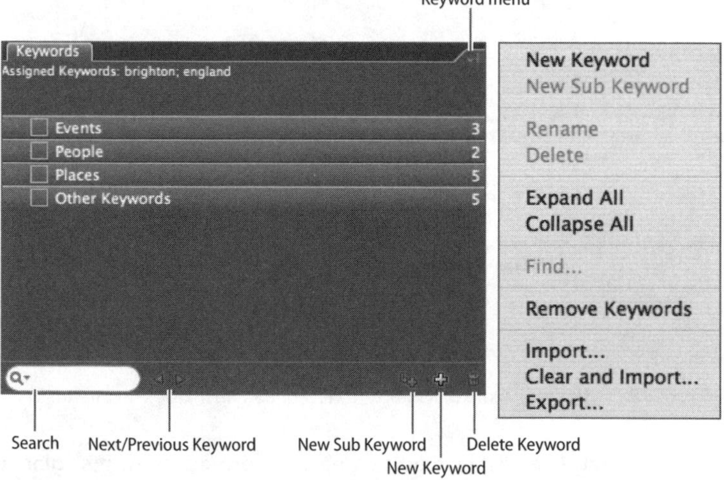

Figure 18c Use the Keywords panel to create keywords or to assign keywords to images.

The top portion of the Metadata panel is occupied by the metadata placard, which displays the settings from the camera when the picture was taken. You'll find information such as the aperture setting, shutter speed, metering mode, ISO, file size, pixel dimensions, and color space. The placard is formatted to resemble the LCD screen on a camera, so you most likely will find it a very useful feature of Bridge (**Figure 18d**).

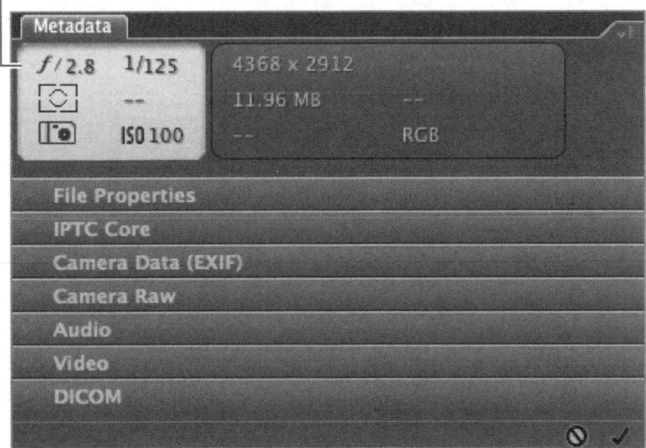

Figure 18d The metadata placard contains an easy-to-understand visualization of valuable information.

Perhaps the most important part of the Metadata panel is the IPTC Core. This is where you can add or modify keywords, copyright, contact information, and more. Click the triangle to the left of the IPTC Core heading to expand the IPTC Core section, select an item, and start typing.

Adding Keywords Training Video

Be sure to check out the free Adobe training video on adding keywords: www.adobe.com/go/vid0095

#19 Using the Loupe Tool

For those times when you need to examine an image closely, the Loupe tool comes in handy. By default, the Loupe tool magnifies a portion of your image to 100 percent (that is, to the level of individual pixels), but you can change the magnification.

To use the Loupe tool:

1. Select an image thumbnail in the Content panel.
2. Click the image in the Preview panel. A virtual loupe appears on the screen, displaying an enlarged view of the portion of the image where you clicked (**Figure 19a**).

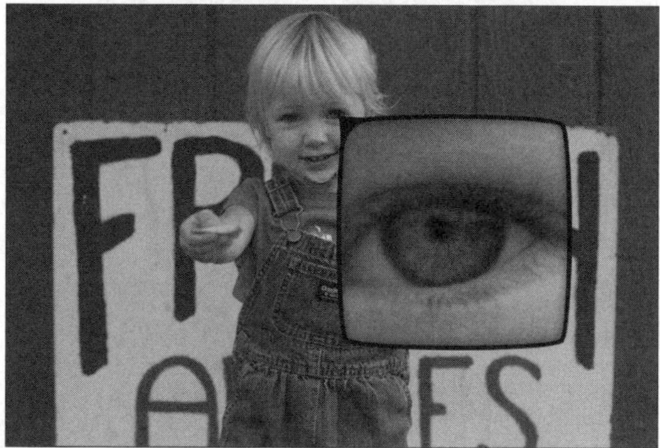

Figure 19a Use the Loupe tool to zoom in on an image preview to check for focus and detail.

3. Drag the Loupe tool to view different areas of the image.
4. If you want a closer look, press the equal key (=). To zoom out, press the minus key (–).
5. To dismiss the Loupe tool, click inside the magnified area.

One of the ways the Loupe tool is most helpful is in examining several images at once. For example, you can use it to compare the sharpness of multiple similar images:

1. In Bridge, Ctrl-click (Windows) or Command-click (Mac) the images you want to compare. The images will appear in the Preview panel.
2. In the Preview panel, click the first of the images you want to compare to open the Loupe tool.
3. Click the second image you want to compare to open another Loupe tool. Continue clicking image previews until you have as many Loupe tools open as you need (**Figure 19b**).

Figure 19b Use the Loupe tool to compare similar images. In this case, both previews look sharp; however, the Loupe tool reveals that the lower image is a higher quality image.

Zoom and Reposition Multiple Loupes

When you have multiple Loupe tools open at the same time, press Ctrl (Windows) or Command (Mac) with the plus key (+) or minus key (–) to zoom all Loupes in and out simultaneously.

To reposition multiple Loupe tools at the same time, hold down Ctrl (Windows) or Command (Mac) and drag one of the Loupe tools. All active Loupes will move simultaneously.

#20 Viewing a Slide Show

There is nothing better than clearing away the clutter, dimming the lights, and watching a slide show of compelling work. Bridge has several features that can make this experience a reality.

Choose View > Slideshow, or press Ctrl + L (Windows) or Command + L (Mac) to launch a slide show of the images in the current folder. Then in Slideshow view, press the H key to display a list of commands for working with the slide show (**Figure 20a**).

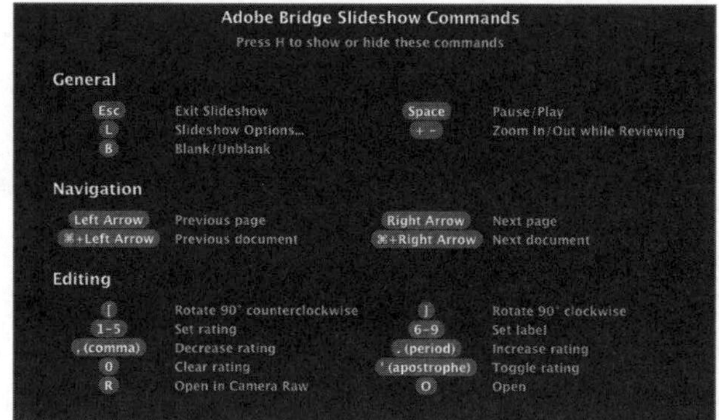

Figure 20a While in Slideshow view, press H to display commands for slide shows.

To customize the slide show, while in Slideshow view, press the L key. The Slideshow Options dialog box appears. Here you can modify options for both the overall display and for individual slides. (**Figure 20b**).

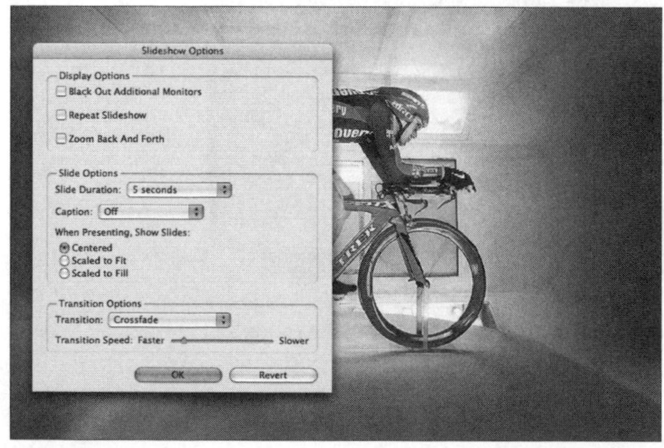

Figure 20b While in Slideshow view, press L to open the Slideshow Options dialog box.

Use Slideshow to See Your Work with Fresh Eyes

When working on images, it's easy to get over-focused on the task at hand. I often return from a shooting session with hundreds and hundreds of images, and if I'm not careful, the sheer volume of images lessens my appreciation of them, as does the fatigue and eye strain that results from being over-focused. Here is what I have found has helped me evaluate my work with fresh eyes: I select my favorite images and begin a looping slide show. Then I walk away from the computer and watch the show from a distance. This gives me invaluable insight into my work.

#21 Using the Photo Downloader

The Photo Downloader is an excellent tool that gives you the ability to import photos from your digital camera or other digital media device. The application lets you specify a location for the downloaded files, rename the images, convert images to DNG (Adobe Digital Negative) format, and save copies to another hard drive if desired (**Figure 21**).

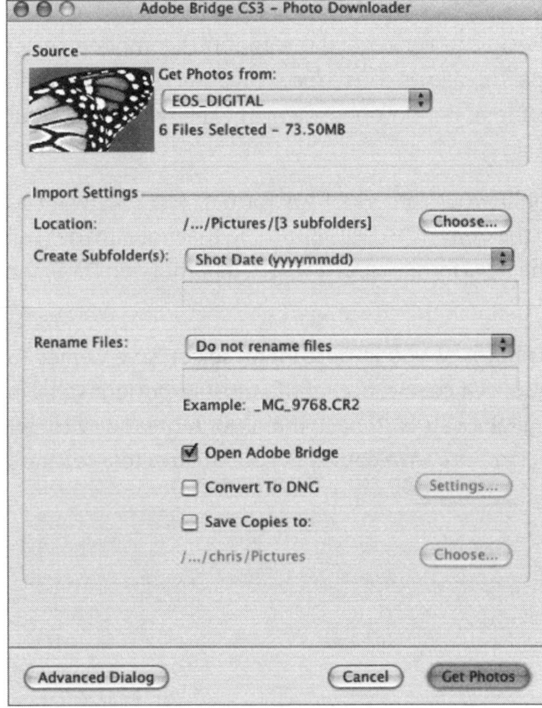

Figure 21 Use the Photo Downloader to download photos from your digital camera or digital media storage device.

To use the Photo Downloader:

1. Connect your camera or card reader to the computer.
2. Choose File > Get Photos From Camera.
3. Select the name of the camera or card reader from the Get Photos From menu. Most likely, the currently attached camera or device will be selected by default.

(continued on next page)

4. Choose the folder location. Ideally, create a folder structure that is consistent, and easy to understand.
5. To rename the files as you import them, choose an option from the Rename Files menu. If you are renaming your images, be sure to use a naming convention that is consistent so that three years from now you'll be able to easily access and find the images you need.
6. If you prefer to have Bridge open once the import is complete, select Open Adobe Bridge. This allows you to focus on other tasks, and when the import is complete, Bridge opens, which likely will direct your attention to the images.
7. If you are shooting in your camera's RAW format, you may want to consider selecting the Convert to DNG option so that your images will be converted to the DNG format upon import. (For more on DNG, see Chapter 4.)
8. To save copies of photos as you import them, select Save Copies To and specify a location. Of course, one of the most important steps in managing your digital assets is to back them up. A great way to get a jumpstart on backup is to save copies of your images to a separate hard drive.

Apply Metadata on Import

If you want to apply metadata to your images as they are imported, click the Advanced Dialog button and type information in the Author and Copyright text boxes, or choose a metadata template from the Template menu. This lets you add your copyright to your images while they're being imported. Now that's what I call optimizing your photographic workflow!

Photo Downloader Training Video

For more info about using Bridge in a photography workflow, be sure to watch this Adobe training movie: www.adobe.com/go/vid0189

#22 Using the "Power Tools" in Bridge

Bridge is equipped with some heavy-duty power tools, which you'll find on the Tools > Photoshop submenu (**Figure 22**).

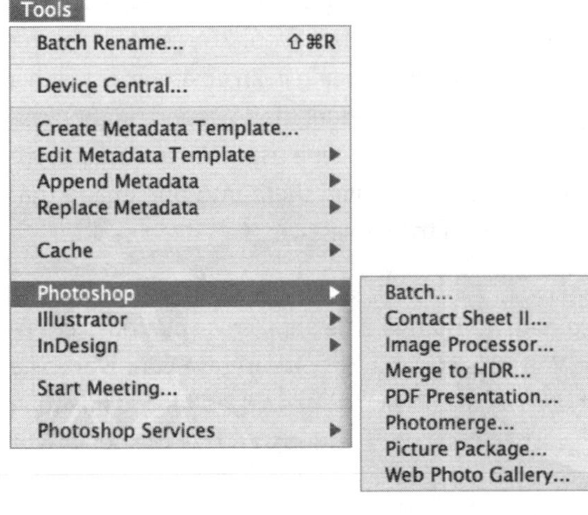

Figure 22 The Tools > Photoshop submenu gives you a direct link to some powerful commands within Photoshop.

You'll find identical commands on the File > Automate submenu in Photoshop, and, in fact, using any of these commands from Bridge will fire up Photoshop, where the operations will actually be carried out. A few of these are covered later in the book, but briefly reviewing them here will help you become aware of their basic functions.

Batch

The Batch command applies a Photoshop action (a saved series of commands) to multiple files.

Contact Sheet

In my own photographic workflow, I regularly make contact sheets for two reasons: to provide visual proofs for clients and for proper digital asset management. Rather than allowing my digital assets to get buried on one of many hard drives, having contact sheets gives me quick visual access to them. In addition, they let me browse through my photos without having to be at a computer. Once I've found the image on the contact sheet, I can quickly navigate to that folder in Bridge.

Image Processor

The image processor provides an effective and efficient way to "batch" resize and convert a small or large number of images. This tool is especially helpful when you need to deliver TIFs or JPEGs to a client (or anyone else for that matter) at a specific size, color space, and dimension.

Merge to HDR

Merge to HDR (High Dynamic Range) combines multiple exposures of the same subject into a single image. The goal with HDR is to achieve a far greater dynamic range of exposure than would be possible in one single exposure. For example, if you're shooting in an environment with a wide range of lighting conditions, such as dark shadows and bright highlights, you can take several images of the scene using different exposure settings and use Merge to HDR to combine them into one image that captures the full dynamic range of the subject.

PDF Presentation

PDF (or Portable Document Format) is a flexible, cross-platform, cross-application file format. With this command, you can save your work as a multi-page document or as a slide show. You can set options to maintain image quality in the PDF, specify security settings, and set the document to open automatically as a slide show if desired.

Photomerge

The majority of panoramic photographs are created with a tool like Photomerge. You take multiple photographs of a panoramic scene and then "stitch" together the images with Photomerge. If you've never tried creating a panorama, I highly recommend it. The format is cinematic and can't be taken in with a simple glance. Instead, it draws viewers in, as they have to visually travel through the photograph.

Picture Package

Picture Package is all about optimizing your printing workflow. Rather than printing a single 4 × 6 on one 8 × 10 sheet of paper and wasting paper and time, Picture Package provides you with a solution to configure and print multiple images on one or more pages. This is incredibly helpful when printing images at various sizes.

Web Photo Gallery

The Web Photo Gallery provides you with an automated way to create a Web site that features a home page with thumbnail images and gallery pages with full-size images.

Photoshop provides a variety of styles for your gallery, which you can select using the Web Photo Gallery command. Each template for gallery styles comes with different options that are customizable.

CHAPTER FOUR

Using Photoshop Camera Raw

The Photoshop Camera Raw plug-in allows you to open raw image files from many different types of digital cameras directly into Photoshop. Using this plug-in is becoming a more and more integral part of one's digital imaging workflow. It is so important that this is actually the longest chapter in the whole book. Camera Raw is flexible and powerful, and it gives you the ability to make nondestructive edits to your images. More than anything, Camera Raw can empower you to accomplish more creative and higher quality results.

In this chapter, you will learn some of the essentials of the Photoshop Camera Raw plug-in. You'll learn how to adjust exposure, color, tone, saturation, sharpness, and more. You'll learn professional tips for creating amazing black-and-white images. You will gain skills in retouching raw images, red eye removal, cropping, and noise reduction. Finally, you'll learn how to apply your new skills in a way that will speed your workflow.

#23 Understanding Photoshop Camera Raw

Learn More About the DNG Format

If you would like more information regarding the DNG format, visit www.adobe.com/products/dng/

The Photoshop Camera Raw plug-in provides a unique and compelling way to process raw, JPEG, and TIFF files from right inside Photoshop. Camera Raw offers a number of different controls to modify exposure, color, tone, contrast, sharpness, and so on. What is unique about Camera Raw is that when you use it to make an adjustment, the data in your image is not changed; rather, the plug-in creates a set of instructions that determine how the pixels in the image are to be displayed.

You can think of a camera raw file as a traditional film negative. If you want to create different types of prints from a film negative, the film negative never actually changes. Rather, you could bring the negative to a photo lab and write down instructions for the lab to print the image brighter, darker, or as a sepia tone. The negative stays the same, but the final output varies based on the written instructions.

In comparison, a raw file (like a negative) isn't ever modified, but the set of adjustment instructions can be infinitely modified. The wonderful thing about this approach is that the image adjustments are not permanent, and they do not drastically increase the file size. Thus, making adjustments with Camera Raw keeps you nimble, creative, and quick.

When you use Camera Raw, the adjustments (or "instructions") you make are stored as metadata. The metadata is saved in one of the following ways:

- As a database (the default storage method)
- As an accompanying sidecar file (an extensible Metadata Platform [XMP] file)
- The file itself (DNG format—a nonproprietary, TIFF-based file format for storing Camera Raw data)

Which option is best? It really depends on your own preferences, so let's discuss the options. By default, Camera Raw is set to save the camera raw "instructions" in a database. This option is best if you are working on only one computer and the image will stay on that computer.

For the majority of amateur and pro imagemakers, this default setting isn't ideal because of the need to store a large volume of images. Multiple hard drives are usually necessary. If this is your situation, you may want to change the default preference to accommodate this need. Open Adobe Bridge and choose Edit > Camera Raw Preferences (Windows) or

Bridge > Camera Raw Preferences (Mac) to display the Camera Raw Preferences dialog box (**Figure 23a**). From the Save Image Settings In menu, choose Sidecar ".xmp" Files. This provides more flexibility, since the raw settings will "travel" with the image rather than stay on the main computer's hard drive.

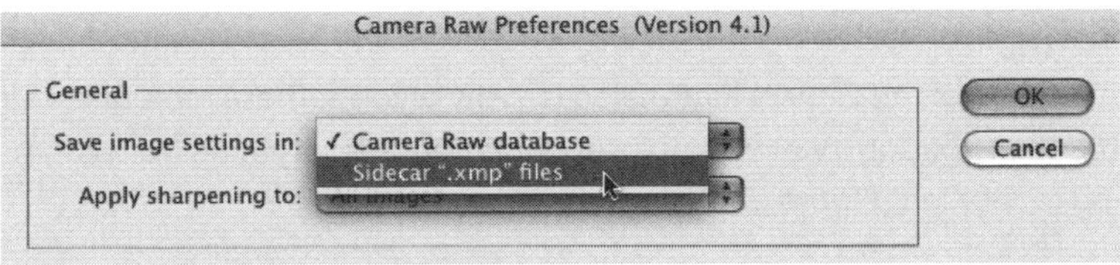

Figure 23a Have Bridge save adjustment changes in sidecar files for more flexibility.

The other option is to convert your images to DNG format, which will store the camera raw settings inside of the file itself. You can convert your images to the DNG format using Adobe's DNG Converter application or by saving them from within Camera Raw as a DNG file.

To use Camera Raw with JPEG and/or TIFF files, open the Camera Raw Preferences dialog box in Bridge and select the checkbox for the appropriate option in the JPEG and TIFF Handling area (**Figure 23b**).

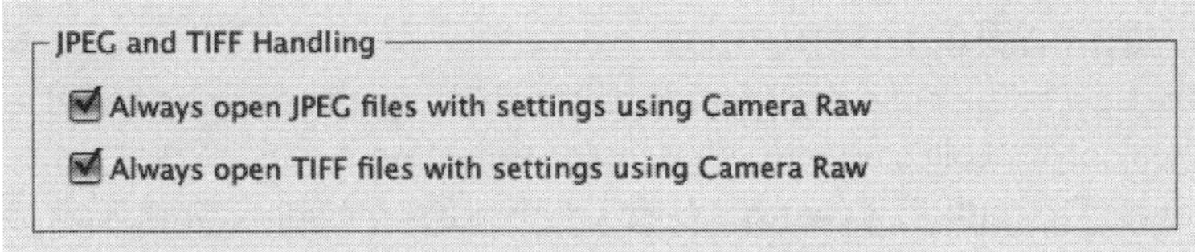

Figure 23b Select one or both of these options to open images in the JPEG or TIFF formats in the Camera Raw plug-in.

Opening Files in Camera Raw

The best way to open JPEGs, TIFFs, or raw files in Camera Raw is to use Adobe Bridge. In Bridge, select an image, and then choose File > Open In Camera Raw.

To open raw images directly into Camera Raw from within Photoshop, choose File > Open, and then navigate to the raw image file.

#24 Learning the Camera Raw Interface

Open an image in Camera Raw from within Photoshop or Bridge. Notice that the interface looks different than Photoshop or Bridge because the plug-in works like a standalone application. To get the most out of Camera Raw, you need to become familiar with the main aspects of its interface.

Tools

At the top of the Camera Raw dialog is a row of tools. These tools give you the ability perform various important functions—everything from zooming to rotating (**Figure 24a**).

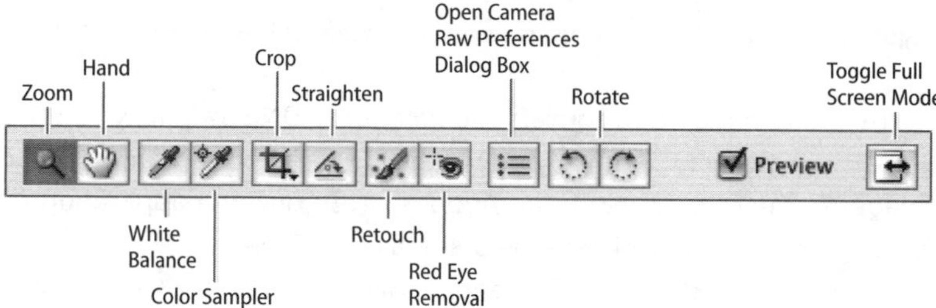

Figure 24a Camera Raw tools.

Image adjustment tabs

The bulk of the power and functionality of Camera Raw can be found in the controls collected into eight image adjustment tabs. Click a tab to access the controls it contains. Each tab uses a somewhat cryptic icon as a label—here's the secret decoder ring (**Figure 24b**):

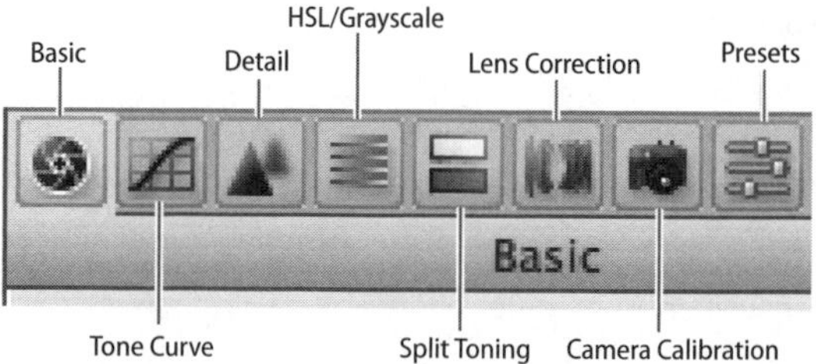

Figure 24b The Camera Raw image adjustment tabs and their functions.

- **Basic.** Adjust white balance, exposure, contrast, saturation.
- **Tone Curve.** Fine-tune tonality.
- **Detail.** Adjust sharpening and reduce noise.
- **HSL/Grayscale.** Convert to color or black and white.
- **Split Toning.** Add color to the highlights and shadows.
- **Lens Corrections.** Fix lens vignetting and chromatic aberration.
- **Camera Calibration.** Customize settings for a specific camera.
- **Presets.** Save and access presets.

Save, Open, Cancel, and Done

When you are finished adjusting your image, click one of the four buttons along the bottom of the Camera Raw window (**Figure 24c**):

- **Save.** Save the raw file in a different file format (PSD, TIFF, DNG, JPEG).
- **Open.** Open the image in Photoshop.
- **Cancel.** Cancel adjustments and return to Bridge.
- **Done.** Apply adjustments and return to Bridge.

Figure 24c When your work in Camera Raw is done, click one of the four buttons.

Devote Your Entire Screen to Camera Raw

When working in Camera Raw, it's a good idea to always work in Full Screen mode. This will help you focus on the image. Click the Toggle Full Screen button or press the F key to go to Full Screen mode; click the button (or press F) again to go back to windowed mode. Camera Raw remembers your setting even if you close the window and open it again.

#25 Setting the White Balance

A correct white balance setting ensures that neutral colors, like grays and white, are actually gray or white rather than tinged with yellow or blue. In addition, by correcting the neutrals, you simultaneously fix any unnatural color shifts that exist in the image.

The Basic tab in the Camera Raw interface has three controls for correcting a color shift in an image: White Balance, Temperature, and Tint. From the White Balance menu, choose a specific lighting environment to fine-tune the color balance (**Figure 25**):

- **As Shot.** Uses the white balance settings chosen by the camera at the moment the picture was taken.
- **Auto.** Camera Raw calculates a new white balance based on the image data.
- **Daylight, Cloudy, Shade, Tungsten, Fluorescent, or Flash.** Camera Raw calculates a new white balance based on the color temperature of the selected lighting condition.

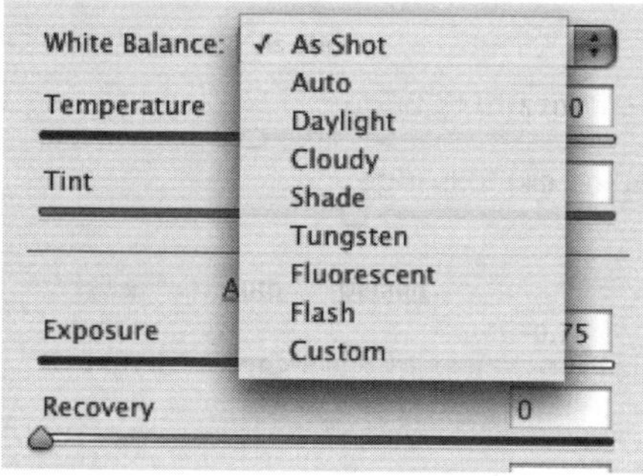

Figure 25 White Balance options.

To fine-tune the white balance, adjust the Temperature and Tint sliders. Adjusting the Temperature slider makes the image warmer or cooler. Adjusting the Tint slider compensates for a green or magenta tint.

Accessing the White Balance setting through the Basic panel to correct white balance works fine; however, one of the quickest and easiest ways to remove color shift in an image is to use the White Balance tool on the main toolbar in Camera Raw. This tool can be used to specify that an object should be white or gray. By doing this, Camera Raw can determine the color of the light in which the scene was shot and then adjust for scene lighting automatically.

Select the White Balance tool and click on an object in the image that you know should be should be a neutral gray or white.

Note
When using the White Balance tool and choosing a white area to click, be sure to choose a white area that contains significant white detail rather than a specular (or shiny) highlight. Sometimes selecting something that is off-white or gray works best.

Tip
You can double-click the White Balance tool icon to reset the white balance to As Shot.

White Balance and the Human Eye

The human eye is incredibly adaptable. Thus, when you first begin to work on digital images, it's difficult to identify color problems. Consider what happens when you wear sunglasses with a yellow tint. After wearing the glasses for a few moments, you actually stop seeing (or noticing) the yellow color shift, but once you remove the glasses you will notice the shift. This is a result of the adaptability of the human eye. Thus, we need some tools like the White Balance tool that will help us notice color inconsistencies. As a side note, an added benefit of using the White Balance tool is that it will train your eye to see color shifts, so you eventually will be able to fix color problems more effectively.

#26 Adjusting Exposure and Tone Automatically

As a professional photographer, I spend the majority of my time in Camera Raw adjusting exposure and tone. There are two options for making these adjustments: Use the Auto option, or you can make custom adjustments using various sliders in the section of the Basic tab that contains tone controls. (The latter is discussed in the subsequent How-To.)

Let's first examine the Auto option.

The Auto button is located at the top of the tone controls section (**Figure 26**). When you click the Auto button, Camera Raw analyzes the raw image data in the file and makes automatic adjustments to tone controls, such as Exposure, Recovery, Fill Light, Blacks, Brightness, and Contrast. Three main situations would make it advantageous to use the Auto option:

- If you shoot a high volume of images and don't have time to dial in specific tone settings, selecting Auto will greatly speed up your workflow.
- If you want an initial idea of the best settings for your image. Auto doesn't always give perfect results, but it can help give you insight into what adjustments may be needed.
- If you are new to Camera Raw, Auto can be used as a starting point. Click Auto and then fine-tune the image with the adjustment sliders.

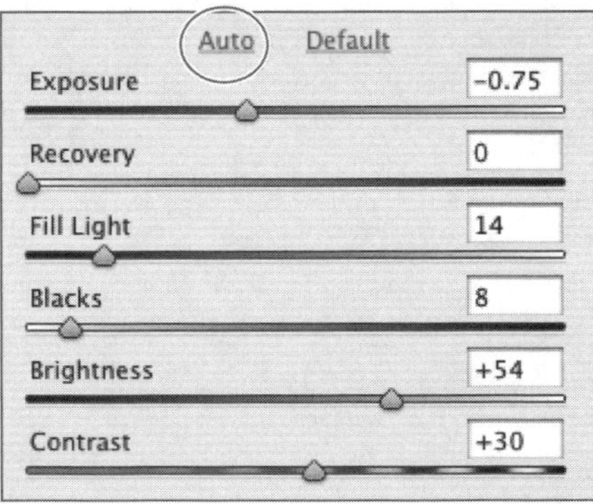

Figure 26 Click Auto to apply tone adjustments automatically.

#27 Adjusting Custom Exposure and Tone

If you want to take your images to the next level, use the exposure and tone sliders located in the Basic tab (**Figure 27**). The sliders are simple and intuitive.

Figure 27 Adjust exposure and tone to taste using these adjustment sliders.

The following are descriptions of each of these controls:

- **Exposure.** Adjusts the overall image brightness so that the image appears to have been exposed correctly. Drag the slider to the left to darken the image and to the right to brighten it.
- **Recovery.** One of the problems frequently encountered with digital capture is overexposure. If the image is overexposed (as a result of incorrect camera settings), the recovery slider can be used to coax details out of its highlights (the brightest part of the image).
- **Fill Light.** In traditional photography. a fill light is used to open up areas of shadow. It is not the key or dominant light source, but a complementary light source. In the same way, the Fill Light slider works to brighten details within shadows, without brightening the deepest blacks.
- **Blacks.** This slider makes a significant change in the darkest shadows, with much less change in the midtones and highlights. As a result, increasing the blacks can increase the contrast in an image. When adjusting the Blacks slider, be careful not to increase its value so much that there is great loss of detail in the dark tones of the image.

(continued on next page)

Reset Sliders to Their Defaults

Here's a handy time-saving tip: Reset any slider in Camera Raw to its default position by double-clicking it.

Reveal Clipping in Camera Raw

The tone sliders constitute an amazing set of adjustments, yet you can overuse them. To see how far you can push the Exposure, Recovery or Blacks values without producing negative results, hold down Alt (Windows) or Option (Mac) while adjusting these sliders to preview where highlights or shadows are clipped. By doing this, you can drag the slider until clipping begins, and then reverse the adjustment slightly.

- **Brightness.** Similar to the Exposure slider, the Brightness slider adjusts the brightness and darkness of the image. However, this slider does not clip (or lose) the image highlights or shadows as aggressively as the Exposure slider. Because of this, it's best to first set the overall tonal scale using the Exposure, Recovery, and Blacks sliders, and then set the brightness. Brightness adjustments also can affect shadow or highlight clipping, so after making a Brightness adjustment, verify and/or readjust the Exposure, Recovery, or Blacks settings as needed.
- **Contrast.** Once you have set the Exposure, Blacks, and Brightness values, it is time to set the contrast. The Contrast slider mainly affects the midtones (although it affects the darktones and highlights somewhat). When you increase contrast, the middle-to-dark image areas become darker, and the middle-to-light image areas become lighter.
- **Clarity.** This setting adds depth and sharpness to an image by increasing local contrast. (You can think of sharpness and contrast as birds of a feather.) When using this setting, it is best to zoom in to 100% or greater. To maximize the effect, increase the setting until you see halos near the edge details of the image, and then reduce the setting slightly.

#28 Enhancing Color with Vibrance and Saturation

The Vibrance and Saturation sliders are located at the bottom of the Basic tab (**Figure 28**).

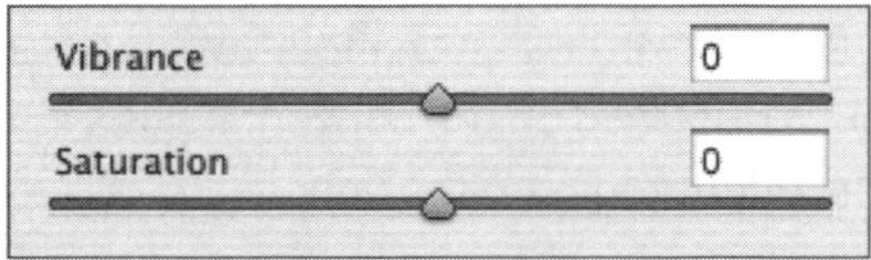

Figure 28 Increase Vibrance to boost less saturated colors. Increase Saturation to boost all color.

By thinking of these settings as teammates, your image enhancements will be better than ever. Both are useful for increasing and decreasing color saturation, yet each creates a different effect. Let's look a little deeper into the strengths and weaknesses of each.

Vibrance

The Vibrance slider is excellent for making nonlinear color adjustments. It analyzes the color in an image, and rather than affecting all the colors in a uniform way, it treats different colors in different ways. For example, if you increase the Vibrance slider, the bright and highly saturated colors will remain relatively unmodified, while the less saturated colors will become more colorful—in essence, brighter and more varied. If you decrease the Vibrance slider, the weaker colors fade away and only the most prominent colors remain.

Tip

The Vibrance slider is especially effective when increasing color in a portrait photograph because of the way it handles skin tones. The tool has built-in logic, which prevents oversaturation of skin tones when vibrancy is increased.

Saturation

The Saturation slider modifies color in a linear fashion, treating all the colors in an image equally. If you decrease the slider to 0, the image turns to grayscale. If you increase the slider to 100, the image becomes oversaturated, and some colors will be clipped (leading to a loss of detail).

Tips

If you want to add a subtle color improvement and at the same time add more color variety, try decreasing the Saturation slider and increasing the Vibrance slider.

Try experimenting with the Saturation and Vibrance sliders in unison with the other Camera Raw color controls. For example, try creating a unique "antique effect" by decreasing the saturation and increasing the color temperature, thus making the image more yellow.

Add Color Variety with Vibrance

The Vibrance slider has many uses; one of my favorites is to increase the Vibrance value to add color variety. I have found this to be especially effective when working on images of fall leaves, sunsets, and sepia-toned images, to name a few.

#29 Using the Tone Curve

It is best to make initial tone adjustments in the Basic tab and then switch to the Tone Curve tab to fine-tune your images. There are two methods of making tone curve adjustments: Parametric and Point. Each has its own tab within the Tone Curve tab. Both let you make changes to the tonal scale of an image. This tonal scale is displayed on the horizontal axis, with the dark tones on the left and the bright tones on the right.

Parametric tone curve

The Parametric tab is divided into four quadrants: Highlights, Lights, Darks, or Shadows (**Figure 29a**). Use the sliders to increase or decrease the darkness or brightness of a particular quadrant. If you would like more specific control, the quadrants can be expanded or contracted by dragging the Region Divider controls along the horizontal axis of the graph.

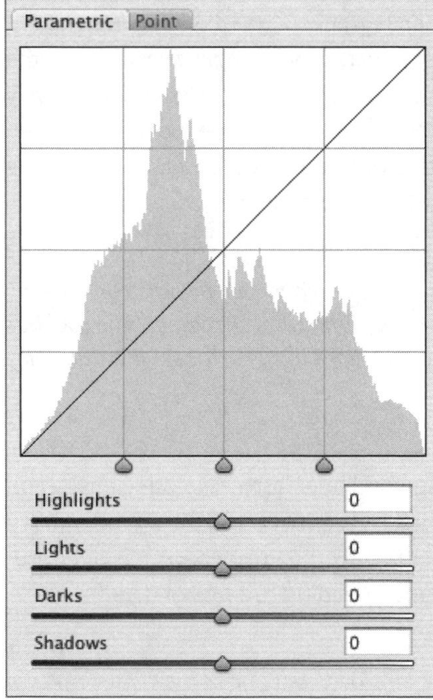

Figure 29a The tone curve in the Parametric tab.

Point tone curve

The Point tab is also divided into four quadrants (**Figure 29b**). However, the modifications are not confined to the quadrant. To make a modification, simply click and drag a point on the curve in the Point tab. Drag the point up to increase brightness. Drag the point down to decrease brightness.

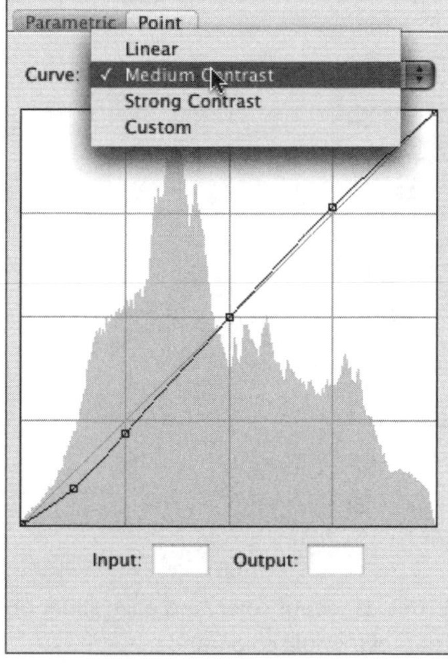

Figure 29b The tone curve in the Point tab.

The Point tab is supplied with presets, which you access via the Curve menu. Try the Medium Contrast (default setting), as it will increase contrast and color saturation.

Note

The changes you make in the Point tab are not reflected in the Parametric tab.

Photoshop Curves vs. Camera Raw Curves

Curves in Photoshop and Camera Raw look similar but act differently. While working in Camera Raw, it is best to change perspectives and think about curves as a way to modify tone, as opposed to the ability to modify tone and individual color channels in Photoshop Curves.

#30 Adjusting Hue, Saturation, and Luminance

The sliders on the HSL/Grayscale tab allow you to make adjustments to a specific range of color. With these controls, you can boost the level of one color relative to others, or increase and decrease saturation and luminance (**Figure 30a**).

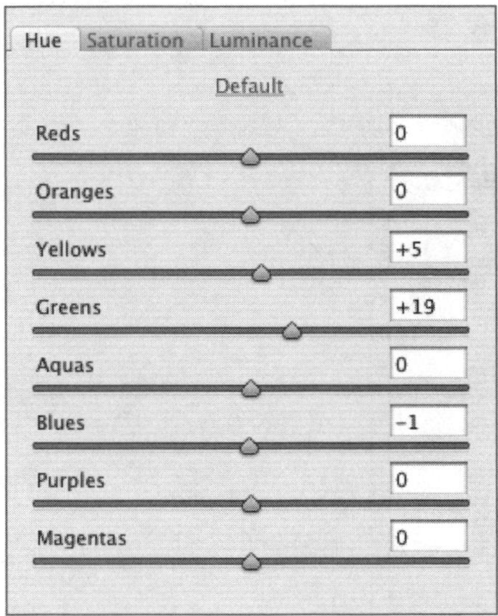

Figure 30a The Hue, Saturation, and Luminance tabs are nested within the HSL/Grayscale tab.

Each of the HSL tabs controls one aspect of color, and each slider on each tab controls the characteristics of a single color range:

- Hue changes the fundamental nature of a color within a limited range. In other words, you cannot change a blue to red, but you can change blue from cyan to purple.
- Saturation changes the vividness of a color. For instance, you can change a blue sky from gray (no color) to highly saturated blue.
- Luminance changes the brightness of the color range.

To get a better handle on HSL, let's consider the following scenario: You have created a beautiful landscape photograph. The image is good, yet you want to enhance the blue sky color. How would you do it?

1. Click the Hue tab and drag the Blues slider to dial in the exact shade of blue you want.
2. Click the Saturation tab and drag the Blues slider to the right to increase the saturation of the blue tones in the image.
3. Click the Luminance tab and drag the Blues slider to the left to make the sky a deeper and darker blue (**Figure 30b**).

Figure 30b The color of the sky in the left half of this image was deepened using the HSL controls.

This scenario is a good example of times when you will utilize all three HSL tabs to produce the desired result. Other times, the best result will be produced by using just one HSL tab.

Why Invest Time in Learning HSL?

With HSL, your creative potential is nearly unlimited, so it's a good idea to spend some time experimenting with it. Because HSL provides a new way to modify and think about color and tone, spending a lot of time with it can help you fine-tune your sense of how color and tone are closely connected. Ultimately, this will help you get the most out of the HSL adjustment sliders.

#31 Creating Black-and-White Images

Software Safety Nets

Suppose you're fiddling with the sliders on the Grayscale Mix tab to create a custom black-and-white conversion, and you decide that you hate what you've come up with. Camera Raw provides two easy ways of starting over. Click Auto at the top of the tab to return to the automatic conversion that Camera Raw produced when you first selected Convert to Grayscale. Alternatively, click Default to reset all of the sliders to their zero position.

Creating stunning black-and-white images is now easier than ever using Camera Raw. If you haven't worked with black and white, now is the time. You can apply an automatic grayscale conversion by selecting the Convert to Grayscale option at the top of the HSL/Grayscale tab (**Figure 31a**).

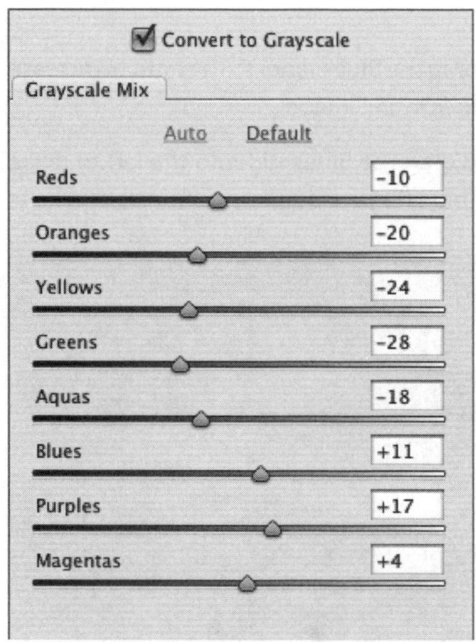

Figure 31a Select Convert to Grayscale to make a custom grayscale conversion.

Camera Raw makes its best guess at a good grayscale conversion based on the image's white balance setting, and the Hue, Saturation, and Luminance tabs are replaced by a single Grayscale Mix tab. The sliders on this tab show the relative proportions of different colors in the image that Camera Raw chose to mix together to create the grayscale image.

Of course, you're not stuck with the choices made by Camera Raw. For the best results, use the Grayscale Mix sliders. Drag these sliders to make specific color ranges lighter or darker to determine the contribution of each color to the grayscale version of the image.

For example, in a photograph of my daughter Annika, I wanted to modify the tonality of her blue jeans overalls. Because the overalls represent the only blue in the image, I was able to modify the tonality using the Blues slider on the Grayscale Mix tab. Dragging the slider to the left darkens the blue in her overalls (**Figure 31b**).

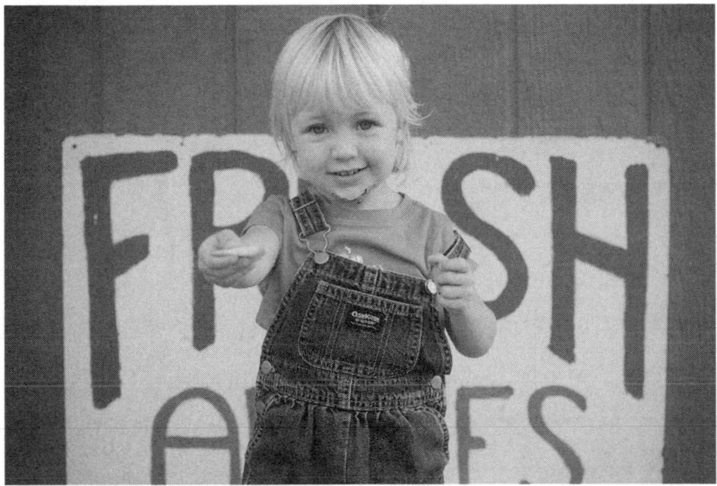

Figure 31b The Blues slider on the Grayscale Mix tab has been dragged to the left, resulting in the darker blue jean overalls.

Dragging the slider to the right has the opposite effect (**Figure 31c**).

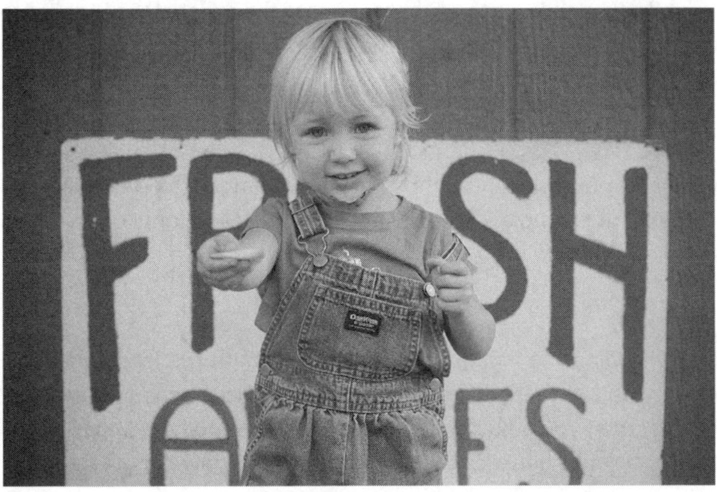

Figure 31c Dragging the Blues slider to the right lightens the overalls.

Creating the Best Black and White

One of the advantages of using the Grayscale Mix sliders to create a black-and-white image is that they don't affect the overall tone, brightness, or contrast in the image. But sometimes you can improve your conversion by using the controls on the Basic and Tone Curve tabs as well.

Once you've adjusted the Grayscale Mix sliders, be sure to revisit the Basic and Tone Curve tabs to make final contrast and tone adjustments.

#32 Using Split Toning

Why Split Tone Color Images?

The primary intent of the Split Toning tab is to modify grayscale images. However, the Split Toning controls can be used to create special effects (like cross-processing) when used to modify color images.

To add color to a grayscale image (or tweak the color of a color image), use the controls in the Split Toning tab. Notice that the Split Toning tab has Hue and Saturation sliders for both highlight and shadow areas. The Balance slider lets you adjust the relative influence of the highlight and shadow controls (**Figure 32**).

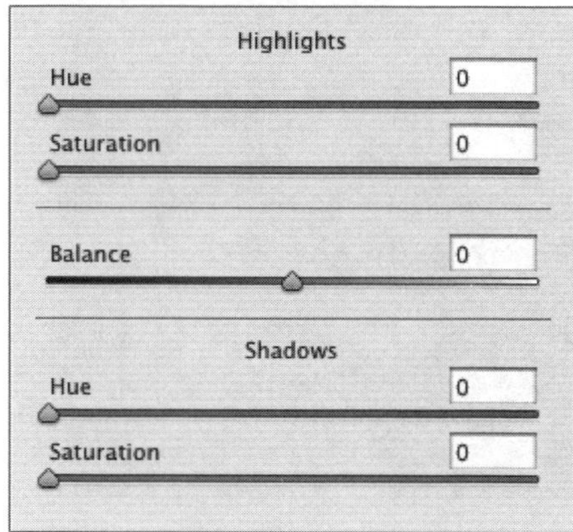

Figure 32 Use the controls in the Split Toning tab to add color to both grayscale and color images.

In either the Highlights or Shadows area, start by dragging the Hue slider to select the color that you would like to add to the image. Then drag the Saturation slider to control the color intensity. Finally, if needed, drag the Balance slider to the right to increase the effect of the Highlights controls on the image; or drag to the left to give the Shadows settings more prominence.

Sepia tone

You can add one color throughout the tonal range—to create a sepia tone effect, for example—by adjusting only the Highlights or Shadows sliders.

Split tone

To create a split tone image, you must adjust both the Highlights and Shadows sliders so that a different color is applied to the shadows and the highlights. Then you adjust the Balance slider to modify the intensity of the toning balance between the Highlight and Shadow controls.

> ***Note***
> *When using the Split Toning sliders, the added tone does not affect the extreme shadows and highlights, as they remain black and white.*

#33 Using Lens Corrections

The Lens Corrections tab is designed to give photographers a tool to fix common problems with photographic hardware, such as lens vignetting and chromatic aberration. However, this tab also provides creative photographic controls that go well beyond the simple functionality of fixing problems.

Fixing lens vignetting

Vignetting is a lens defect that occurs with certain lenses (especially wide angle lenses), causing the edges and especially the corners of an image to be darker. In many instances, especially in architectural photography, the result of lens vignetting is undesirable. You can use the Lens Vignetting sliders to compensate or remove the vignetting (**Figure 33a**).

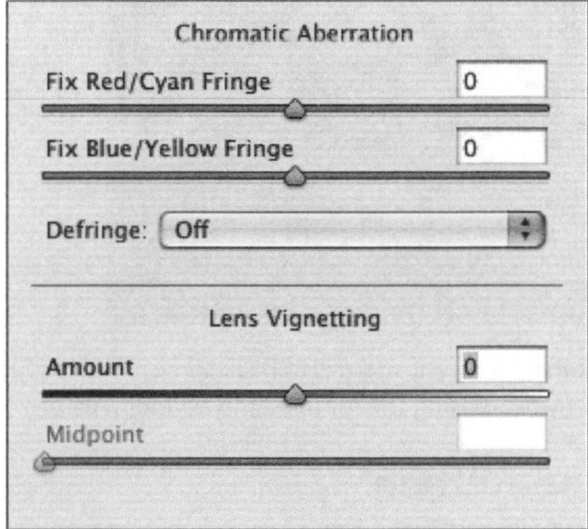

Figure 33a Use the controls on the Lens Corrections tab for creative results or to fix lens vignetting or chromatic aberration.

Drag the Amount slider to the right to lighten the corners, or drag to the left to darken the corners.

Use the Midpoint slider to expand or contract the vignetting effect. For example, you might drag the Amount slider to the left to darken the corners. Then you might decrease the Midpoint value to increase the "reach" of the vignetting so that the darkening extends from the corners toward the center of the image. Conversely, you could increase the Midpoint value to restrict the darkening adjustment to an area closer to the corners.

Adding creative lens vignetting

Many photographers are now using the Lens Vignetting controls to darken the corners of images (**Figure 33b**). This special effect adds a unique look and feel. Adding a lens vignette will affect the overall tone of an image. Thus, once you have applied the effect, be sure to go back to the Basic and Tone Curve tabs to make final tone adjustments.

Figure 33b This photograph was taken on a recent surf trip to Baja, Mexico. The lens vignetting was added in Camera Raw by decreasing the Amount and Midpoint values.

Correcting chromatic aberration

Chromatic aberration is a lens defect that results in images with *color fringing*, in which the details near the corners of an image have a red or cyan fringe. To identify chromatic aberration, zoom in to an area near the corner of an image and look for color fringing. While color fringing isn't all that common, except when using wide angle lenses, it's worth noting how to fix it in case you encounter it.

In the Camera Raw Lens Corrections tab, adjust either of the Fix Red/Cyan Fringe or Fix Blue/Yellow Fringe sliders. As you adjust these controls to the left and right, watch the fringe in the image increase or decrease until you find the correct setting. The goal is to remove as much of the color fringing as possible.

> ***Tip***
>
> *When adjusting one of the Chromatic Aberration sliders, press and hold Alt (Windows) or Option (Mac) to hide fringes of other colors. This way you can focus in on the color fringing that you are attempting to fix.*

#34 Retouching

Camera Raw is equipped with a Retouch tool, which is very effective at general retouching. You can use it to remove or reduce unwanted distractions, blemishes, dust, scratches, and so on. However, keep in mind that it's better to perform fine retouching in Photoshop, since that program provides more detail control. The advantage of retouching in Camera Raw is that it is nondestructive and doesn't drastically increase your file size.

To begin retouching in Camera Raw, follow the steps below:

1. Choose the Retouch tool in the Camera Raw toolbar and choose from the Type menu the kind of retouching you want to do: Heal or Clone (see the sidebar) (**Figure 34a**).

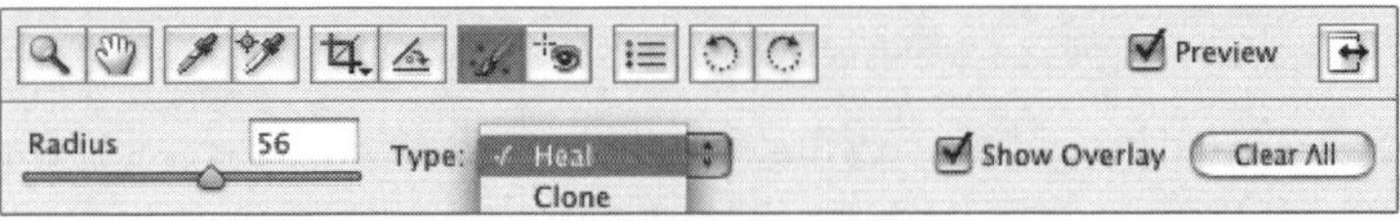

Figure 34a Choose the Retouch tool and then choose Heal or Clone.

2. Move the Radius slider to the right or left to increase or decrease the area affected by the tool.

3. In the image, click the spot to be retouched. Two circles will appear: a red circle shows the area being retouched, and the green circle indicates the source area for retouching.

4. To reposition either circle, simply drag within it. To increase or decrease the size of either circle, hover over the circle edge until the cursor becomes a double arrow, and then drag (**Figure 34b**).

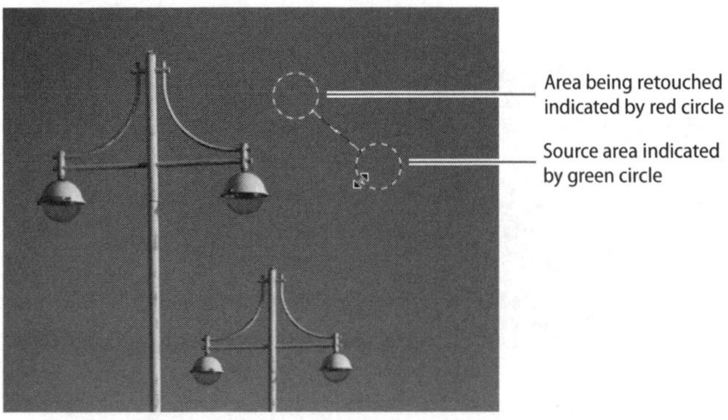

Figure 34b Resize the Retouch tool by dragging the edge of either circle. You can also drag either circle to reposition it.

Clone and Heal in Camera Raw

The Camera Raw Heal and Clone tools work identically to the Healing and Cloning tools in Photoshop. Both tools sample and copy pixels to another area in the image. The main difference between the tools is that the Healing tool carefully blends the texture of the copied area (the source) with the pixels in the area being retouched, while the Clone tool copies and pastes pixels from the source without the careful blending.

#35 Removing Red Eye

Most cameras today come equipped with a red-eye reduction flash setting. However, this feature doesn't always do the trick, especially when using small point-and-shoot cameras whose flash units are very close to their lenses.

To remove red eye using Camera Raw:

1. Choose the Red Eye Removal tool from the toolbar (**Figure 35a**).

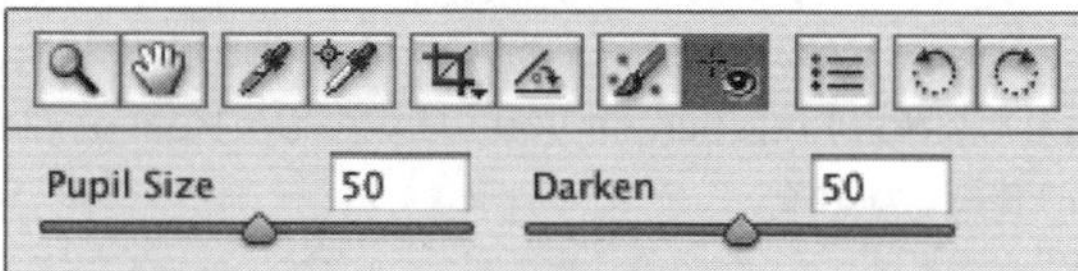

Figure 35a The Red Eye Removal tool.

2. Drag a rectangle around the eye. It is best to create a rectangle that is slightly bigger than the iris (**Figure 35b**).

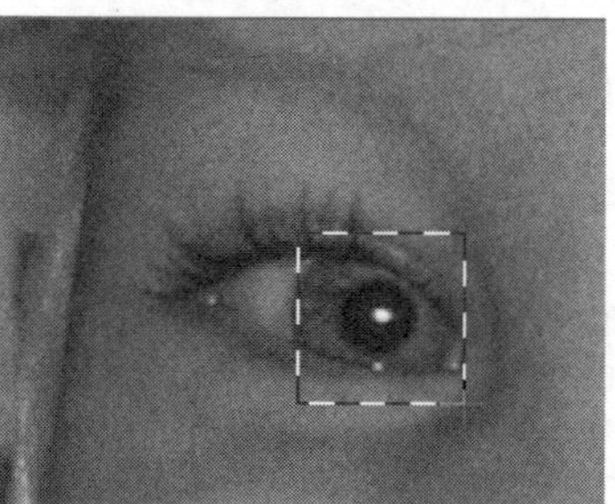

Figure 35b Drag to create a rectangle a bit bigger than the iris of the eye.

3. When you release the mouse button, the selection will reduce to the size of the red area (**Figure 35c**).

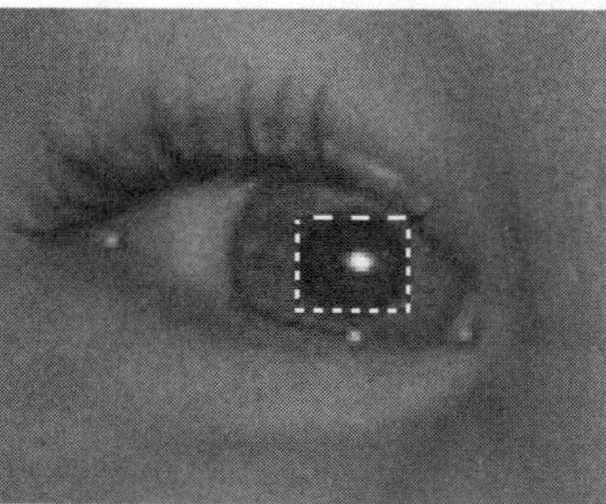

Figure 35c The red area is selected.

4. Modify the Pupil and Darken sliders to fine-tune the correction.

   Repeat these steps for other eyes that need correction.

#36 Cropping, Rotating, and Straightening

The advantage of cropping, rotating, and straightening in Camera Raw is simple: What would be destructive in Photoshop can be done nondestructively in Camera Raw. The ability to reconstruct the image to its pre-cropped, rotated, or straightened state provides a creative "safety net" that is helpful for the amateur and pro alike.

Arbitrary Rotation

You can also arbitrarily rotate an image using the Crop tool:

1. First create a crop area as described on this page.
2. Next, move the cursor toward one of the four corner points of the crop. When you see the cursor change appearance so that is it has two arrows, drag to rotate the crop area.

Cropping and rotating

To crop an image in Camera Raw:

1. Open an image in Camera Raw. Click and hold on the Crop tool to choose a preset aspect ratio for your crop area. You can also use this menu to clear a current crop.
2. To define a crop area, drag out a rectangle around the area that you want to preserve. The part of the image that will be cropped is grayed out (**Figure 36a**).

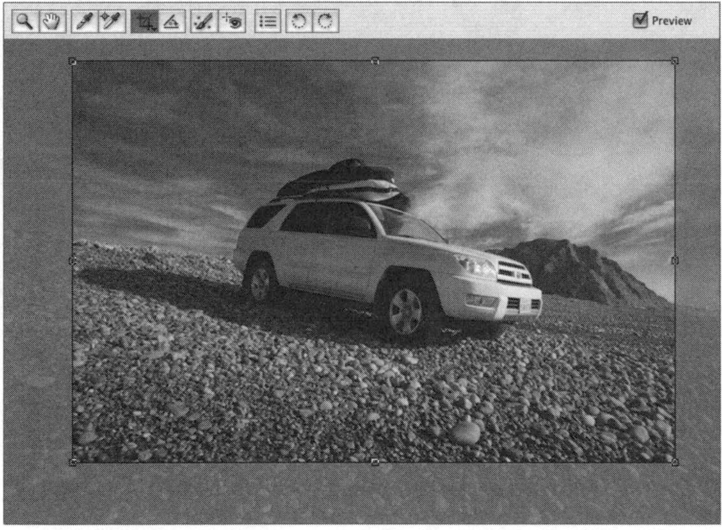

Figure 36a Drag a rectangle around the area you want to keep.

3. To modify the size of the crop, drag any of the middle or corner anchor points.
4. To reposition the crop area, click anywhere inside it and drag.

(continued on next page)

If You Change Your Mind

You can clear the crop area, or cancel a rotation or straightening operation at any time by pressing the Esc key.

5. When you are satisfied with your crop, click one of the buttons in the bottom right corner:
   - Open Image to view the cropped image in Photoshop
   - Done to return to Bridge. The image thumbnail will be updated to reflect the new crop.

Straightening

An important element of a photograph is a level horizon line. The Straighten tool can help you level or straighten your image in no time at all. Choose the Straighten tool on the toolbar and drag along an object in the image that should be level. This will automatically rotate the image so that the line that you created is straight (**Figure 36b**).

Figure 36b Drag with the Straighten tool along a line that ought to be horizontal.

#37 Sharpening and Reducing Noise

The Sharpening and Noise Reduction controls are located on the Detail tab (**Figure 37**).

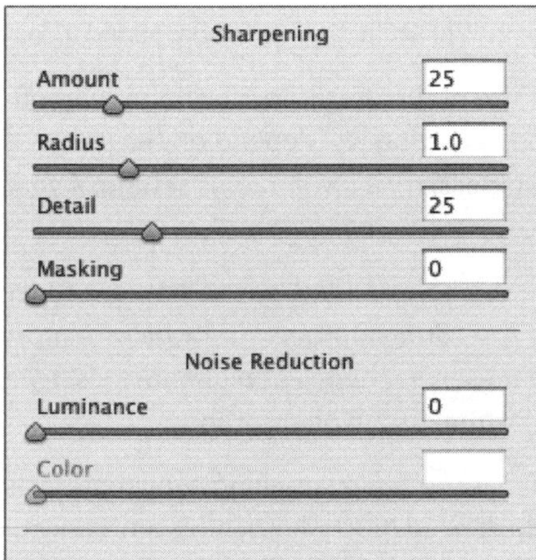

Figure 37 The Detail tab.

To achieve the best results with these controls, be sure to change your zoom level to 100%. Choose the zoom level from the menu on the lower left of the Camera Raw window.

Tip
The quickest way to change your zoom to 100% is to double-click the Zoom tool button in the toolbar.

Sharpening

The type and intensity of sharpening that you apply is contingent upon the image itself. Because of the many variations in photographs, sharpening is more of an art than a formula. To sharpen effectively, you need to learn about the basic principles and then apply those to a particular image. In Camera Raw, the Sharpening sliders affect only the luminosity information in the image; that is, the light and dark values of each pixel. Color information is not changed.

Typically, it is best to begin your adjustments using the Amount and Radius sliders on the Detail tab, which control how much sharpening is applied to the entire image and how it is applied. Then move on to the Detail and Masking sliders to dial back the sharpening in certain areas:

Advanced Sharpening

While adjusting any of the Sharpening sliders, hold down Alt (Windows) or Option (Mac) to get a grayscale display of the results of your work. What is displayed is not the same for each slider, though:

- When dragging the Amount slider, the grayscale image shows the full effect on the Luminosity channel of all the sharpening adjustments you've made.
- Dragging the Radius or Detail slider reveals the degree to which the image is being sharpened (dark areas are sharpened more, light areas less).
- The grayscale image displayed when dragging the Masking slider shows the actual mask, applied to the image, in which black corresponds to no sharpening and white corresponds to sharpening.

- The Amount slider adjusts edge definition. A value of zero equals zero sharpening. Increase the Amount value to sharpen the whole image. Typically, it is best to set a lower value for this control, because high values tend to create "halos," or visible artifacts around sharpened areas.
- The Radius slider adjusts the size of the details to which the sharpening is applied. The correct Radius setting will depend on the image. If you have an image with fine details, try a lower radius setting; if your image is dominated by large objects, try a higher radius.
- The Detail slider tones down the halos added by the Amount slider while keeping edges sharp. A setting of 0 gets rid of halos almost entirely, and a setting of 100 preserves them. For blurry images, try a lower setting. To emphasize texture, try a higher setting.
- The Masking slider applies a mask to the sharpening, which protects relatively smooth areas that don't need much sharpening, and concentrates the sharpening along the edges of items. (I'll talk about masks in chapter 5, but for the moment just remember that in Photoshop, a mask is a technique for protecting part of an image from a editing, like masking tape). In the Masking slider, a setting of zero means everything in the image receives an equal amount of sharpening. With a setting of 100, sharpening is mostly limited to the strongest edges.

Noise reduction

The Noise Reduction sliders can be used to improve images that have noise (visible artifacts that degrade the image). Noise often occurs as a result of shooting with a high ISO, improper exposure, or a low-quality digital capture. These sliders are not a cure-all for noise, but for many of us, they are a regular step in our photographic workflow.

Drag the Luminance slider to the right to reduce grayscale noise. This will smooth out the irregular shape and size of noise. Drag the Color slider to the right to reduce color noise. When reducing noise, be careful not increase the settings so high as to over-soften the image.

Tip

If an image has a high amount of noise, using Noise Reduction in Camera Raw is a good starting point. If you need to reduce further, try the Reduce Noise Filter in Photoshop or one of the many Noise Reduction plug-ins that you can purchase separately.

#38 Processing Multiple Images

One of the many advantages of working with Camera Raw is that it speeds up your workflow. In particular, Camera Raw enables you to make edits to multiple images in a relatively short amount of time.

Synchronizing settings

In Adobe Bridge, select multiple files and open them in Camera Raw. Thumbnails of your selected images will appear in a vertical column—the Filmstrip pane—on the left side of the Camera Raw window (**Figure 38a**).

Figure 38a The Filmstrip displays multiple images at once.

At this stage, there are multiple strategies for processing the images. Choose the strategy that best fits your workflow needs:

- Make a selection of images from the Filmstrip pane or click the Select All button to select all of them. Now when you modify any of the Camera Raw controls, the modification will be applied to all the images.

(continued on next page)

Save Photoshop Camera Raw Settings

As you develop your Camera Raw workflow, you may discover that you tend to use specific adjustments over and over again. In this case, saving those adjustments as a preset can be a real time-saver. Open the Camera Raw Settings menu (click the icon in the upper right of the image adjustment tab area), and choose Save Settings. There are also a number of resources where you can download or purchase prebuilt Camera Raw settings, such as http://getit.davidjay.com/

Copy and Paste Settings

You can also use Bridge to apply Camera Raw settings to multiple files by copying and pasting:

1. In Bridge, select an image that has been edited in Camera Raw.
2. Choose Edit > Develop Settings > Copy Camera Raw Settings.
3. Select one or more files, and choose Edit > Develop Settings > Paste Settings.

- Select a single image. Click the Select All button and then click the Synchronize button. This opens the Synchronize dialog box, which allows you to choose which adjustments will be applied to all selected images. Select the check boxes for the specific settings (such as exposure, white balance, and so on) that you would like to synchronize (**Figure 38b**).

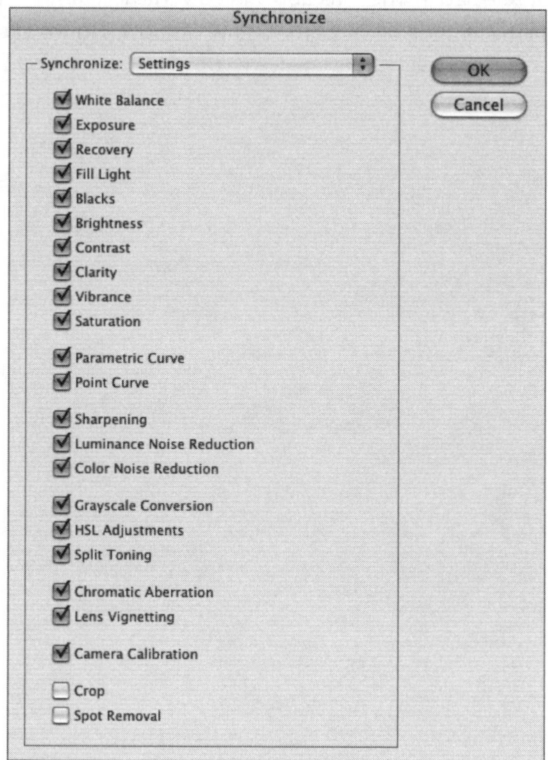

Figure 38b The Synchronize dialog box.

Tip

In Bridge, the quickest way to access the Copy and Paste Camera Raw Settings commands is to use the context menu. Right-click (Windows) or Control-click (Mac) the thumbnail of the image whose settings you want to copy and choose Copy Camera Raw Settings from the Develop Settings submenu. You can then use the context menu to apply the settings to any images you want.

CHAPTER FIVE

Working with Layers

Layers are integral to working in Photoshop. They allow you to keep image elements and adjustments separate from one another so that you can move them independently and enable or disable them at will. You can think of layers as being like sheets of clear transparent film stacked one on top of the other.

Here's a quick example of how layers work: Say you have a single layer Photoshop document that contains an image, and you want to add text on top of the image. To do this, you choose the Type tool and click within the document window. This adds a type layer above the image. The result is a document that contains two layers: the bottom layer contains the image, and the top layer contains the type. Each of these layers can be dealt with individually.

Layers can be used for a wide array of tasks, such as compositing multiple images, adding text to an image, adding vector graphics, making color and tone adjustments, converting an image to black and white, adding special effects to an image, and more. The advantage of a layers-based workflow is that you can make edits nondestructively. For example, if you're using a color image as the background layer, you can add an adjustment layer to convert that background layer to black and white. This type of edit is nondestructive because it is not permanent. If you decide that you don't like the black-and-white adjustment, you can simply hide or delete the layer.

Because layers are essential to nondestructive image editing, you should strive to become adept at using them. Layers are an integral part of a sound photographic workflow. Getting into the habit of using them can help you work more efficiently, with more creative results.

#39 Using the Layers Palette

The Layers palette displays the layer structure of your Photoshop file. It also includes controls for manipulating layers, including creating new ones and deleting old ones, changing the layer stacking order, changing the visibility of layers, collecting layers into groups, and adding layer effects.

To view the Layers palette, choose Window > Layers or press F7 (**Figure 39a**).

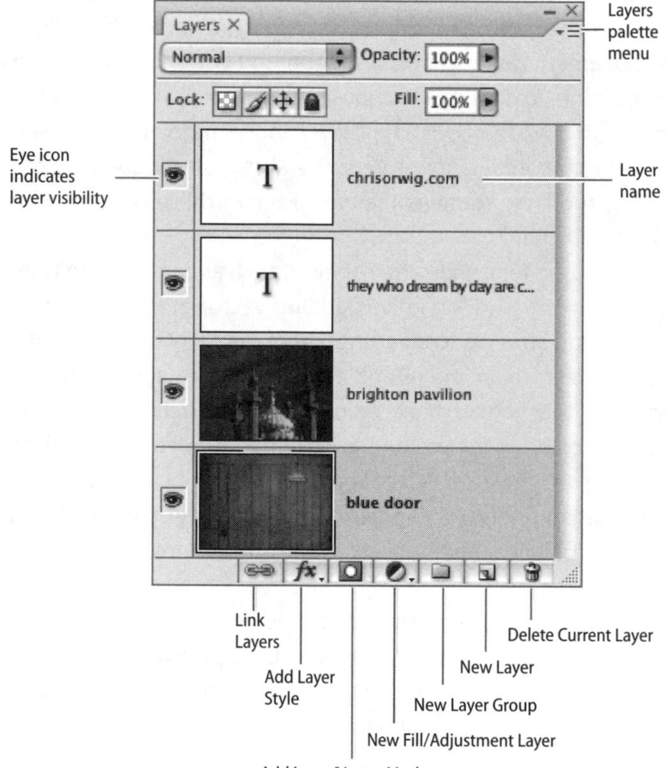

Figure 39a The Layers palette.

The buttons located along the bottom of the palette perform these functions:

- **Link Layers.** Links two or more layers. When one linked layer is repositioned or transformed, all linked layers are simultaneously repositioned or transformed.

Background Information

Most Photoshop images start off with a single layer called *Background*. This layer has very special properties: It can't have any transparent pixels, its opacity can't be adjusted, it can't be moved (either dragged within the image frame or by restacking), and its blending mode can't be changed.

But it's easy to convert the background into a normal layer: Double-click it in the Layers palette, and the New Layer dialog box opens. Type a name for the converted layer in the Name field and click OK.

Fun Fact

How many layers can be created in one Photoshop document? The layer limit per document is a whopping 8,000 layers!

- **Add Layer Style.** Creates a variety of effects, such as shadows, glows, and bevels, that change the appearance of a layer. Layer effects are linked to the layer contents.
- **Add Layer Mask.** Creates a mask, which can be used to show or hide portions of the layer and reveal the layers below. Masking layers is a valuable technique for combining multiple photos into a single image or for making local color and tonal corrections.
- **New Adjustment Layer.** Adds an adjustment layer to the image, which allows you to edit color and tone nondestructively (see the next How-To for more information).
- **New Layer Group.** Organizes selected layers by placing them in a folder.
- **New Layer.** Creates a new layer above the currently targeted layer. To create a layer below the currently selected layer, press Ctrl (Windows) or Command (Mac) while clicking the New Layer button.
- **Delete Current Layer.** Deletes the currently selected layer(s).

You can toggle the visibility of layers on or off by clicking the Eye icon to the left of a specific layer. Rename a layer by double-clicking its name (in the Layers palette) and then typing.

Layers are indispensable when creating composite images, such as the one shown in **Figure 39b**, which illustrates the combination of text and image layers shown in Figure 39a.

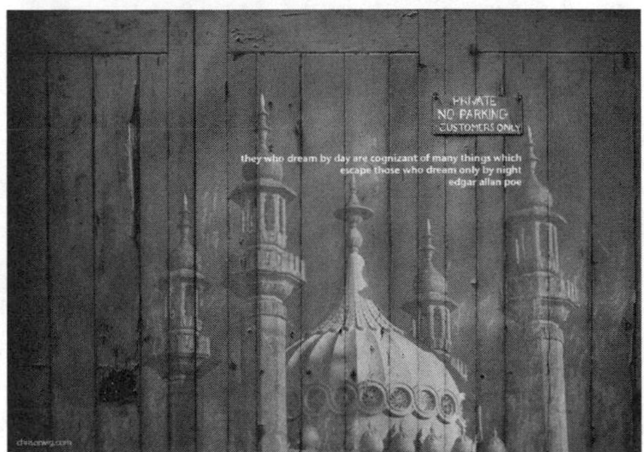

Figure 39b The image that results from the combination of the layers shown in Figure 39a.

Duplicating Layers

If you want to try out some edits on an image, but you want to preserve the original, make a duplicate of the layer you're working on first. Select the layer (or Background) and press Ctrl + J (Windows) or Command + J (Mac).

Worried About Layers and File Size?

If you're new to using layers, you may find yourself concerned about creating too many layers and unnecessarily increasing the file size. While this is a valid concern—we always need to be concerned about file sizes—keep it mind that layers expand your creative potential. In many cases, the benefits you gain by expanding and experimenting with layers far outweigh the extra file size.

#40 Using Adjustment Layers

Chapter 9 introduces you to the various commands on the Image > Adjustments submenu that you'll use to alter the tone and color characteristics of your pictures. There's one problem with those commands, though: Their effects are permanent. They change the actual pixels in your image, and if you change your mind later, you're stuck (unless you use the Undo command immediately, of course).

Now, one of the most celebrated aspects of digital photography is flexibility, and adjustment layers provide this in spades. Adjustment layers apply color and tonal adjustments to your image nondestructively; that is, without permanently changing pixel values. The advantages of nondestructive adjustments are twofold: First, they give you the ability to undo or remove an adjustment and restore the image to its original state. Second, the ability to undo can act as a safety net, which allows for more creative experimentation.

To add an adjustment layer to an image, click the Create New Adjustment Layer button at the bottom of the Layers palette and choose a type of adjustment layer from the menu (**Figure 40**). The dialog box for the particular adjustment you chose displays.

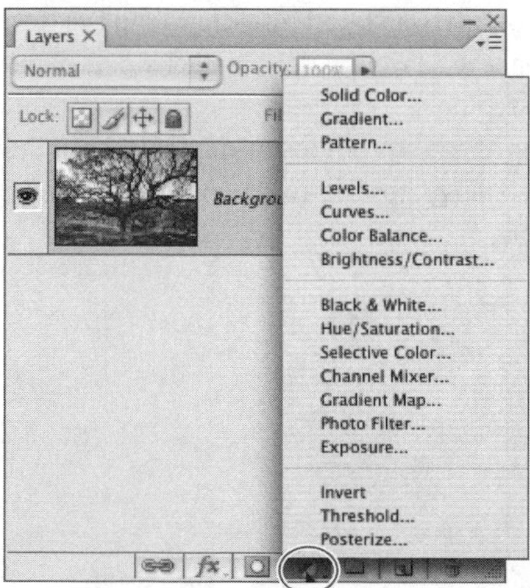

Figure 40 Click the Create New Adjustment Layer button to open the menu showing the available types of adjustment layers.

Note

Adjustment layers have built-in layer masks that give you the ability to use the paint or fill tools to specify what part of the image will be modified. For more on masking, read Chapter 10.

Modifying Adjustment Layers

You can reopen the settings dialog box for an adjustment layer by double-clicking the adjustment layer thumbnail in the Layers palette. This allows you to change the layer settings after you've created it.

Adjustment layers have many of the same properties as other layers. For example, you can turn their visibility on and off to apply their effect or to preview the effect. Or try lowering the opacity of an adjustment layer to lower the intensity of the effect.

#41 Using Shape Layers

You can create a wide array of shapes in Photoshop by using shape layers. Shape layers are useful because their contours are defined by vectors rather than pixels. A *vector* is a graphic element that is defined mathematically, and creates a crisp, smooth outline no matter its resolution.

To create a Shape layer:

1. Click the Shape tool button and select one of the shape tools (**Figure 41a**).

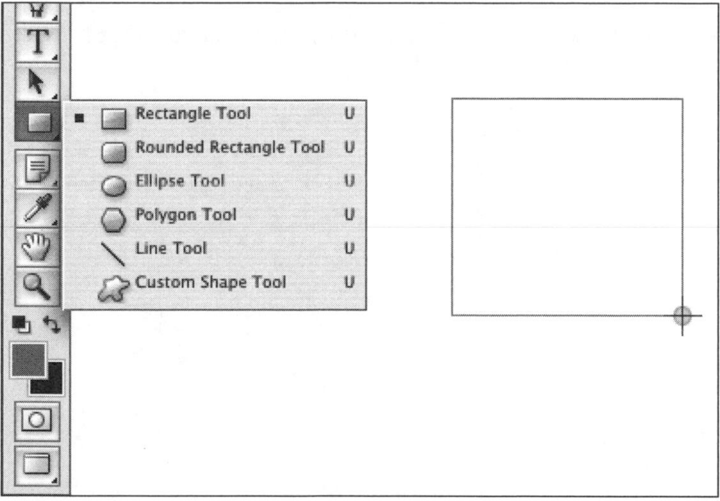

Figure 41a Choose the desired shape tool from the Toolbox. In this example, the Rectangle tool is selected. Drag with the tool in your image to create a shape.

2. Click the Shape Layers button in the options bar (**Figure 41b**).

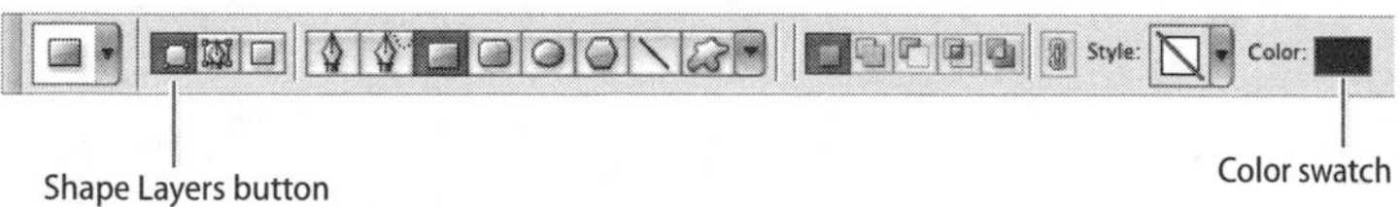

Figure 41b The options bar when a shape tool is active.

3. Click the color swatch in the options bar, and then choose a fill color for the shape from the Color Picker.

(continued on next page)

Editing Shapes

A shape is a fill layer linked to a vector mask. To change the fill or outline, do one of the following:

- Change the color of a shape by double-clicking the shape thumbnail in the Layers palette. Next, choose a different color using the Color Picker.
- To change the outline of a shape, begin by clicking the shape vector mask thumbnail in the Layers palette or Paths palette. Next, modify the shape using one of the shape and/or Pen tools.
- Move a shape without modifying its appearance by holding down the spacebar and dragging the shape to a new location.

4. Drag over your image to draw a shape. To constrain the shape, hold the Shift key as you drag. Doing so constrains a rectangle or rounded rectangle to a square, an ellipse to a circle, or a line angle to a multiple of 45 degrees.

Notes

You can set tool options in the options bar. Be sure to click the inverted arrow next to the shape buttons to access additional options for each tool.

To apply a style to the shape, select a preset style from the Style menu in the options bar.

#42 Using Type Layers

In Photoshop, text elements reside on their own layers, separate from bitmap image elements. A type layer is a vector layer (like a shape layer), so it can be scaled without losing any quality or detail. The type also remains editable, so you change the words or other attributes (like typeface, font size, or font color) at any time.

To add text to an image:

1. Choose the Text tool from the Toolbox or press the T key.
2. From the options bar, choose a font and set the size and color of the font (**Figure 42a**).

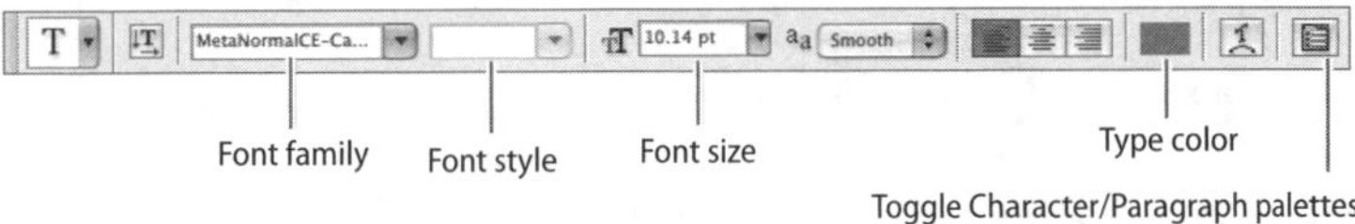

Figure 42a With the Type tool active, the options bar displays commands for formatting text.

3. Click in the document window and start typing to add text—a new type layer is created automatically.
4. When you've finished entering text, press the Enter key on the numeric keypad to commit your changes to the type layer.

Edit text just like you would in a word processing document. Choose the Text tool and click anywhere within the text to place the insertion point. Either start typing to add new text, or select existing text by double-clicking or by dragging (**Figure 42b**). Selected text can be replaced by typing, or reformatted by choosing new options from the options bar.

Figure 42b Selected text can be formatted or edited.

A wider range of text formatting options than you get in the options bar is available in the Character palette. Make sure a text layer is selected,

Text Speed Tip

The quickest way to select and modify text is by way of the Layers palette. When you create a text layer, it is marked in the Layers palette with a "T" icon. Double-click the text layer icon "T" in the Layers palette to select all the text on that layer. Make any needed changes and then press the Enter key on the numeric keypad to commit your changes.

and then click the Toggle Character/Paragraph palettes button on the options bar, or choose Window > Character (**Figure 42c**).

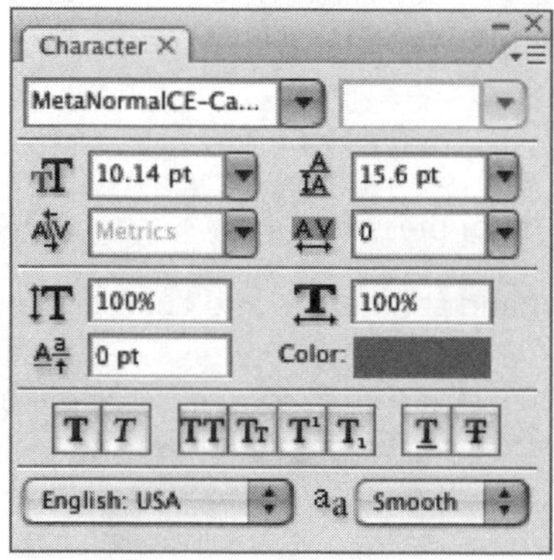

Figure 42c For an exhaustive set of text formatting controls, use the Character palette.

> ***Note***
>
> *To perform some operations on type, including applying some filters and painting with brushes, you must first* rasterize *the type layer. Rasterizing type converts it from vector art to pixel-based art (like ordinary photographic data), rendering the text uneditable. To Rasterize type, select the type layer and choose Layer > Rasterize > Type.*

#43 Using Layer Effects and Styles

In Photoshop, you'll find a whole arsenal of special *layer effects* that you can use to dress up the contents of a layer. These effects take the form of shadows, glows, 3-dimensional appearances, overlays, and many more. You can apply more than one effect to a layer—all of the effects applied to a layer taken together constitute a *layer style*.

Layer effects are linked to layers in the sense that they conform to the contents of the layer. Because of this, when you move or edit the layer, the effects adapt to the modified content. For example, if you add a drop shadow effect to a type layer, you can then edit the text or modify the characteristics of the font and the effect will be applied to the newly modified type. This flexibility makes layer effects and layer styles practical tools in anyone's workflow.

To create a layer style, start by adding a layer effect to a layer. Click the Add Layer Style icon at the bottom of the Layers palette and choose an effect from the menu (**Figure 43a**).

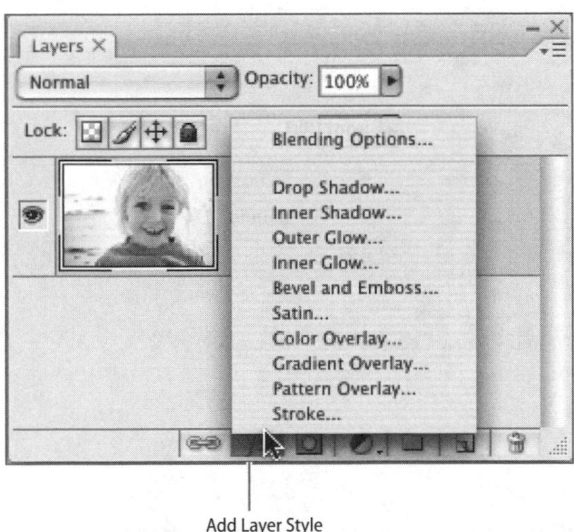

Figure 43a Click the Add Layer Style icon to choose a layer effect.

Choose one of the following effects:

- **Drop Shadow.** A shadow that appears behind, and offset from, the layer contents.

(continued on next page)

- **Inner Shadow.** A shadow that appears just inside the edges of the layer's content, giving the layer a hollowed-out appearance.
- **Outer Glow and Inner Glow.** Glows that project out from the content, or hug the inside edges of the layer's content.
- **Bevel and Emboss.** Highlights and shadows that create a 3-dimensional appearance.
- **Satin.** Interior shading that creates a smoothly textured finish.
- **Color, Gradient, and Pattern Overlay.** Overlays the layer content with a color, a gradient, or a pattern.
- **Stroke.** Draws an outline around the layer contents.

The Layer Style dialog box opens, with the chosen layer effect selected (**Figure 43b**).

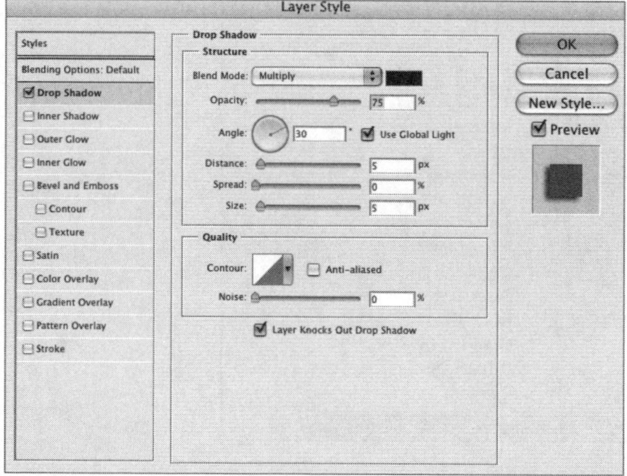

Figure 43b Choose options in the Layer Style dialog box for the selected effect. Click the checkboxes next the names of other effects to add those to the layer style.

To choose options for a layer style:

1. In the list on the left, add effects to the style by selecting the checkboxes next to their names.

2. Click the name of a layer effect to access the options for that effect.

3. To apply the effect, click OK.

In the Layers palette, the list of layer effects appears underneath the layer. Click the Eye icon to show or hide the effects. To the right of the layer name, the *fx* icon will show that one or more effects have been applied. Click the arrow on the far right to expand or collapse the list of effects (**Figure 43c**).

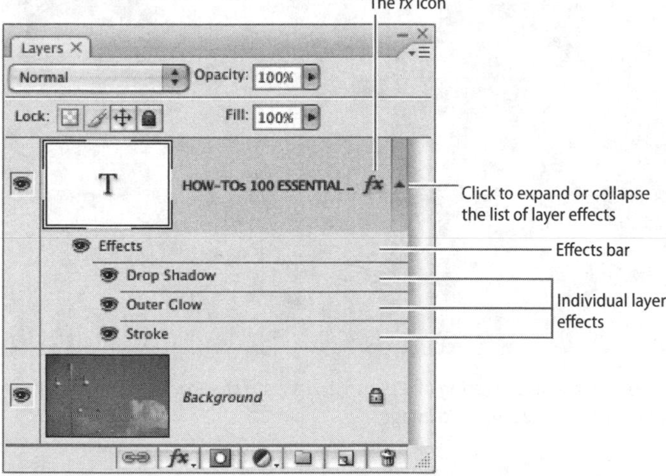

Figure 43c The *fx* icon indicates that effects have been applied to a layer. Click the arrow to the right of the *fx* icon to expand or collapse the view of the layer effects. Click the eye icon to show or hide each individual effect.

Quickly Copy Layer Styles

In certain instances, you will want to apply the same layer style to multiple layers. An example might be a document with five text layers that all need to have the same Stroke and Drop Shadow effects.

The most effective way to accomplish this is to apply the Stroke and Drop Shadow effects to one layer and then copy the layer style to the remaining four layers.

In the Layers palette, press Alt (Windows) or Option (Mac) and drag a single layer effect from one layer to another to another. To copy an entire layer style, hold Alt (Windows) or Option (Mac) and drag the effects bar from one layer to another.

If you were to carry out either of these drag operations without holding down the modifier key, you would move the effect or layer style from one layer to another, rather than duplicate it.

Create Layers from Layer Styles

Say that you've worked up an elaborate Photoshop file containing many layers using layer styles, and then you find that you need to use that image in an application that can't "read" Photoshop layer styles. You could flatten the image, but then you would lose all of the flexibility that a layered image affords you.

If the target application supports Photoshop layers, there's a compromise solution available to you: You can separate each layer style into a stack of layers, in which each layer effect is rasterized onto its own layer (see the note accompanying How-To #42 about rasterization). To do this, choose Layer > Layer Style > Create Layers to parse the various effects into separate layers.

Using layer styles can greatly enhance your work. In the following example, I have applied Stroke and Drop Shadow effects to the type layers to help separate the text from the background image (**Figure 43d**).

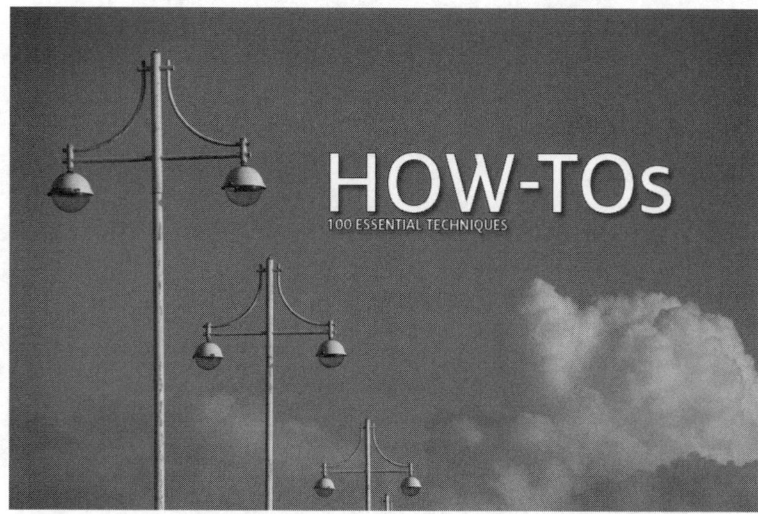

Figure 43d A layer style consisting of a stroke and a drop shadow help this type layer to stand out against the background image

Tip
In the Layers palette, double-click anywhere in the layer effects list (or the fx *icon itself if the layer effects list is closed) to reopen the Layer Style dialog box.*

#44 Working with Layer Groups

I recently completed a layered composite image of one of the fastest cyclists in the world: Ivan Basso of the Trek Discovery Team. I was really excited about the image, so I put in a lot of work into it. When I was finished, I counted 57 layers!

The only way to organize a complex image like that is using layer groups. Layer groups provide the capability to collect layers into folders. While not all images will have that many layers, just about any image can use some organization.

To create a new layer group using default options, do one of the following:

- Click the New Layer Group button in the Layers palette (see Figure 39a).
- Choose Layer > New > Group.
- Choose New Group from the Layers palette menu.

You may find it helpful to put similar layers in groups. For example, if you are retouching an image and you have multiple layers for clean up, multiple layers for enhancements, and multiple layers for color and tone adjustments, you might create layer groups named Clean Up, Enhance, and Color and Tone to organize and simplify your layers. Then rather than having to scroll through numerous layers, you can click on the group layer triangle icon to expand and collapse a particular folder (**Figure 44**).

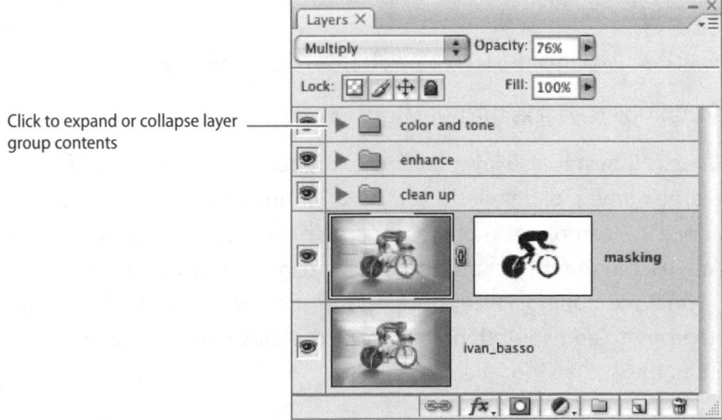

Figure 44 In this Photoshop file, layers are gathered into groups by function. To see the contents of a layer group, click the triangle next to its folder icon.

New Layer Group Speed Tip

When creating a new layer group, you can use a shortcut that enables you to open a dialog box and define a few settings. Simply press and hold Alt (Windows) or Option (Mac) while clicking the New Layer Group button in the Layers palette to display the New Group dialog box where you can set your layer group options:

- **Name.** Specifies a name for the group.
- **Color.** Assigns a color to the group in the Layers palette. This is for organizational purposes only. It will not affect the color of the layer group contents.
- **Mode.** Specifies a blending mode for the group.
- **Opacity.** Specifies an opacity level for the group.

When you are finished making your selections, click OK.

#45 Locking Layers

Locked or Not Locked?

When a layer is locked, a lock icon appears to the right of the layer name. The lock icon is solid when the layer is fully locked and hollow when the layer is partially locked.

Working with multiple layers can get tricky because it is possible to accidentally make changes that you did not intend to make. Fortunately, once you have made revisions to a layer, you can lock the layer (fully or partially) to protect its contents. Select the layer and click one of the layer locking icons located near the top of the Layers palette (**Figure 45**).

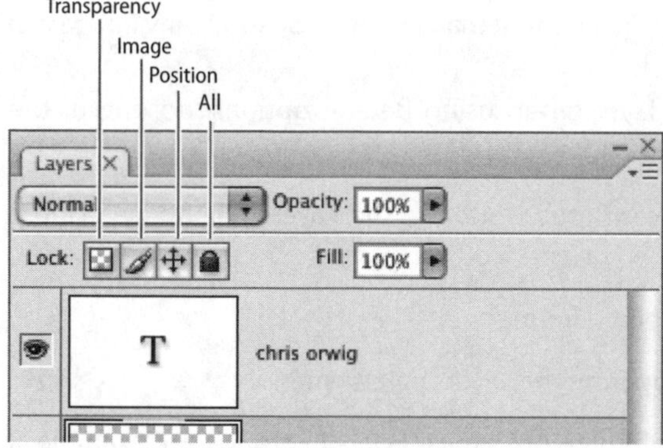

Figure 45 Layer-locking options.

You can choose from the following options in the Layers palette:

- **Transparency.** Preserves transparency by confining editing to the opaque portions of the layer.
- **Image.** Protects the layer's pixels by preventing modification with the painting tools.
- **Position.** Prevents the layer's pixels from being moved.
- **All.** Completely locks the layer from any type of editing.

When is it best to use layer locking? It depends on the image. If there are a large number of detailed layers, you will find it helpful to lock a layer fully once it is complete. In other scenarios, you may want to lock a layer partially if it has the correct transparency and image but you are uncertain of the final positioning. Finally, locking transparency is especially helpful if you desire to add something to a layer that has transparency without affecting the underlying layers.

#46 Using Auto-Align and Auto-Blend

Combining multiple exposures into one composite typically presents some challenges. In particular, exposure differences between source images may create seams or inconsistencies in the combined image. However, Auto-Align and Auto-Blend are two of the most exciting features in Photoshop CS3. Auto-Align lets you align two or more images that have similar content, whereas Auto-Blend lets you blend multiple images that have overlapping content in order to create a panoramic image. Together, these two features let you combine multiple exposures with ease and create the appearance of smooth transitions in the final images. These features are helpful for a wide range of photographic subject matter, such as architecture, people, panoramic landscapes, and more.

To combine two exposures into one composite image using the Auto-Align and Auto-Blend commands:

1. Copy or place the images you want to combine into the same document, keeping each image in a separate layer (**Figures 46a, 46b, 46c**).

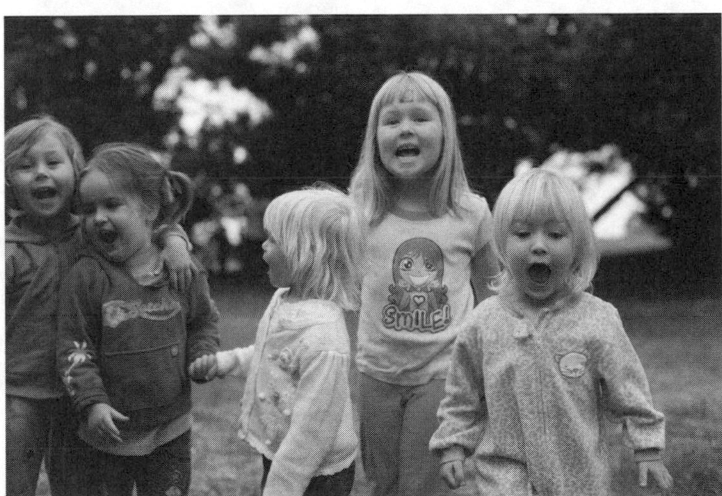

Figure 46a Original exposure 1.

(continued on next page)

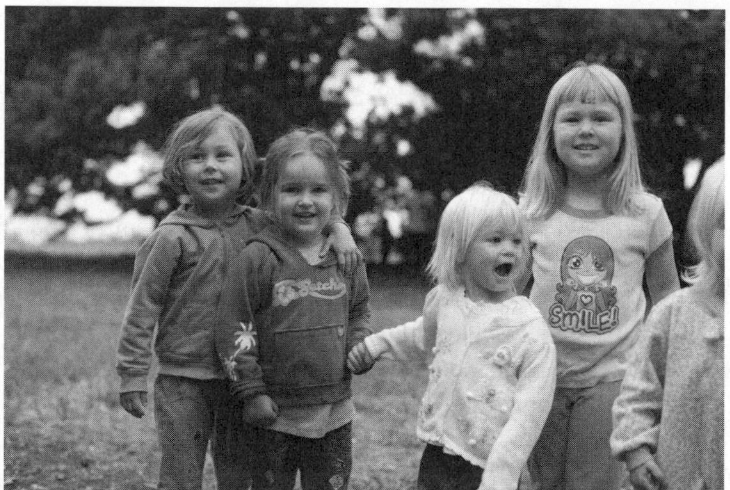

Figure 46b Original exposure 2.

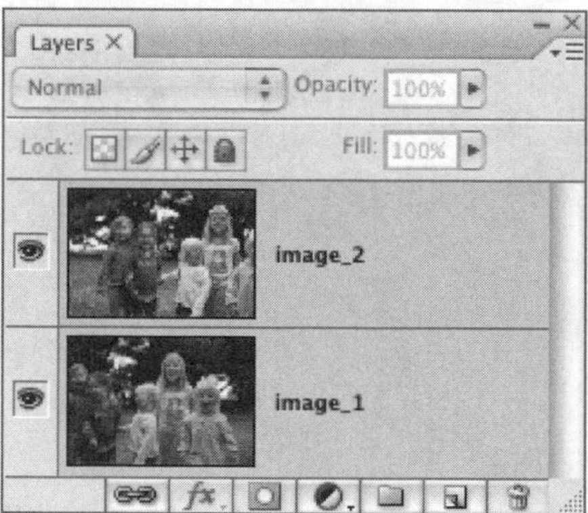

Figure 46c The original images combined in the one document. Both layers are unlocked.

2. Select both layers by Ctrl-clicking (Windows) or Command-clicking (Mac). Both layers are highlighted in the Layers palette.
3. Choose Edit > Auto Align Layers. The Auto-Align Layers dialog box appears.
4. The Auto-Align Layers dialog box offers several Projection options for combining the images. For most images, select Auto. This will scale, transform geometrically, and position the images so that they are aligned.

5. With the layers still selected, choose Edit > Auto-Blend Layers. Here is where the final touch of magic happens: Photoshop applies layer masks as needed to each layer to produce a seamless composite image (**Figures 46d, 46e**).

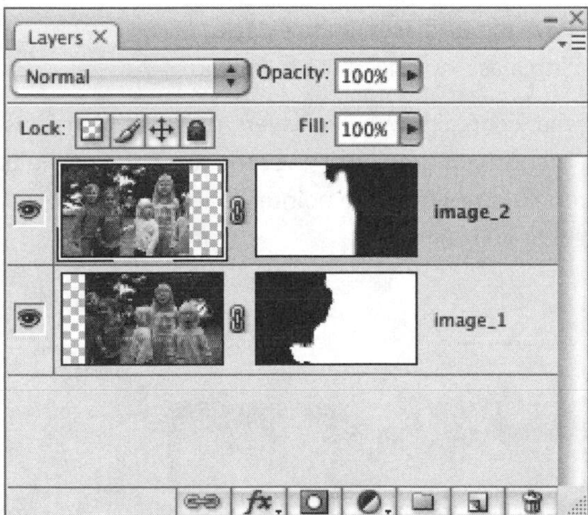

Figure 46d The Edit > Auto-Blend Layers command adds a layer mask to each layer base to seamlessly combine multiple layers.

Figure 46e The result of auto-alignment and auto-blending.

Note

Auto-Blend Layers is only available for RGB or grayscale images.

#47 Creating a Clipping Mask

If you've ever seen a picture in which text or a geometric shape is filled with photographic imagery, you've probably seen a *clipping mask* in action. A clipping mask is a stack of two or more layers in which the non-transparent content of the bottommost (or *base*) layer clips the content of the layers above it like a cookie cutter. A clipping mask can contain many layers, but they all have to be adjacent in the stack.

To create a clipping mask, do one of the following:

- If your clipping mask contains only two layers, press Alt (Windows) or Option (Mac), and position the cursor over the top edge of the base layer in the Layers palette. When the pointer changes to two overlapping circles, click (**Figure 47a**).

Alt-click (Windows) or Option-click (Mac) here to create a clipping mask.

Figure 47a A two-layer image in which the top layer is a photograph and the bottom layer contains type.

- If your clipping mask contains more than two layers, in the Layers palette, select the layer(s) you want to include in the clipping mask (do not select the base layer), and choose Layer > Create Clipping Mask.

Adding to a Clipping Mask

If you create a new layer between layers in a clipping mask, or drag an unclipped layer between layers in a clipping mask, the layer becomes part of the clipping mask.

No matter which method you use, the name of the base layer will be underlined, and the rest of the layers in the clipping mask will be indented and marked with a right-angle arrow pointing down (**Figure 47b**).

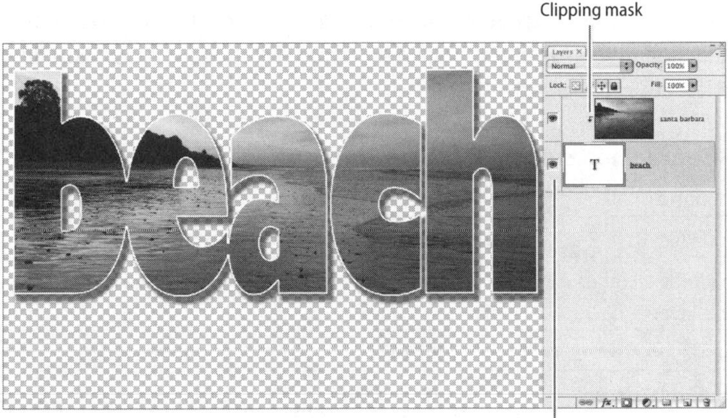

Figure 47b The beach layer now clips the santa barbara layer, and photographic imagery from the latter fills the word *beach*.

Note

Layers in the clipping mask acquire the opacity and blending mode of the base layer.

Clipping Mask Speed Tip

Speed up your work by learning this shortcut: To quickly create or release a clipping mask, select the layers you want to include in the mask and press Ctrl + Alt + G (Windows) or Command + Option + G (Mac).

#48 Using Layer Shortcuts

This chapter began by explaining that layers are integral to working in Photoshop. One way to take your layer skills to the next level is to use keyboard shortcuts. A word of caution, however: The following shortcuts are not for the faint-of-heart or even the average Photoshop user. But who wants to be average anyway? Learn these shortcuts to become a Photoshop power-user, and to gain skills that will speed up your workflow and lead to more creative results.

Keyboard Shortcuts for Working with Layers

Command	Windows Shortcut	Mac Shortcut
Copy layer	Ctrl + J	Command + J
Show/hide all other visible layers	Alt-click the eye icon	Option-click the eye icon
Group layers	Ctrl + G	Command + G
Merge visible layers	Ctrl-Shift + E	Command + Shift + E
Select next layer down/up	Alt + [or]	Option + [or]
Move target layer down/up	Ctrl + [or]	Command + [or]
Merge down	Ctrl + E	Command + E
Merge copies of all visible layers into target layer	Ctrl + Shift + Alt + E	Command + Shift + Option + E
Select all type; temporarily select type tool	Double-click type layer thumbnail	same
Select/deselect multiple contiguous layers	Shift-click	same
Select/deselect multiple discontiguous layers	Ctrl-click	Command-click
Create a clipping mask	Alt-click the line dividing two layers	Option-click the line dividing two layers

CHAPTER SIX

Making Selections

One of my great privileges in life is having the opportunity to teach Photoshop at the Brooks Institute of Photography. From the get-go, the students are typically eager about learning how to make image modifications, adjustments, and corrections. My job is to redirect this enthusiasm and get them to realize that what they should be most interested in is learning how to make good selections. When working in Photoshop, you must select elements in the image before you can correct them. The quality of the selection often directly equates with the quality of the final adjustment.

A selection isolates one or more parts of an image. Making a selection allows you to edit and apply effects and adjustments to a specific part of your image. For example, when retouching a portrait, it is common to add a bit of sparkle to the eyes. To accomplish this effect, you select the eyes and then sharpen them. In this way, the eyes can be sharpened separately from the rest of the image.

You can make selections in Photoshop in numerous ways. This chapter discusses Photoshop's main selection tools, how to modify and customize selections, and how to make selections based on color. As you read through it, keep in mind that no single selection technique is best. Rather, the best technique is contingent upon the task at hand.

#49 Selecting with the Marquee Tools

The marquee tools let you select rectangles, ellipses, and single-pixel rows and columns. To begin using one of the marquee tools, select the tool in the Toolbox. Four tools share a single icon space; normally, only one is visible, with three more hidden behind it. To access the hidden tools, click and hold on the visible marquee tool until the hidden tools appear (**Figure 49a**).

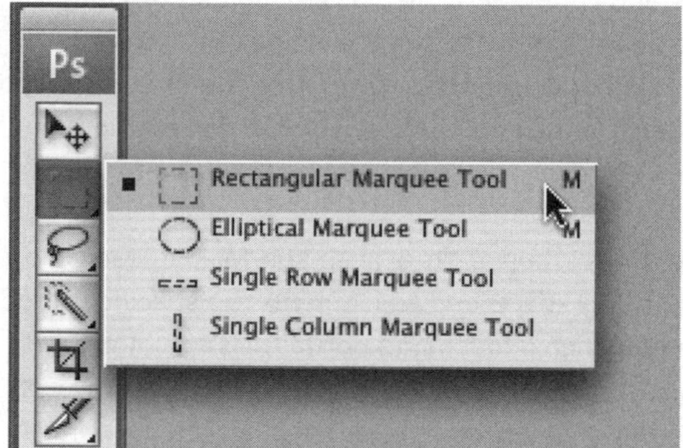

Figure 49a In the Toolbox, tool icons that are marked with a small triangle in the bottom-right corner conceal more tools that can be accessed by clicking and holding on the icon.

Choose the appropriate marquee tool to make a selection:

- **Rectangular Marquee.** Makes rectangular selections.
- **Elliptical Marquee.** Makes an elliptical selection.
- **Single Row or Single Column Marquee.** Selects columns a single pixel wide or rows a single pixel high.

Once a tool is selected, make a selection by dragging in the image. A selection is marked by small dashes that move around the selected area. In Photoshop circles, these are called "marching ants." To show or hide the marching ants, press Ctrl + H (Windows) or Command + H (Mac) (**Figure 49b**).

Repositioning Marquee Selections

When making marquee selections, it can be difficult to place the selection in the correct position. Follow these steps to reposition selections:

1. Create the selection.
2. Continue to hold down the mouse button.
3. Press and hold down the spacebar and drag the selection to the desired position.

Figure 49b Marching ants surround the three lights that have been selected in this image, each of which has been selected with the Elliptical Marquee tool.

When you choose a marquee tool, options specific to the tool appear in the options bar. (The general options for the various selection tools will be discussed later in this chapter.) For the Rectangular and Elliptical Marquee tools, you can choose how the relationship between the height and width of the area you select is constrained. The choices are on the Style menu (**Figure 49c**):

- **Normal.** No constraint.
- **Fixed Ratio.** Constrains the selection to a fixed ratio between width and height, but the size is variable.
- **Fixed Size.** Constrains the selection to a size chosen by you. The size can be measured in pixels (px), inches (in), or centimeters (cm).

Figure 49c The Rectangular Marquee tool options as displayed in the options bar.

Tip

The Single Row or Single Column Marquee tools are useful for making a 1-pixel-wide selection or line. To make a 1-pixel-wide selection, select either tool, and then drag. To convert the selection to a line, choose Edit > Fill.

Practice Constraint

When dragging with either the Rectangular or Elliptical Marquee tool, holding down the Shift key constrains the selected area so that its height and width are equal. In other words, holding down Shift while using the Rectangular Marquee tool gives you a square selection, and doing the same while using the Elliptical Marquee tool gives you a perfectly round one.

One more keyboard tip that will help you position your selection more precisely: Holding down the Alt (Windows) or Option (Mac) key while dragging centers the selection on the spot where you started dragging.

#50 Using the Lasso Tools

Yeehaaa! In the Wild West, cowboys used lassos to catch and corral cows. In Photoshop, the lasso tools are used to make freeform, polygonal (straight-edged), and magnetic (snap-to) selections. For both the cowboy and the Photoshop user, the lasso can be a bit tricky. Once you get the hang of it, however, you'll find yourself reaching for the rope quite often.

To use the Lasso tool, select it in the Toolbox, or press and hold on the tool to view the three hidden lasso tools, of which each performs a different function (**Figure 50a**).

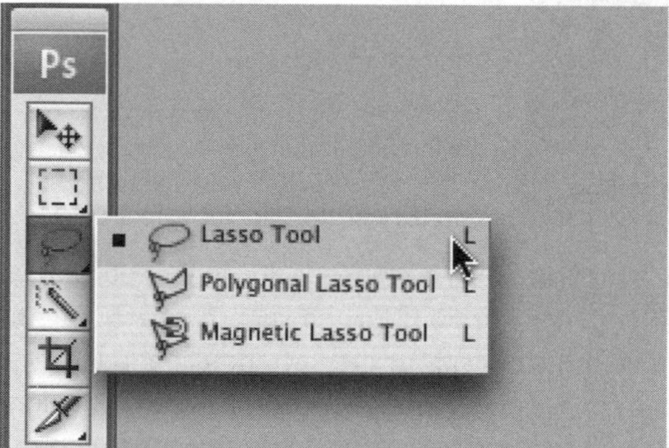

Figure 50a Select one of the three lasso tools in the Toolbox.

The Lasso tool is useful for making freeform selections. The Polygonal Lasso tool is useful for making selections that consist of a series of straight lines (but that can't be made by the Rectangular Marquee tool). And the Magnetic Lasso tool is useful for making quick selections of objects outlined by strong edges set against high-contrast backgrounds.

To use the Lasso tool, simply drag with it around the area you wish to select. Then return to your starting point to close the loop.

To use the Polygonal Lasso tool:

1. Click on the image to set the first point.
2. Reposition the cursor and click again. This will create a straight line between the two points.

3. Continue creating straight lines and loop back to the first point (**Figure 50b**).

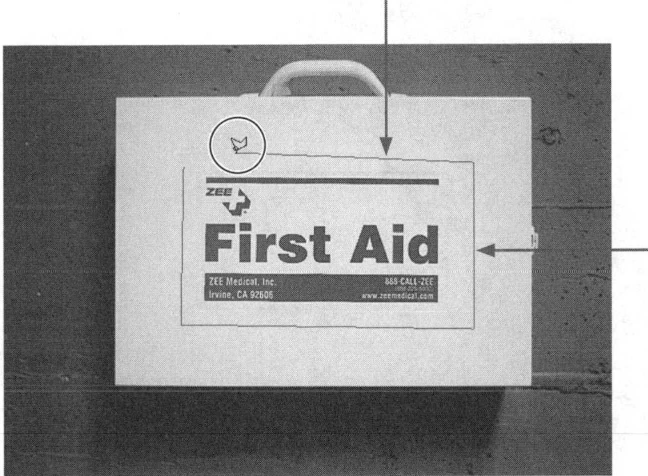

Figure 50b In this image, I am using the Polygonal Lasso tool to select the "First Aid" graphics.

4. Click the first point to complete the selection.

The Magnetic Lasso tool is the most complex of the lasso tools. To use this tool:

1. Click to set the first anchor point.
2. Move the cursor along the edge you want to select (**Figure 50c**). The tool will automatically attempt to snap to the edge and create anchor points.

(continued on next page)

Fine-Tuning: The Magnetic Lasso Tool Options

Setting the appropriate options for the Magnetic Lasso tool will help you create the best selection:

- **Width.** Enter a pixel value in the Width field so that the Magnetic Lasso tool only detects edges within the specified distance from the pointer.
- **Contrast.** The edge sensitivity is controlled by contrast. A low percentage detects low-contrast edges. A high percentage detects high-contrast edges.
- **Frequency.** To specify the rate at which the lasso sets anchor points, enter a value between 0 and 100 in the Frequency field. With a higher value, the selection border conforms to the edge you're trying to follow more quickly.
- **Stylus Pressure.** If you have a stylus tablet, select this option to use stylus pressure to adjust the edge width. For example, an increase in stylus pressure decreases the edge width.

Closing the Selection Border

To close the selection border, you have a couple of options:

- To close a border created by any of the three tools, drag back over the starting point and click.
- To close the border with a straight segment, hold down Alt (Windows) or Option (Mac) and double-click.
- To close the border with a freehand Magnetic segment, double-click, or press Enter or Return (Magnetic Lasso tool only).

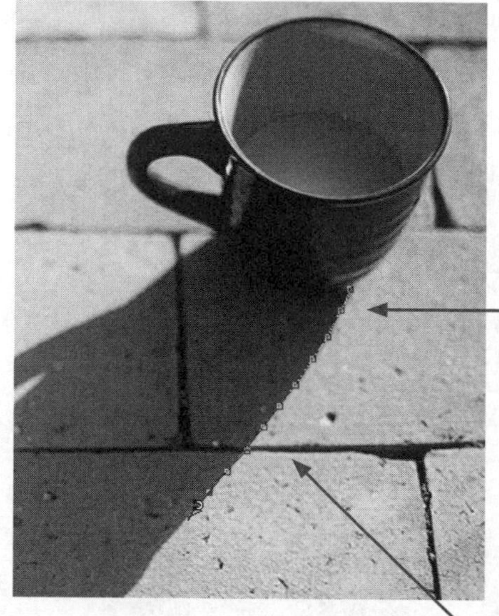

Figure 50c In this example, I have moved the Magnetic Lasso Tool along the edge of the shadow to begin to make a selection of the shadow.

3. Continue moving the cursor along the edge and complete the selection by looping back and clicking on the first anchor point.

Tip

To make sure the Magnetic Lasso selects the correct edge, you can increase or decrease the width detection value while using the tool. To do this, press the right bracket (]) to increase the Magnetic Lasso edge width by 1 pixel; press the left bracket ([) to decrease the width by 1 pixel.

#51 Using the Quick Selection and Magic Wand Tools

The Quick Selection and Magic Wand tools make selections based on image characteristics. The advantage of using these tools is that you don't have to create or trace outlines. Rather, you set options, make a selection, and the tool does the rest.

Although what each of these tools accomplishes is similar, they go about it in different ways. The Quick Selection tool, as the name implies, lets you *quickly* "paint" a selection using an adjustable round brush tip. The tool is brilliant in that when you paint, it analyzes the surrounding pixels and grows the selection to include similar pixels (within clearly defined edges). The Magic Wand tool selects similar pixels based on color.

To use either tool, select it in the Toolbox (**Figure 51a**).

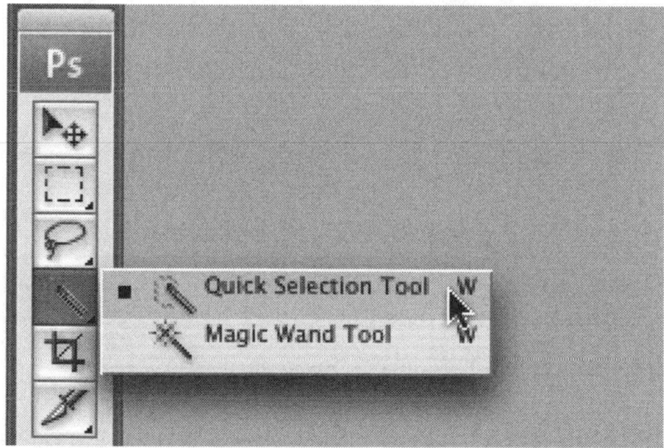

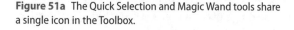

Figure 51a The Quick Selection and Magic Wand tools share a single icon in the Toolbox.

To use the Quick Selection tool, choose it and modify the options in the options bar (**Figure 51b**).

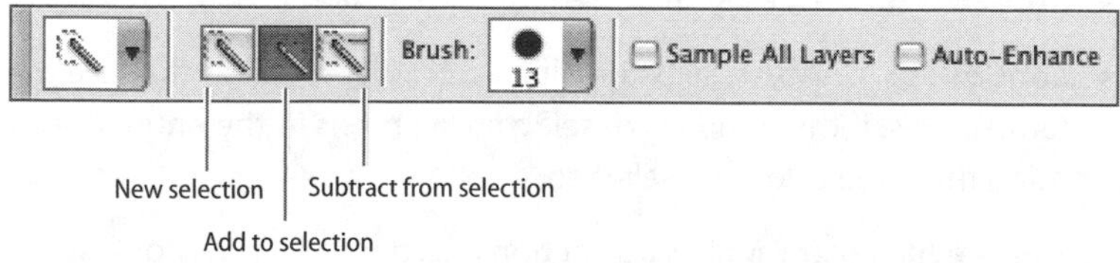

Figure 51b The options bar when the Quick Selection tool is active.

Quick Selection Modification

- To enlarge a selection once you have stopped clicking, click the Add to Selection button in the options bar and paint in another area. The selection will grow to include this new area.
- To subtract from a selection, click the Subtract from Selection button, and then drag over the area you wish to deselect.

A Tip on Brush Tips

When creating a selection, press the right bracket (]) to increase the diameter of your Quick Selection brush tip; press the left bracket ([) to decrease it.

The options include the following:

- **Brush Size.** Choose the diameter of your brush (in pixels). Use a small brush size for smaller detailed selections, and a larger brush size for broader selections.
- **Sample All Layers.** The selection will be based on information from all layers instead of just the currently selected layer.
- **Auto-Enhance.** Automatically refines the selection edges. Leave this deselected if you wish to have more manual control of the edge and intend to refine the edge by hand.

Once you have chosen your options, paint inside the area of the image that you want to select. As you paint, the selection will automatically extend to the edge of the image area. Marching ants will surround the selected area.

To use the Magic Wand tool, select it and specify the options in the options bar (**Figure 51c**).

Figure 51c For more control, specify Magic Wand options in the options bar.

The options include the following:

- **Tolerance.** Defines the range of color that will be included in the selection. A low tolerance means that only pixels whose colors are very close to those clicked by the tool will be selected. A high tolerance value means that pixels with a broader range of colors will be included.
- **Anti-aliased.** Creates a smoother-edged selection.
- **Contiguous.** Creates a selection only with adjacent areas that use the same colors. If the option is deselected, all pixels in the entire image using the same colors are selected.
- **Sample All Layers.** Makes a selection based on all layers, not just the current layer.

Once you have specified the options, click the area you want to select. The selected area will be surrounded by marching ants.

#52 Modifying Selections

Many of the selections that you make will need to be modified, and each selection tool is equipped with different options to enable this. The options bars for the marquee tools, lasso tools, and the Magic Wand tool have a set of four buttons in common: New, Add To, Subtract From, and Intersect With. When the New button is selected, every time you click with the mouse, a new selection is created, and any current selection is lost. If the Add To or Subtract From button is selected, each click of the mouse adds to, or subtracts from, the current selection. When the Intersect With button is selected, new selections are retained only where they overlap previously selected pixels (**Figure 52**).

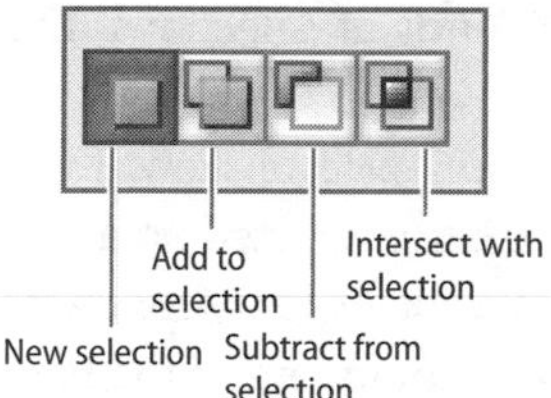

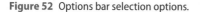

Figure 52 Options bar selection options.

Another way to modify a selection is using the Anti-Alias option, which is available for the lasso tools, the Elliptical Marquee tool, and the Magic Wand tool in the options bar. Anti-aliasing is the process of filling in the gaps between the square pixels (by mixing together some of the color from outside the selection with the selected area) to create a smoother edge. This option is ideal for subtle, softer edged selections. For harder edge selections, you'll want to deselect anti-aliasing. Whatever choice you make, you'll need to select or deselect anti-aliasing before making a selection—you can't add it after the fact.

Tip

Anti-aliasing is useful when cutting, copying, and pasting selections to create composite images.

Feathering is available for the marquee and lasso tools. It works to blur edges of a selection by creating a transition area between the selection and its surrounding pixels by selecting some pixels only partially. This blurring can cause some loss of detail at the edge of the selection. The loss of detail can be helpful when retouching or blending multiple images or adjustments.

Selection Speed Tip

To quickly modify selections, right-click (Windows) or Control-click (Mac) the active selected area to open a context menu where you can choose from the following:

- Deselect
- Select Inverse
- Feather
- Refine Edge
- Save Selection
- Make Work Path
- Layer Via Copy
- Laver Via Cut
- New Layer
- Free Transform
- Transform Selection
- Fill
- Stroke
- Smart Sharpen
- Fade

To feather a selection, specify the amount of feathering in the options bar. Alternatively, you can choose Select > Modify > Feather, and then choose the amount.

The other commands on the Select menu can also be used to refine selections after you've made them:

- The **Expand and Contract** commands can be used with all types of selections. Choose Modify > Expand or Contract and specify a number between 1 and 100 pixels. This will uniformly increase or decrease the size of your selection based on the specified number, which comes in handy when you need to make small modifications.
- **Transform Selection** can be used with all kinds of selections. This allows you to reshape the geometry of the selection border by subjecting it to transform operations such as rotate, scale, or skew. If you are going to significantly increase or decrease the selected area, it is best to transform the selection (as opposed to using Expand/Contract). Choose Select > Transform Selection, and then drag one of the handles on the bounding box that surrounds the selection. The Transform Selection command also allows to you make free transformations.
- The **Grow and Similar** commands can be used with all selections. Both work to enlarge the selection; however, they accomplish this in different ways. Choose Select > Grow to enlarge the selection by adding contiguous pixels—in other words, those pixels surrounding the original selection. Choose Select > Similar to add pixels with similar color values from anywhere in the image. The Select > Similar command uses the tolerance setting in the Magic Wand tool. For more information, see How-To #51.

Table 52 lists each selection tool and its different options.

Table 52 Selection Tool Options

Tool	Add to	Subtract from	Intersect	Anti-Alias	Feather	Tolerance
Rectangular Marquee	√	√	√		√	
Elliptical Marquee	√	√	√	√	√	
Lassos	√	√	√	√	√	
Quick Selection	√	√	√			
Magic Wand	√	√	√	√		√

#53 Using the Refine Edge Tool

When you make a selection, you do not always know if the selection is a good one until you have applied an adjustment. If it isn't, you have to undo the adjustment and begin again. The Refine Edge tool takes selection precision to the next level. This tool lets you quickly view a selection against different backgrounds for fine-tuned editing.

To use the Refine Edge tool, first create a selection using one of the selection tools. Then click Refine Edge in the selection tool's options bar or choose Select > Refine Edge.

The Refine Edge dialog box opens (**Figure 53**).

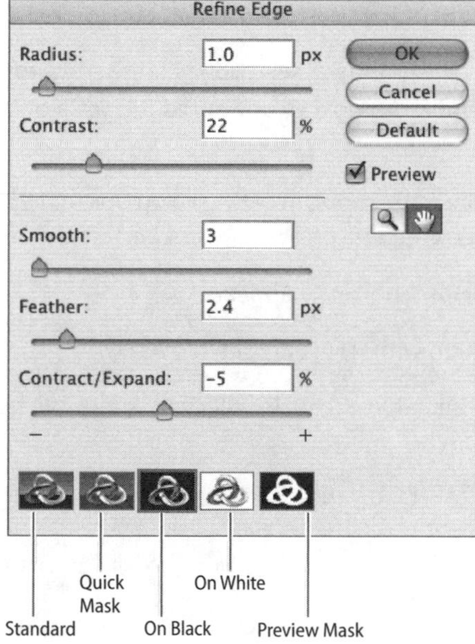

Figure 53 Modify the sliders to fine-tune the selection. Choose a preview mode to quickly identify problematic areas in the selection.

The sliders in this dialog box include the following:

- **Radius.** Defines the width of the zone around the selection boundary that will be affected by the Refine Edge dialog box. A higher radius creates a more exact selection boundary. Increase the radius to improve edges with soft transitions or fine detail.
- **Contrast.** Sharpens soft selection edges. Increase contrast to remove excessive noise near selection edges.
- **Smooth.** Smoothes irregular or jagged selection edges.
- **Feather.** Creates a uniform, soft-edged selection edge.
- **Contract/Expand.** Shrinks or expands a selection. Contracting (or shrinking) is particularly useful for removing unwanted fringes along the selection edge.

Use the preview mode buttons at the bottom of the dialog box to help identify problematic areas in the selection:

- **Standard.** View the selection as it normally appears.
- **Quick Mask.** View the selection with transparent red overlay.
- **On Black/White.** View the selection against a black or white background.
- **Preview.** View the selection as a black-and-white mask.

#54 Selecting a Color Range

Using the Color Range command lets you make color-based selections. Color Range lets you target a specific color and dynamically adjust the reach of the selection to other colors.

To use the Color Range command:

1. Choose Select > Color Range to open the Color Range dialog box (**Figure 54a**).

Figure 54a The Color Range dialog box. Because the color yellow had been sampled in the image, using the Eyedropper tool, the yellow bike is now selected and shows up as white in the preview area in the dialog box.

2. Choose Sampled Colors from the Select menu (**Figure 54b**) and move the mouse pointer over the image, where it becomes an eyedropper.

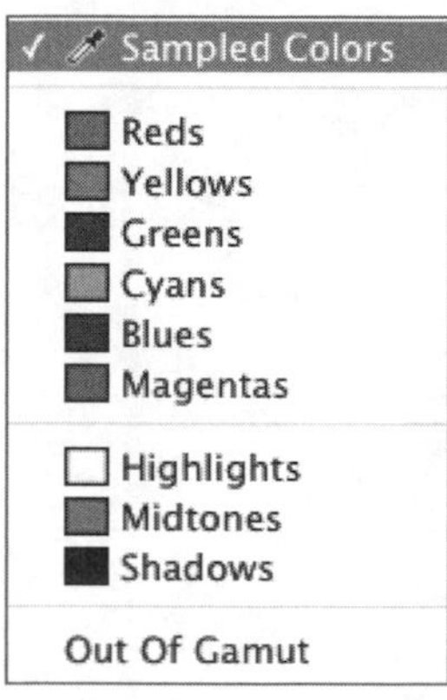

Figure 54b The Select menu in the Color Range dialog box.

(continued on next page)

Pick a Color

You can also choose a specific color or tonal range from the Select menu in the Color Range dialog box. This method has a serious drawback, however: You can't adjust the selection, so its usefulness is limited.

Reset and Undo

In the Color Range dialog box (as well as in other places in the Photoshop interface), you can undo any adjustments you've made by resetting the values to their default values. To do this, press and hold down Alt (Windows) or Option (Mac) to turn the Cancel button into to a Reset button. Then click Reset.

3. Click an area in the image that has the color you want to select. All instances of that color in the image will be selected. The preview area in the center of the dialog box displays the selected area according to the options directly beneath the preview:
   - **Selection.** Displays the selection depending on the option chosen from the Selection Preview menu. The default is a grayscale mask, in which white represents selected pixels, and shades of gray represent partially selected pixels.
   - **Image.** Reveals the entire image. This is helpful if you want to sample from a part of the image that isn't onscreen.
4. To adjust the range of colors selected, use the Fuzziness slider on the left side of the dialog. Drag the slider to the right to increase the color range and thus expand the selected area.
5. To add colors to the selection, choose the eyedropper icon with the plus (+) symbol and click additional colors in the image. To remove colors from the selection, choose the eyedropper icon with the minus (–) symbol, and then click in the image.

CHAPTER SEVEN

Using Blending Modes

I'll never forget the day when my artist Mom taught me about mixing paint—it was magic! I mixed some blue and yellow paint together and all of a sudden I had created green! I was able to create something that was previously completely unimaginable. The same and more can be said about Photoshop's blending modes. They give you the ability to control not only how color blends together, but also how images, tone, type, and shapes blend. More specifically, blending modes enable you to control how the contents of one layer blend with the layer(s) below it.

We'll spend the first part of this chapter exploring how Photoshop blending works, and then we'll begin applying this knowledge to a number of scenarios. Hopefully, by the time you're finished reading and experimenting, you'll have a head start in using blending, which will catapult your creativity to previously unimaginable heights!

#55 Understanding Blending Modes

There are over two dozen blending modes in Photoshop, so the sheer quantity of options can be intimidating. Fortunately, though, because of the many similarities between blending modes, the options are not as complex as they first appear. Searching for the right blending mode is often a snap because the modes are grouped together based on their overall functionality, such as darkening, lightening, comparing, and color (**Figure 55a**).

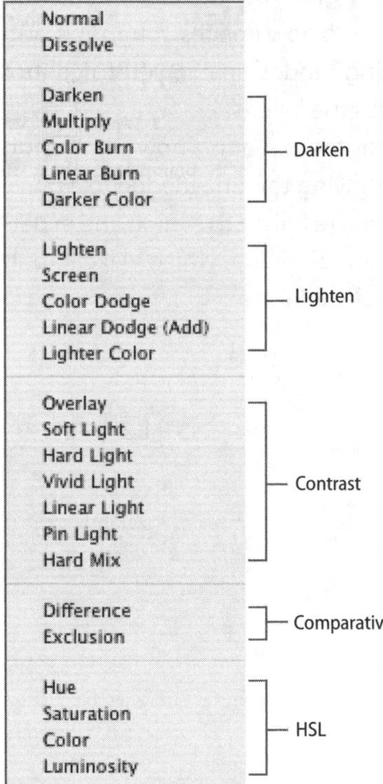

Figure 55a While categorizing blending modes according to their functionality oversimplifies matters a bit, it will help you become familiar with how blending modes work.

When learning about the different blending modes and visualizing a blending mode's effect, it's helpful to be familiar with a couple of terms (**Figure 55b**):

- **Base color.** The original color in the image; the color of the bottom layer.
- **Blend color.** The color being applied; the color of the top layer.

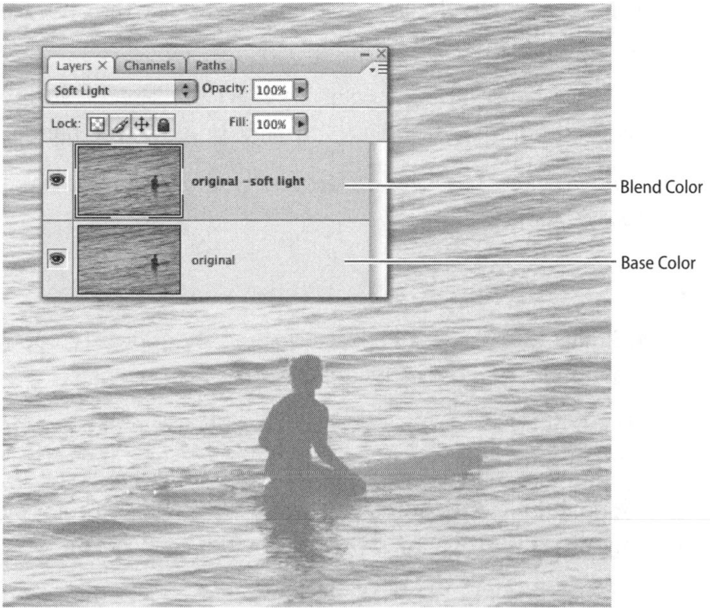

Figure 55b In this example, an image has been duplicated into a new layer, and the upper layer has been set to a blending mode. In scenarios such as this, the bottom layer can be referred to as the base color and the top layer as the blend color.

To get a handle on the specifics of blending modes, it's helpful to become familiar with the brief descriptions of the blending modes that follow.

Normal or dissolve

- **Normal.** Default mode without blending.
- **Dissolve.** Blends with a random replacement of the pixels.

Darken

- **Darken.** Selects the base or blend color—whichever is darker—as the result color.
- **Multiply.** Multiplies the base color by the blend color. Black always produces black, and whites are unchanged.

(continued on next page)

- **Color Burn.** Uses the blend color to darken by increasing the contrast. Blending with white produces no change.
- **Linear Burn.** Darkens the base color to reflect the blend color by decreasing the brightness. Blending with white produces no change.
- **Darker Color.** Darkens based on all channels; only the lighter pixels on the blend layer remain.

Lighten

- **Lighten.** Similar to Darken, Lighten selects the base or blend color—except that it selects whichever is lighter—as the result color.
- **Screen.** Lightens in a similar way to projecting multiple photographic slides on top of each other.
- **Color Dodge.** Brightens the base color to reflect the blend color by decreasing the contrast. Blending with black produces no change.
- **Linear Dodge (Add).** Lightens the base color to reflect the blend color by increasing the brightness. Blending with black produces no change.
- **Lighter Color.** Lightens based on all channels; only the lighter pixels on the blend layer remain.

Contrast

- **Overlay.** Multiplies or screens the colors, depending on the base color. Blending with 50% gray has no effect.
- **Soft Light.** Darkens or lightens the colors, depending on the blend color. Blending with 50% gray has no effect.
- **Hard Light.** Multiplies or screens the colors, depending on the base color. Hard Light works like Overlay, but the blending is more intense. Blending with 50% gray has no effect.
- **Vivid Light.** Color dodges or burns, depending on the blend color. Blending with 50% gray has no effect.

- **Linear Light.** Color dodges or burns the colors by decreasing or increasing the brightness, depending on the blend color. Blending with 50% gray has no effect.
- **Pin Light.** Uses the Lighten blending mode for lighter colors and the Darken Blending mode for darker colors. Blending with 50% gray has no effect.
- **Hard Mix.** Creates a posterized image comprised of up to eight colors: red, green, blue, cyan, magenta, yellow, black, and white. The blended color is a result of the base color and luminosity of the blend layer.

Comparative

- **Difference.** Subtracts either the blend color from the base color or the base color from the blend color, depending on which has the greater brightness value. This mode is useful for creative effects and determining alignment of similar layers.
- **Exclusion.** Similar to Difference mode, yet a bit more muted and with less contrast. Blending with white inverts the base color values. Blending with black produces no change.

HSL

- **Hue.** Creates a result color with the luminance and saturation of the base color and the hue of the blend color.
- **Saturation.** Creates a result color with the luminance and hue of the base color and the saturation of the blend color.
- **Color.** Combines the luminance of the base color and the hue and saturation of the blend color. This mode is incredibly useful for coloring monochrome images and for tinting color images because the color is mapped to the grayscale tone of the image. So in effect you can see through the color to the image details.
- **Luminosity.** The blend layer is blended with luminance and does not affect the base color. This mode creates the opposite effect of Color blending mode.

#56 Working with Blending Modes

Scroll Through the Blending Modes

Sometimes you will know exactly which blending mode will work best. Other times, it is helpful to try different modes. The best way to do this is to scroll through the different modes:

1. Select the layer to be blended (the blend layer).
2. Select the Move tool (shortcut key: V). (This actually works with most of the tools—not just the Move tool.)
3. Press Shift and the plus key (+) to scroll down or the minus key (-) to scroll up through the layer blending modes.

Even though you may be able to access a particular blending mode in any of several areas of Photoshop—whether it's through the Layers palette, using the Fade, Fill, or Stroke commands, or any of the layer styles—it works the same regardless of how you access it. The trick is to learn where to find which blending mode in the different areas of Photoshop. Let's take a look at a few examples.

Blending via the Layers palette

The most common way to apply a blending mode is from the Layers palette:

1. Select a layer on the Layers palette.
2. From the Blend Mode menu at the top of the Layers palette, choose a blending mode (**Figure 56a**).

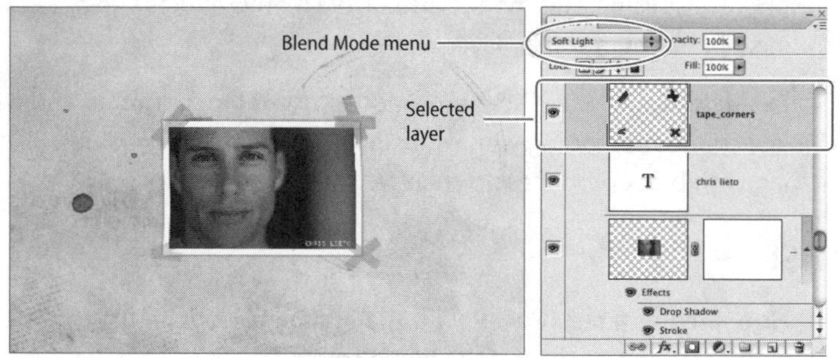

Figure 56a Here I wanted to blend the top layer into the underlying layers. I selected the top layer, "tape_corners." Then I chose the Soft Light blending mode, which blends the tape graphics into the underlying layers.

Blending via the Fade command

The Fade command can be used to change the opacity or blending mode of a filter operation, painting-tool application, or color adjustment after the fact.

For example, if you used the Brush tool to paint on your image and you wanted to modify that brush stroke, before you do anything else you would choose Edit > Fade, drag the Opacity slider, and/or choose a blending mode from the Mode menu (**Figure 56b**).

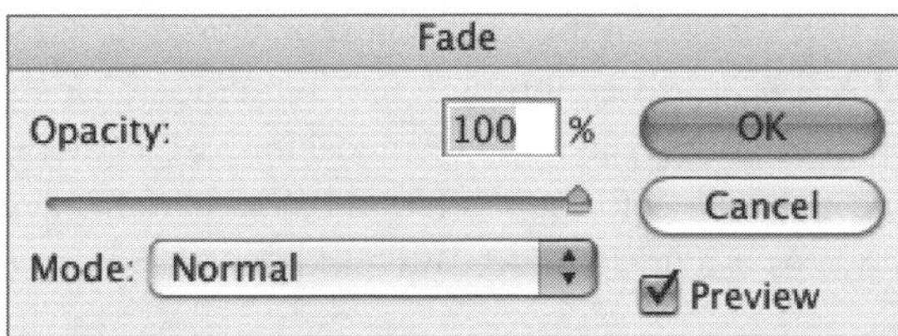

Figure 56b In the Fade dialog box, adjust the opacity, or choose a blending mode, or both.

Note
The Fade command works only if invoked immediately after using a filter, painting tool, or color adjustment.

Blending via the Brush tool

When using the Brush tool, you can choose a blending mode from the options bar. If you wanted to modify the color of someone's eyes, for example, you could do the following:

1. Choose the Brush tool and choose a color in the Color Picker.
2. In the options bar, choose Color from the Mode menu (**Figure 56c**).

Figure 56c With the Brush tool active, choose a blending mode from the Mode menu in the options bar.

3. Paint with the brush directly on the eyes.

Because the Color blending mode is selected, painting with the brush changes the color of the eyes, but leaves the luminance (the grayscale texture information) intact. The end result is an eye color that looks realistic. In contrast, painting with the brush without using the Color blending mode would result in a color brush stroke on top of (and not blended into) the image.

Blending Mode Shortcuts

Most of the time, selecting blending modes from a menu suffices. But if you want to take your skills to the next level, it's a good idea to learn the following shortcuts for selecting some of the more common blending modes:

1. Select a layer.
2. Choose the Move tool.
3. Press Shift + Alt (Windows) or Shift + Option (Mac), and then press one of the following letters:
   - N = Normal
   - M = Multiply
   - S = Screen
   - F = Soft Light
   - C = Color

#57 Using the Multiply Blending Mode

The Multiply blending mode is one of the most commonly used darkening modes. The effect is similar to viewing two photographic transparency slides laid on top of each other. In more technical terms, this mode darkens by multiplying the base color by the blend color. Black always produces black, and whites are unchanged. The end result is a darker image.

To understand how the Multiply blending mode works, follow the steps below:

1. Choose the Move tool and drag two images into one Photoshop document. Each image will be on its own layer.
2. Select the image in the top layer and change the blending mode to Multiply.

In **Figure 57a,** the image with the streetlights and the bright sky has been dragged on top of the image of the dark wall and set to Multiply mode. The resulting image is darker than either of the original pictures. Note especially how the whiter tones in the sky image have less impact.

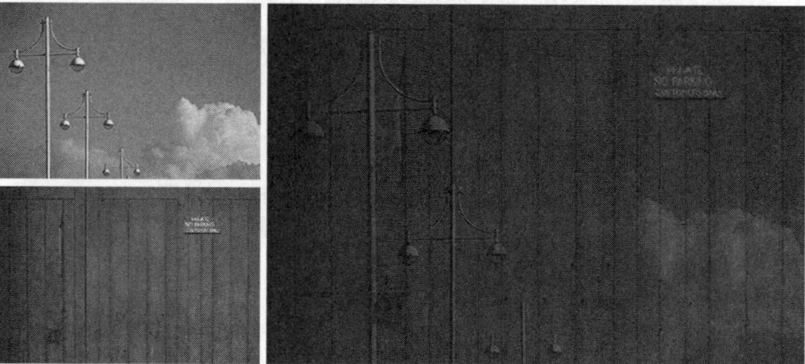

Figure 57a The two original images shown at left are blended using Multiply mode, producing the result seen at right.

One practical use for the Multiply blending mode is to darken an over-exposed area of an image. Let's take **Figure 57b** as an example, in which the exposure of the image on the left needs to be corrected.

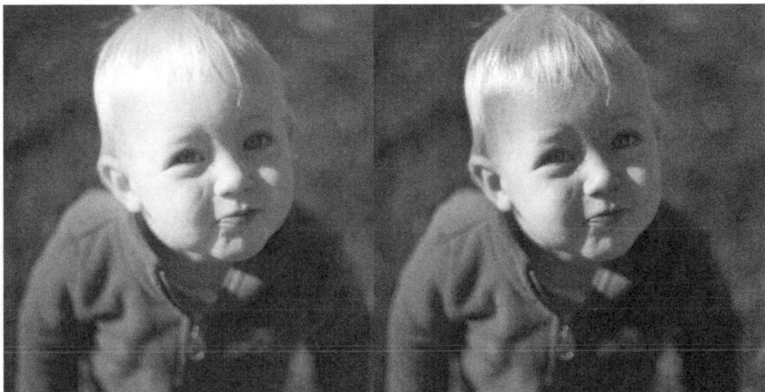

Figure 57b The original image (left) is overexposed. The exposure on the final image (right) has been corrected.

1. Working in the Layers palette, select the Background layer. Choose Layer > Duplicate.
2. With the newly duplicated layer still selected, choose Multiply from the Blend Mode menu. The image darkens noticeably.
3. To limit the darkening to the overexposed area of the face and hair, add a layer mask to the upper layer. Choose Layer > Layer Mask > Hide All. This will create a black mask that conceals the darkening effect.
4. Choose the Brush tool.
5. Click the Foreground Color box in the Toolbox to open the Color Picker and choose white.
6. Back in the Layers palette, click the layer mask to select it.
7. Paint with white on the bright areas of the subject's face to allow the darkening effect to show through the layer mask.

The final result is an image with a more correct and darkened exposure on the face of the subject.

Note
This sequence of steps is just one of several ways that you can correct overexposure in an image. To execute this technique, it is helpful to have a good understanding of masking. For more information on masking, be sure to read Chapter 10.

Removing a White Background

Removing an object from a white Background can be quite a complex and time-intensive task. Before diving in, try using the Multiply blending mode to get a quick (and rough) preview of what the object on a white background would look like removed from the background.

For example, consider a two-layer document in which the Background layer contains an image of a picnic table, and the top layer contains an image of an apple photographed on a white background. The goal is to remove the apple from the white background, and place it on the table. To get a rough preview of how this might look, do the following:

1. Select the apple layer and choose the Multiply blending mode. This will remove the white area so that only the apple remains.
2. If the apple is too faint, duplicate the apple layer to increase its density.

Following these steps can help you determine whether it would be worthwhile to invest the time in using selections, masks, and so on to separate the apple from the background.

#58 Using the Screen Blending Mode

The Screen blending mode is one of the most commonly used of the lightening modes. Its effect is similar to projecting multiple photographic slides on top of each other and results in an overall lightening of an image (**Figure 58a**).

Original Screen

Figure 58a The original images on the left are blended together on the right using the Screen blending mode.

In contrast to the Multiply blending mode, the Screen blending mode modifies mainly the brighter tones in an image. In **Figure 58b,** for example, I created a few grayscale gradients and placed them in a layer above a background, as shown in the original image (top). I then changed the layer containing the gray items to Screen mode. The result (bottom) is that the brighter tones become brighter, whereas the blacks seem to disappear.

Original

Screen

Figure 58b The original gray gradient (top) is blended using the Screen mode (below).

One practical use of Screen mode is to brighten an underexposed area of an image. Here's how you might correct the exposure in (**Figure 58c**).

Figure 58c The original image on the left is underexposed. The exposure was corrected by stacking a duplicate of the image set to Screen mode on top of the original, and then using a layer mask to protect part of the image from the lightening effect.

To correct the exposure, follow the steps below:

1. Select the Background layer. Choose Layer > Duplicate.
2. In the Layers palette, choose Screen from the Blend Mode menu. This will brighten the overall image.
3. To limit the lightening to the underexposed area of the sky, add a layer mask to the upper layer. Choose Layer > Layer Mask > Reveal. This will create a white mask that reveals the brightening effect.
4. Choose the Brush tool.
5. Click the Foreground Color box in the Toolbox to open the Color Picker and choose black.
6. Back in the Layers palette, click the layer mask to select it.
7. Paint with black on the sky to remove the lightening effect.

The final result is an image with a more correct and appealing exposure.

#59 Using the Soft Light Blending Mode

As a photographer, you'll probably find that Soft Light is one of the blending modes you will use most often. This blending mode targets the darker and brighter tones but doesn't modify the middle grays. Because of this, there are many creative and practical photographic uses for Soft Light, such as combining multiple images, increasing contrast, color saturation, and burning and dodging (see the next How-To). For example, **Figure 59a** illustrates how you can use blending to combine multiple images and add more contrast.

Figure 59a The original images on the left blended together on the right using the Soft Light blending mode.

To increase color saturation and contrast in an image using Soft Light mode, follow the steps below:

1. Select the Background layer. Choose Layer > Duplicate.

(continued on next page)

2. With the new layer still selected, choose the Soft Light blending mode. This will increase the contrast and color saturation of the image (**Figure 59b**).

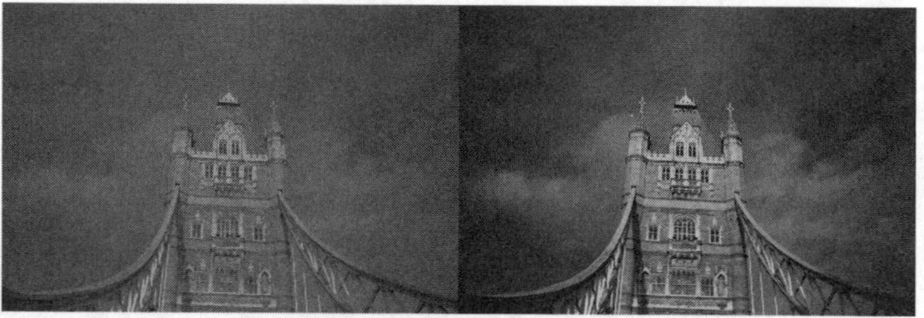

Figure 59b The final image (right) was created by duplicating the Background layer and changing the blending mode of the copy to Soft Light.

3. In the Layers palette, adjust the opacity of the Soft Light layer to achieve the effect you want.

#60 Burning and Dodging Using Blending Modes

Burning and Dodging are photographic terms used to describe the technique of darkening or brightening tones in an image to create visual impact. There are a number of different ways to burn and dodge in Photoshop, such as using the Burn and Dodge tools in the Toolbox. However, the best approach is to use the Soft Light blending mode in combination with the Brush tool (**Figure 60**).

Figure 60 On the right, the corners of the image have been darkened or burned.

Using the Soft Light mode is useful because you can dodge and burn nondestructively. In other words, you will be able to have flexibility to undo or reduce the intensity of the dodging and burning. To effectively burn and dodge, follow the steps below:

1. Select the Background layer. Choose Layer > New Layer.
2. With the duplicate layer still selected, choose the Soft Light blending mode.
3. Choose the Brush tool.
4. Press D to choose the default foreground and background colors, black and white, respectively.
5. Paint with black to darken (burn) or paint with white to brighten (dodge). (Press X to switch between black and white.)

In Figure 60, the original image (left) was modified using Soft Light and then painted with black to burn in details.

#61 Using Advanced Blending Techniques

In this chapter, we have thus far examined how to use blending modes as a way to blend entire layers. In most cases, these techniques will suffice. Yet, there are times when you may need blend only parts of layers together, perhaps only areas containing pixels within a certain tonal range. That is where the Advanced Blending feature comes into play.

For example, you can use Advanced Blending to make a selection of a subject's skin to soften the texture. To achieve this, follow the steps below.

1. Open an image of a portrait.
2. Select the Background layer. Choose Layer > Duplicate Layer.
3. Click on the Eye icon on the Background layer to hide the original Background layer.
4. Select the top layer, in other words, the new duplicate layer.
5. Click the *fx* icon at the bottom of the Layers palette and choose Blending Options from the menu. The Layer Style dialog box opens to the Blending Options: Custom pane (**Figure 61a**).

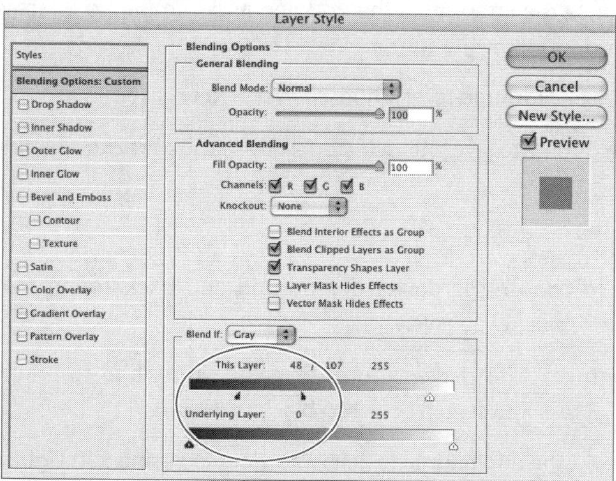

Figure 61a The Layer Style dialog box, open to the Blending Options: Custom pane. The Advanced Blending controls occupy the bottom portion of the dialog box.

6. In the Advanced Blending area of the Layer Style dialog box, find the Blend If sub-area. Drag the left This Layer slider to the right to remove (or blend) the dark tones.
7. Alt-drag (Windows) or Option-drag (Mac) the left slider to split it into two smaller sliders.
8. Drag each triangle to create a smoother removal (or blending) of the dark tones. Click OK.

   The final result (on the right) is a layer that contains only the brighter tones in the original image (**Figure 61b**).

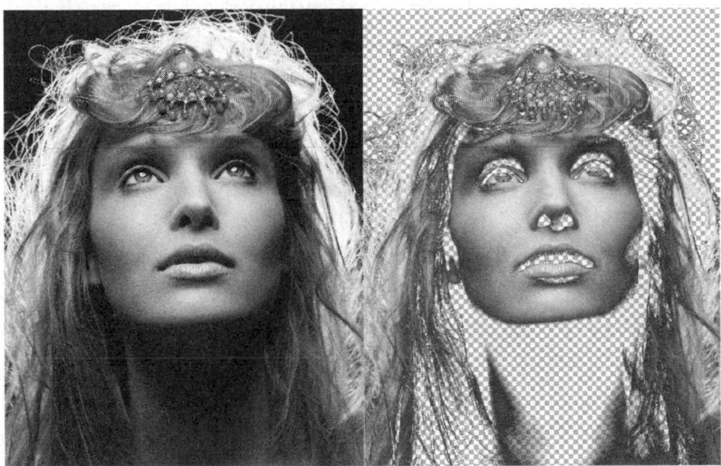

Figure 61b In this example, Advanced Blending was used to select the brighter tones of the image. By blending away the darker tones, only the brighter skin tones remained.

9. Choose Filter > Blur > Surface Blur to soften the entirety of the Advanced Blending selection.
10. To limit the softening to the skin, choose the Eraser tool from the Toolbox. In the options bar, select a medium-size, soft-edged brush and 100% opacity. Erase any areas where the smoothing is not needed.
11. Click the Eye icon on the Background layer to make it visible again.

Note

Keep in mind that Advanced Blending is complicated, but it is well worth learning!

Tip

To quickly access the Advanced Blending controls, double-click on the layer to the right of the layer name.

Recovering Shadow Detail with Advanced Blending

Another common use of the Advanced Blending options is to recover shadow tones for printing. This is especially helpful when using the Soft Light blending mode (as described in the previous How-To). A negative side effect of using this blending mode is a darkening of the shadow detail to the extent that detail is lost.

If you follow the procedure in How-To #60 and you find that you've lost some shadow detail, follow these steps:

1. Select the layer that has the Soft Light blending mode applied.
2. Open the Layer Style dialog box and switch to the Advanced Blending controls.
3. Move the left This Layer slider to the right. As you move the slider, watch the shadow detail and stop when you see an appropriate amount of it.
4. Alt-drag (Windows) or Option-drag (Mac) the slider to split it into two sliders and adjust them to create a smooth transition.

#62 Creating a Blending Composite

One of the most powerful uses of blending modes is for creating expressive, artistic or commercial visual composite images. If blending for expressive outcomes is something you haven't tried, you'll definitely want to try this after reading this How-To.

One of the nice things about creating a blending composite is that there are no rules, no limitations, and no such thing as common sense. As Picasso once said: "Common sense is the chief enemy of creativity." Having this type of attitude when it comes to creating blending composites can be incredibly freeing and lead you to new creative heights.

1. Open three images to be composited. In this example, from left to right: a poem, a photograph of a leaf, and a photograph of a tree (**Figure 62a**).

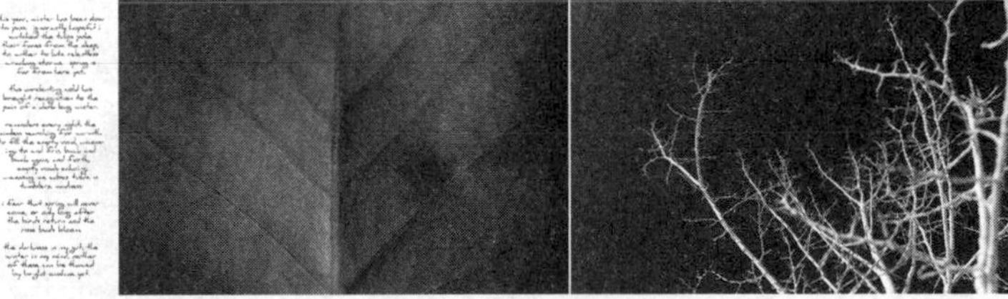

Figure 62a Three elements, before compositing.

2. Select the Move tool. Drag one or two of the images into the other image. In this example, the poem and tree were dragged into the leaf image. As you drag in the images, each one will be placed on a new layer.
3. Name the layers appropriately. In this example, appropriate choices would be "poem," "leaf," and "tree."
4. Position the images to create an interesting composition.
5. Select the "tree" layer and choose the Soft Light blending mode.
6. Press Ctrl-I (Windows) or Command-I (Mac) to invert the "tree" layer.
7. Select the "poem" layer.

(continued on next page)

8. Click the Layer Style Effect icon in the Layers palette and choose Drop Shadow.

9. Click OK to apply the Drop Shadow effect.

The final result (**Figure 62b**) is a composite image that expresses a visual idea that could not have been communicated without blending.

Figure 62b The final composite image.

Creating an Expressive Composite

For this example, I was interested in creating a visual piece that expressed my response to a poem. In particular, a line in the poem, which describes the slow passing of winter, struck me. With this thought in mind, I sought to create a visual that expresses my appreciation for the poem. To create your own expressive composite, look for things that inspire you.

CHAPTER EIGHT

Using Filters

In traditional photography, a filter is a glass element that you put on the front of the lens to affect the final image. In Photoshop, a filter works in a similar way in that it creates a new way to display the image. In contrast to traditional photography, with Photoshop you can apply and blend multiple filters in unique ways, which delivers unlimited filtering possibilities.

Photoshop filters are used for a wide array of functions, from practical production tasks like sharpening to creative special effects like adding motion blur. Regardless of the task at hand, you use the same basic workflow steps to add and apply any kind of filter.

It's important to keep in mind that filters are multifaceted and can be applied in many different scenarios. To address them comprehensively would require many pages. This chapter focuses on only the essentials of filtering. However, as you're reading through it, try to get into the habit of continually envisioning other scenarios in which you might use a particular filter. When you have completed the chapter, take the time to experiment with the other filters—experimenting is the best way to learn the many facets of each.

#63 Using Smart Filters

The Smart Filters feature gives you the ability to apply just about any Photoshop filter in a nondestructive manner. Exceptions include the Extract, Liquify, Pattern Maker, and Vanishing Point filters.

Nondestructive Smart Filters do not permanently modify pixels. Instead, when you apply a Smart Filter to an image, a set of "instructions" is recorded; when the image is displayed onscreen or output in some other manner, the output image is altered according to the instructions. The original pixel data, however, is preserved. You can modify, hide, or delete the instructions, and the filter effect is removed without affecting the original image.

To apply a Smart Filter, follow these steps:

1. Select a layer in the Layers palette.
2. Choose Filter > Convert for Smart Filters, and click OK in the dialog box that appears.
3. Apply a filter. For example, choose Filter > Noise > Add Noise.
4. Choose settings for the filter and click OK (**Figure 63a**).

Figure 63a Choose your settings in the filter dialog box.

When a layer has a Smart Filter applied, the filter appears below the layer in the Layers palette (**Figure 63b**). By default, the Smart Filter contains a mask filled with white that reveals the entire filter effect. To collapse or expand the list of Smart Filters, click the triangle at the right edge of the layer to which the Smart Filter is applied.

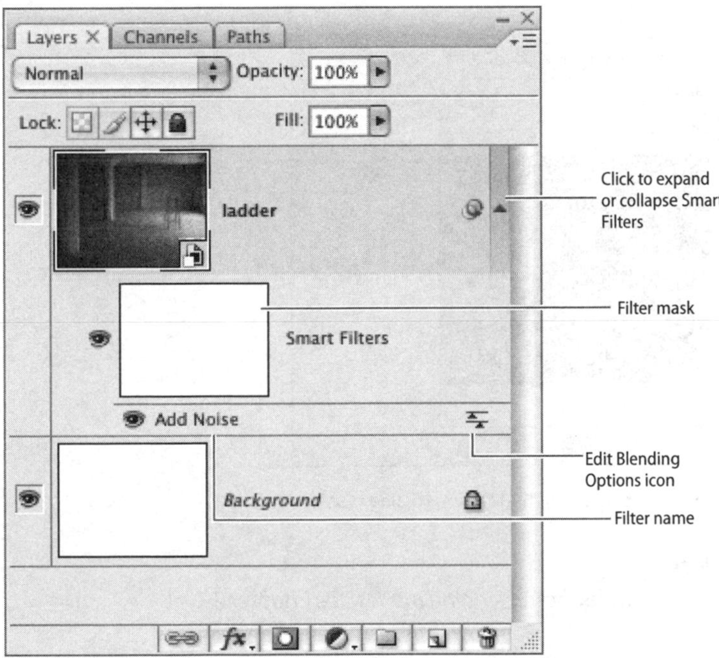

Figure 63b Smart Filters appear below the layer to which they are applied.

To restrict the effect of the filter to a portion of the image, paint with black on the filter mask (for more on masking, see Chapter 10). To edit the filter settings, double-click the name of the filter to re-open its dialog box.

To Be or Not To Be . . . Smart

There are definite pros and cons to using Smart Filters.

On the positive side, Smart Filters are very flexible, with built-in masks and controls to fine-tune the filter's strength and blending. Smart Filters also allow you to make nondestructive edits and adjustments. Having this "safety net" may help you to take more visual risks knowing that any adjustment can be reduced or completely removed.

At the same time, the flexibility and freedom of Smart Filters come at the price of file size and speed. Using Smart Filters can dramatically increase the size of your file and create longer save times depending on your particular computer configuration. In sum, while Smart Filters are designed to be flexible and save time, if you have an older computer, it may be best to reserve their use for situations when you feel the extra flexibility is helpful.

You can also choose a blending mode for each Smart Filter:

1. Double-click the Edit Blending Options icon for the filter. The Blending Options ([*filter name*]) dialog box opens (**Figure 63c**).
2. Choose a blending mode from the Mode menu and/or change the Opacity setting.

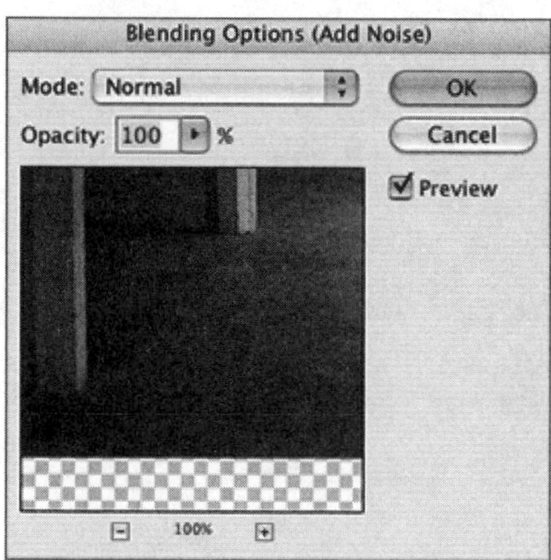

Figure 63c The Blending Options dialog box.

Note
To learn more about blending modes, see Chapter 7.

#64 Adding Blur

A plethora of techniques exists for adding blur in Photoshop. Rather than cover all of these techniques, this chapter focuses on a few Photoshop blur filters that seek to replicate photographic blur: Gaussian Blur, Motion Blur, and Radial Blur.

Gaussian Blur

Gaussian Blur is useful for softening details in an image.

1. Select a layer in the Layers palette.
2. Choose Filter > Blur > Gaussian Blur to open the Gaussian Blur dialog box.
3. Drag the Radius slider to the right to increase the softening and blurring effect. The actual amount of the radius will depend on the image resolution. For low-resolution images like the one pictured in Figure 64a, try a low radius. For a high-resolution image, try a higher setting.
4. Click OK to apply the Gaussian Blur. Not surprisingly, the image becomes blurry (**Figure 64a**).

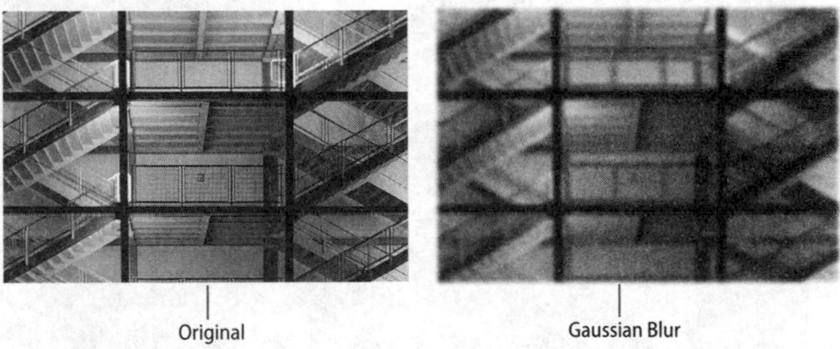

Figure 64a Applying a Gaussian Blur with a radius setting of 10 produced the image on the right.

Note

Too much Gaussian Blur can be overpowering. Try using Gaussian Blur with a low radius setting to create a soft focus portrait, or make a selection and apply the blur to a specific area of an image.

Motion Blur

Traditional photographers create motion blur by taking a photograph of a moving object with an extended exposure time.

In Photoshop, the Motion Blur filter can be used to produce a similar blur effect. Here's how:

1. In the Layers palette, select the layer to which you want to apply motion blur.
2. Choose Filter > Blur > Motion Blur. The Motion Blur dialog box opens.
3. Specify a blur direction by entering a value in the Angle field (between –360º and +360º), and an intensity value in the Distance field (between 1 and 999). For this image, I have chosen a 21-degree angle and an intensity of 14.
4. Click OK to apply Motion Blur (**Figure 64b**).

Figure 64b An image to which the Motion Blur filter has been applied.

Radial Blur: Spin

The Radial Blur filter using the Spin option simulates the soft blur created by a rotating camera.

1. Select a layer in the Layers palette.
2. Choose Filter > Blur > Radial Blur to open the Radial Blur dialog box.
3. Specify the amount and quality of the blur you want, and select the Spin Blur Method. The actual amount setting will depend on the image resolution. For my image, I have set the amount to 17 and selected Good for the Quality setting.
4. Click OK. The filter applies a rotational blur to the image (**Figure 64c**).

Figure 64c The image with a Spin Radial Blur applied.

Radial Blur: Zoom

The Radial Blur filter with the Zoom option selected simulates the effect of a zooming camera to produce a soft blur.

1. Select a layer in the Layers palette.
2. Choose Filter > Blur > Radial Blur to open the Radial Blur dialog box.
3. Select the Zoom Blur Method, choose an amount, and select a quality option. The actual amount will depend on the image resolution. In the example image below, I have chosen 17 for the amount, and Good for the Quality setting.

(continued on next page)

4. Click OK. The filter applies a blur that mimics the effect of a camera zooming in on the image (**Figure 64d**).

Figure 64d The image with a Zoom Radial Blur applied.

#65 Adding Film Grain

Recently, a friend of mine and editor of one of the world's major adventure sport magazines said, "Sometimes, digital is too perfect. I miss the texture, the personality, the grit, the life of film grain." Certain images can benefit from adding film grain, which sometimes adds more personality, dimension, depth, and nostalgia to an image. One way to reproduce the effect of film grain is to use the Film Grain filter, which applies an even pattern of noise to the image; a smoother pattern is used in the highlight areas.

1. In the Layers palette, select a layer.
2. Choose Filter > Artistic > Film Grain. The Filter Gallery opens, with the Film Grain filter selected (**Figure 65a**).

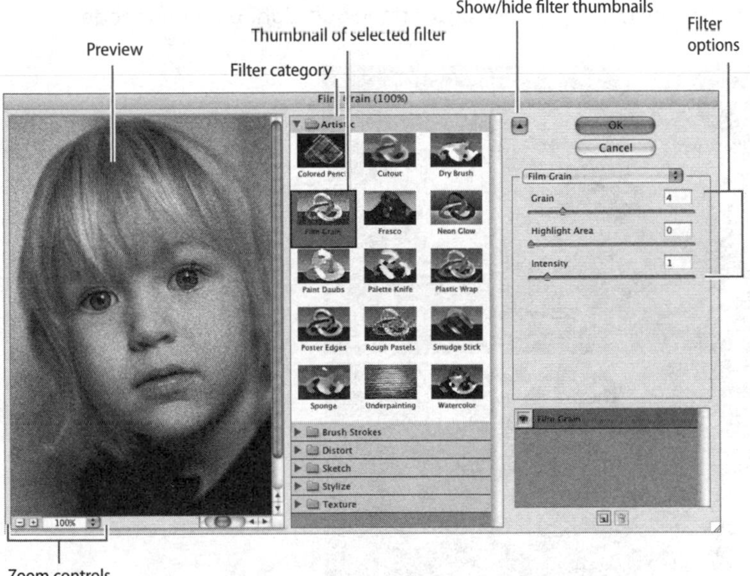

Figure 65a The Filter Gallery.

3. Change the image preview zoom amount by clicking on the plus (+) or minus (–) icons in the lower left corner of the dialog box.
4. Adjust the Filter options by dragging these sliders:
   - **Grain** to increase or decrease the density of the grain.

(continued on next page)

Film Grain Plug-Ins

Film grain can be added using Photoshop filters (as described in this How-To) or using third-party plug-ins, which need to be purchased separately. Two of my favorite film-grain plug-ins are Exposure from Alien Skin (www.alienskin.com) and Color Efex Pro from Nik Software (www.niksoftware.com).

- **Highlight Area** to increase or decrease the percentage of the image treated as highlights.
- **Intensity** to control the degree of the highlight brightening

The actual slider values will depend on the image resolution. To create a more subtle effect, use lower values. In my example image, I have chosen Grain, 4; Highlight, 0; and Intensity, 1.

5. Click OK to apply the Film Grain filter.

After applying the Film Grain filter to a new layer, try using one of the blending modes on a duplicate layer (Chapter 7) or painting on the filter mask (Chapter 10) to limit the grain to specific areas. This will make the grain look more realistic. In **Figure 65b**, I duplicated the Background layer, added film grain, and then applied the Soft Light blending mode.

Figure 65b The bottom image shows the result of using the Film Grain filter on a duplicate layer, and then applying the Soft Light blending mode.

#66 Using the Lens Correction Filter

In this chapter, so far we have covered enhancement and effect filters. Now we will shift gears and examine a corrective filter.

The Lens Correction filter fixes common lens flaws, such as barrel and pincushion distortion, vignetting, and more. This filter is especially helpful with architectural photography or in general when shooting with wide-angle lenses or when shooting at a low position looking up (or a high position looking down). The results of this filter can be dramatic or subtle. Keep in mind that often it is the subtle improvements that differentiate a decent photograph from an amazing one.

For example, in **Figure 66a**, the Lens Correction filter was used to correct the image on the bottom. This is especially noticeable when you look at the difference in the wood paneling on the left side of the before and after versions of the image.

Figure 66a The lower (and much more valuable) architectural image was corrected with the Lens Correction filter.

To apply the Lens Correction filter:

1. Select a layer in the Layers palette.
2. Choose Filter > Distort > Lens Correction. The Lens Correction dialog box opens (**Figure 66b**).

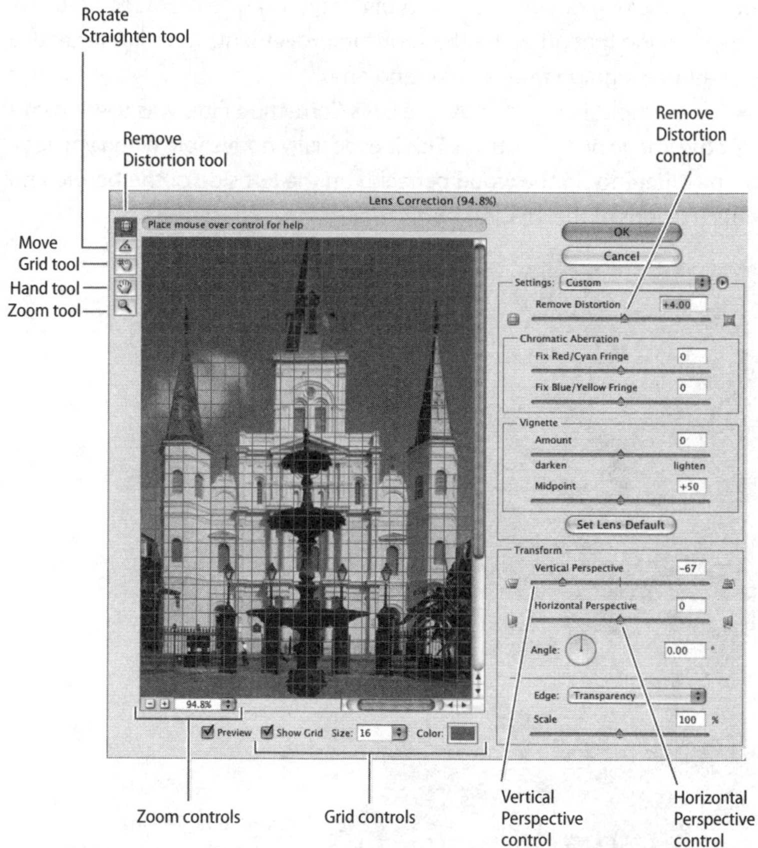

Figure 66b The Lens Correction dialog box.

3. Select Show Grid at the bottom of the dialog box.
4. Use the Size setting to adjust the grid spacing and the Color box to change the color of the grid.

5. Choose the Move Grid tool and drag the grid so that it aligns with the lines in the image. By comparing the grid with the lines in your image, you can determine how much correction is needed.

6. Adjust the Lens Correction sliders to correct the image. Below are the slider controls you will use most often:

   - **Remove Distortion** corrects two of the most common problems of lens distortion: barrel or pincushion distortion. Barrel distortion is a lens defect that causes straight lines to bow out toward the edges of the image (**Figure 66c**). Pincushion distortion is the opposite effect, in which straight lines bend inward (**Figure 66d**). Drag the slider to the left to correct pincushion distortion, or to the right to correct barrel distortion.

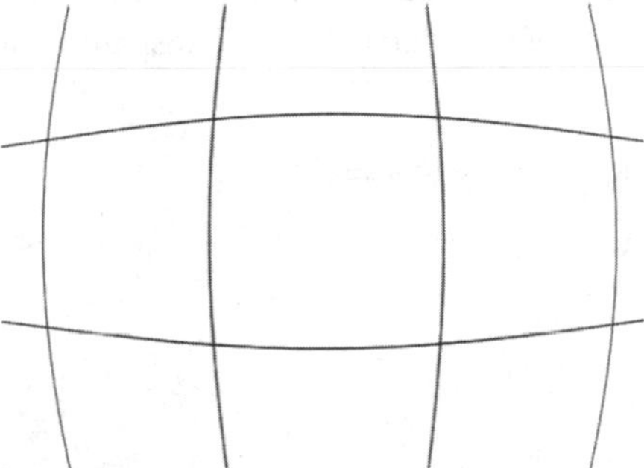

Figure 66c A grid showing barrel distortion.

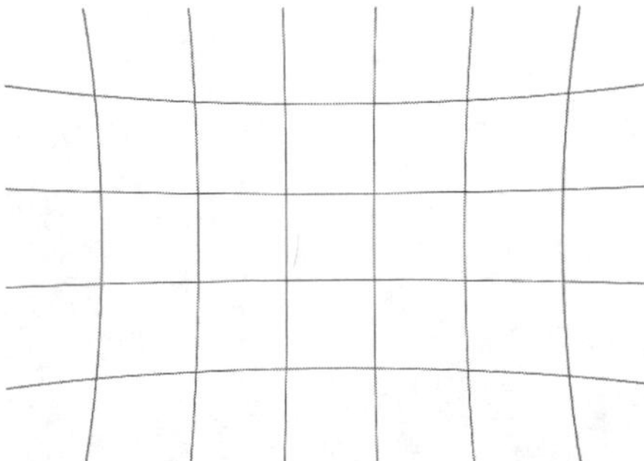

Figure 66d A grid showing pincushion distortion.

(continued on next page)

Lens Correction and Wide-Angle Lenses

The following corrections are particularly helpful when shooting with extreme wide-angle lenses. You can make these corrections using the Lens Correction filter or in Adobe Camera Raw (Chapter 4). When possible, make them in Camera Raw, since it provides more accuracy and flexibility.

- **Chromatic Aberration** corrects color fringing. Zoom in on the image preview to get a closer view of the fringing as you make the correction.
- **Vignette** corrects images that have darkened edges. This can also be used for the creative purpose of intentionally darkening the corners to create a vignette.
- **Amount** sets the amount of lightening or darkening along the edges of an image.
- **Midpoint** specifies the width of area affected by the Amount slider. Specify a lower number to affect more of the image. Specify a higher number to restrict the effect to the edges of the image.

Lens Correction and People

Distortion is easy to identify in the "straight and level" world of architectural photography. Thus, the Lens Correction filter is primarily used to correct distortions that occur in photography of structures, building, objects, and so on. At the same time, when used delicately, the Lens Correction filter can be a great asset when working on portraits. I have found that reducing lens barrel distortion on close-up headshots is a particularly effective portrait enhancement.

Tip

Choose the Remove Distortion tools and drag on the image toward the center to correct for barrel distortion and toward the edge of the image to correct for pincushion distortion.

- **Vertical Perspective** corrects image perspective caused by tilting the camera up or down. This correction is especially helpful when shooting tall buildings from a low perspective. Drag the slider to make vertical lines in an image parallel.
- **Horizontal Perspective** corrects image perspective, making horizontal lines parallel.
- **Angle** rotates the image to correct for camera tilt.
- **Edge** specifies how to handle the blank areas that result from corrections. For the majority of situations, choose Transparency for the best results.
- **Scale** increases or decreases the image size.

7. Click OK to apply the filter.

CHAPTER NINE

Modifying Color and Tone

Color and tone evoke. Red can be fierce and full of passion. Yellow can be warm and nostalgic. Blue can be cold and isolating. Deep and dark tones can draw in the viewer. Flat and dull tones can stir up distant vague memories. Take both of the forces of color and tone, mix them together, and you have the capability to create inexplicable visual impact. This chapter delves into the wonderful world of using Photoshop to modify color and tone.

While Photoshop's strengths are broad and deep—similar to an athlete who performs well in multiple sports—perhaps the arena where Photoshop excels most is in color and tone. No other digital imaging application comes close to rivaling the color and tone tools in Photoshop. This chapter shows you how to use essential tools like Levels, Curves, Hue/Saturation, Color Balance, Photo Filters, and more so that you can begin to make profound color and tone enhancements to your images.

Keep in mind, however, that because of the inherent wonders and complexities of color and tone, it can take a lifetime to learn how to approach them. The best artists often learn the essential skills and then approach color and tone as a mystery to be experienced rather than a problem to be solved. Just as Picasso once pondered, "Why do two colors, put one next to the other, sing? Can one really explain this?"

The techniques you learn in this chapter should provide a foundation from which to work as you explore the power of color and tone. They should also help you create images that connect more vividly with your viewers.

#67 Adjusting Levels

What Is a Histogram?

You may remember our discussion of histograms in Chapter 2, where we glanced briefly at the histogram in the Levels dialog box. Histograms are found on certain high-end cameras and in various other places in Photoshop, such as in the Curves dialog box, the Camera Raw dialog box, the Histogram palette, and so on. Here's a quick refresher on the histogram and its importance:

- A histogram illustrates how pixels in an image are distributed by graphing the number of pixels at each brightness level.
- Histogram information is helpful because it reveals whether the image contains enough detail in the shadows, midtones, and highlights.
- Histogram information can be used to correct exposure and color.

Almost all images need some fine-tuning using levels or curves, so let's begin by discussing levels. You can use the Levels dialog box to correct the tonal range and color balance of an image by adjusting the intensity levels of image shadows, midtones, and highlights.

1. To adjust the key tones in an image, select the layer you want to work on, and then choose Image > Adjustments > Levels. The Levels dialog box appears (**Figure 67a**).

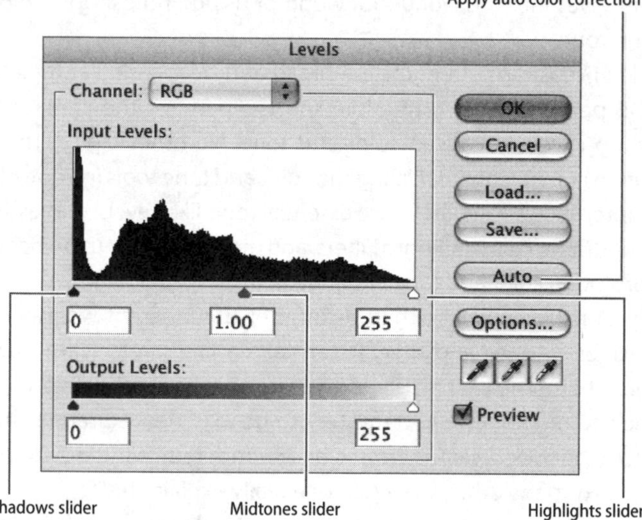

Figure 67a Think of the Levels dialog as a way to visually adjust color and tone.

2. Move the Shadows, Midtones, or Highlights sliders to make adjustments. Think of the Levels dialog as a visual guide for controlling and correcting exposure:

   - If an image is underexposed, move the Shadows slider to the right to increase the darker tones.
   - If an image is overexposed, move the Highlights slider to the left to decrease the brighter tones.

- To control the overall brightness of an image, move the Midtones slider to the left to lighten it or to the right to darken it. It may be helpful to think of the Midtones slider as a dimmer switch. While it doesn't turn the lights on or off, it does control the overall brightness.

One of the most common reasons to use the Levels dialog box is to fix images that are "flat" and lack tonal variety and contrast. For example, **Figure 67b** is a washed-out image, with limited contrast. It was much improved by opening the Levels dialog box and dragging the Shadows slider to the right to increase the darker tones, and dragging the Highlights slider to the left to decrease the brighter tones. This produced an enhanced image (**Figure 67c**).

Figure 67b The original image before any adjustments.

Figure 67c In the Levels dialog box, the Shadows slider was dragged to the right, and the Highlights slider was dragged to the left to create a more natural tonal range in the image.

Levels Shortcut

Because making Levels adjustments is a common practice, it's worth learning the shortcut to the Levels dialog box: In the Layers palette, select the layer you want to adjust and press Ctrl + L (Windows) or Command + L (Mac).

#68 Using the Curves Dialog Box

Both the Curves and Levels dialog boxes can be used to adjust the entire tonal range of an image. However, the difference between the two boils down to precision. While the Levels dialog box contains three sliders for making adjustments, the Curves dialog lets you adjust up to 14 different points throughout an image's tonal range (from shadows to highlights). As one of my fellow teachers once said, "Curves is Levels on steroids."

To apply a Curves adjustment:

- Select the layer you want to work on. Choose Image > Adjustments > Curves. The Curves dialog box opens (**Figure 68a**). From here you can make your adjustments.

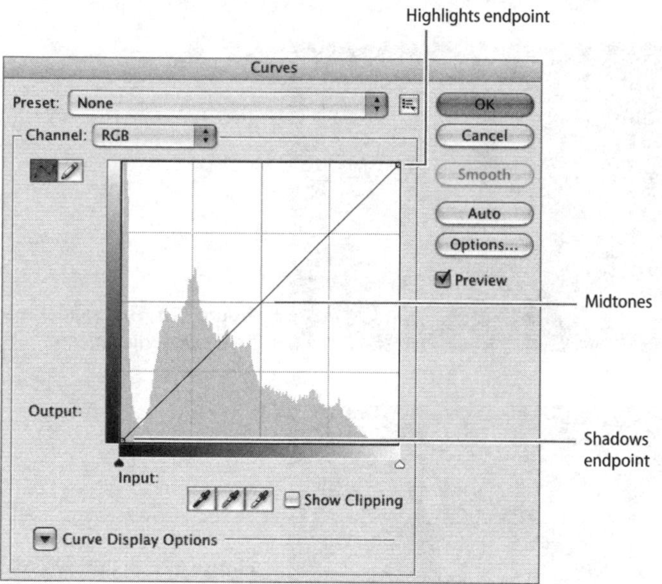

Figure 68a Curves lets you make precision adjustments to the color and tone of an image.

At first glance, the Curves dialog box can be intimidating. But once you begin, you'll find that applying an adjustment is easier than you thought it would be. I tend to apply a Curves adjustment to almost all of my images.

One of the most commonly applied and classic Curves adjustments is the *S* curve. In the Curves dialog, the shape of the curve can be modified to change the color saturation, contrast, and tone of your image.

To apply an *S* curve:

1. In the Curves dialog box, do any of the following:
   - Click the curve line near the top (near the Highlights endpoint) and drag up to strengthen the highlights.
   - Click the curve line near the bottom (near the Shadows endpoint) and drag down to darken the shadows.
   - Click the curve line near the middle (in the Midtones area) and drag up or down to adjust the overall brightness.

   Figure 68b shows an image in desperate need of an *S* curve because the image lacks contrast and color saturation.

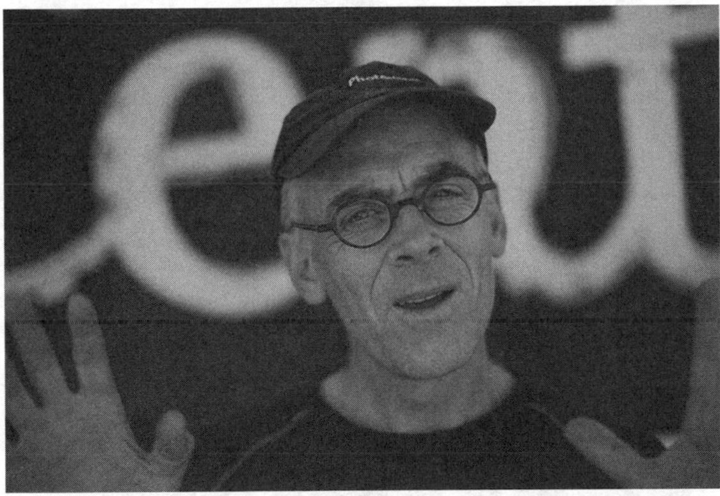

Figure 68b This image needs a Curves adjustment to increase contrast and color saturation.

(continued on next page)

Advanced Color with Curves

One of the most powerful aspects of Curves is that it gives you the ability to make precise adjustments to the different color channels of your image:

1. In the Curves dialog, choose an individual color channel from the Channel menu. If you are working on an RGB image, for example, choose one of the following:
   - Red to modify: Red and Cyan
   - Green to modify: Green and Magenta
   - Blue to modify: Blue and Yellow
2. Once you have chosen a specific channel, click the Curve line and drag it up to lighten that channel's color and down to lighten the channel's complementary color. For example, in the Red channel, drag up to add red. Drag down to add cyan.

Curves Shortcut

If you make a lot of Curves adjustments—and chances are you will—here's a shortcut you may find helpful: Select a layer in the Layers palette and press Ctrl + M (Windows) or Command + M (Mac) to open the Curves dialog box.

Curves Precision

For more precise control of curves, press Alt (Windows) or Option (Mac) while clicking anywhere inside the grid area to change a 4 × 4 grid to a 10 × 10 grid.

Figure 68c shows how the curve was adjusted in an effort to fix the image.

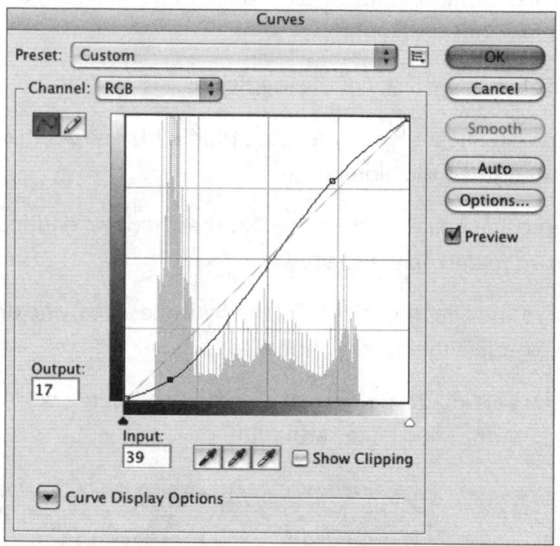

Figure 68c Darkening the shadows and brightening the highlights produced the classic *S* curve.

2. Click OK to apply the adjustment and view the final result.

   Figure 68d shows the result of applying an *S* curve adjustment to Figure 68b.

Figure 68d The final image as a result of the *S* curve adjustment.

#69 Adjusting Hue and Saturation

The Hue/Saturation command lets you adjust the hue (color), saturation (color intensity), and brightness of an image. These controls are some of those rare tools that "cross party lines," being of equal value to both technical and creative imagemakers.

To apply a Hue/Saturation adjustment:

1. Click the desired layer, and choose Image > Adjustments > Hue/Saturation. The Hue/Saturation dialog box appears (**Figure 69**).

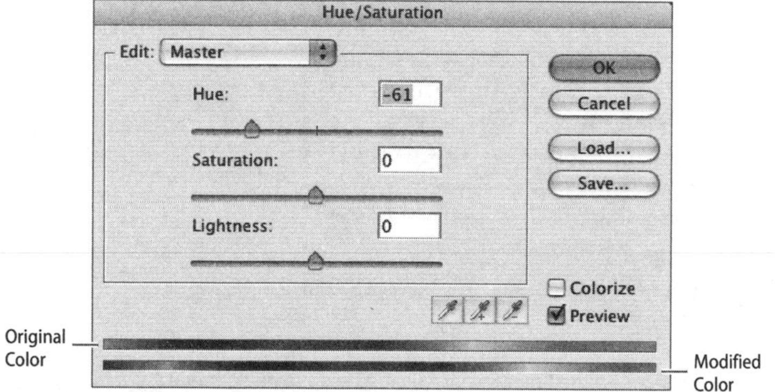

Figure 69 The Hue/Saturation dialog provides controls to modify color, saturation and brightness.

2. Do any of the following:
   - Drag the Hue slider to shift all the colors in the image around the color wheel. As you drag, the colors in the Modified Color bar at the bottom of the dialog box move in relation to the Original Color bar.
   - Move the Saturation slider to the right to increase saturation, or to the left to decrease or remove saturation.
   - Move the Lightness slider to the right to increase lightness, or to the left to decrease lightness.

Tip
Hue/Saturation adjustments are particularly well suited to fine-tuning colors in a CMYK image to bring them within gamut of a specific output device.

Advanced Hue/Saturation Technique

By default, the Master channel is selected in the Edit menu of the Hue/Saturation dialog box. This default setting is great when making global adjustments. However, for more precise control, you can choose a specific color from the menu to adjust only that color. For example, in a recent photograph I shot of a woman in a red dress, the dress was overexposed. To adjust only the color of the dress, I chose the Red channel and then decreased the Saturation and Lightness sliders by 5 points. This corrected the exposure of only the reds in the image, but left the rest of the colors intact.

#70 Adjusting Color Balance

If you are a visually oriented person, you will really like the Color Balance command because it is both intuitive and visually easy to understand. In more particular terms, Color Balance changes the overall colors in an image. If you are looking for a tool to make strong global color adjustments, Color Balance is your tool.

To apply a Hue/Saturation adjustment:

1. Select the desired layer and choose Image > Adjustments > Color Balance. The Color Balance dialog box appears (**Figure 70**).

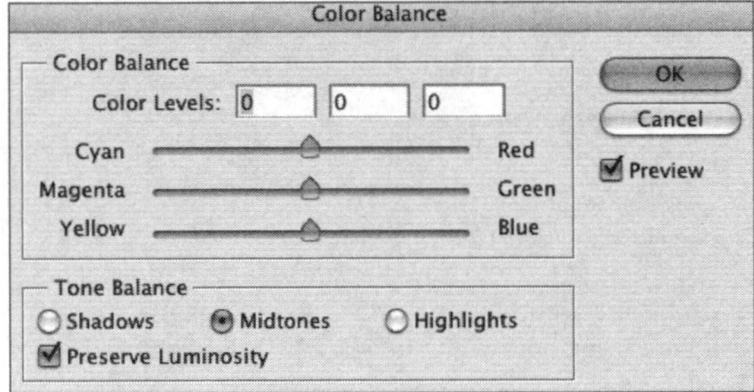

Figure 70 Use the Color Balance dialog box to make general color corrections and modifications to the shadows, midtones, and highlights in your image.

2. To maintain a tonal balance in the image, leave the Preserve Luminosity option selected to prevent changing the luminosity values in the image while changing the color.
3. Select the Shadows, Midtones, or Highlights radio button to indicate the tonal range where you want to focus the changes.
4. Drag each slider toward a color that you want to strengthen in the image and away from a color that you want to weaken in the image.

Color Balance and Sunsets

The Color Balance command can be used for a wide array of color modifications. To learn more about how this tool works, try using the command on a photograph of a sunset. You will be amazed at the results!

1. Open the Color Balance dialog box and increase the Red by 40 points.
2. Modify Yellow or Blue, depending on the image. Try adding 40 points to one or the other.

I've applied this Color Balance adjustment to many photographs of the sunset, and the subtle boost in color makes all the difference in the world.

#71 Replacing Color

The Color Replacement tool is a good choice when you need to replace the color of a specific object with another one, whereas the Replace Color command is a good choice when you need to make a global color change.

Using the Color Replacement tool

To use the Color Replacement tool:

1. Choose the Color Replacement tool from the Toolbox (it's hidden behind the Brush tool) (**Figure 71a**).

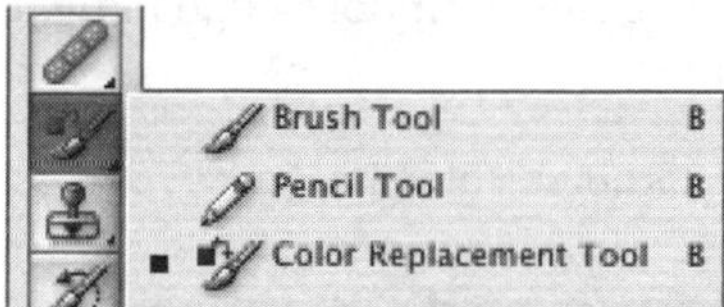

Figure 71a The Color Replacement tool shares a spot on the Toolbox with the Brush tool.

2. Configure the following settings in the options bar (**Figure 71b**):

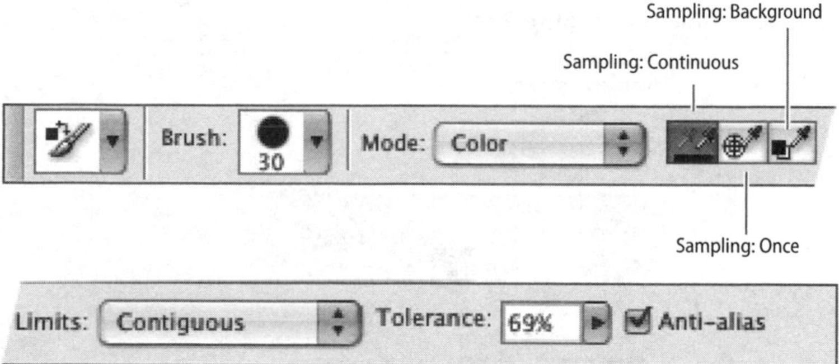

Figure 71b The options bar for the Color Replacement tool.

- **Brush.** Modify the size of the brush to match the size of the color object you want to change.
- **Mode.** The Color setting typically works best.
- **Sampling.** To sample colors continuously as you drag, choose Continuous. To replace the targeted color only in areas containing the color that you first selected, choose Once. To replace only the areas containing the current background color, choose Background Swatch.

(continued on next page)

- **Limits.** To replace the sampled color wherever it occurs under the pointer, choose Discontiguous. To replace colors that are part of a continuous area, including the color immediately under the pointer, choose Contiguous. To replace connected areas containing the sampled color while better preserving the sharpness of shape edges, choose Find Edges.
- **Tolerance.** Choose a low percentage to replace colors very similar to the pixel you click, or raise the percentage to replace a broader range of colors.
- **Anti-alias.** Select this option to define a smooth edge in the corrected areas.

3. Paint in the image to replace the targeted color.

Using the Color Replace command

To use the Color Replace command:

1. Choose Image > Adjustments > Replace Color to open the Replace Color dialog box (**Figure 71c**).

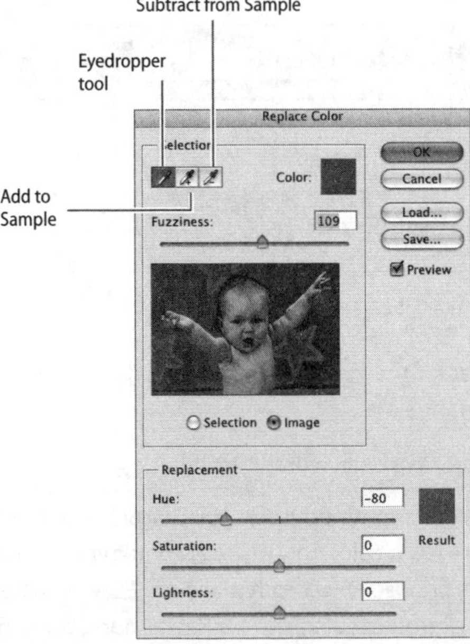

Figure 71c The Replace Color command works effectively when you need to make global color replacements.

2. Select a display option by choosing either the Selection radio button, which displays the mask in the preview window, or the Image radio button, which displays the image in the preview window.
3. Use the Eyedropper tool and click the area of the image or the preview box where you want to replace the color. If you need to add areas of color, use the Add to Sample tool. If you need to subtract areas of color, use the Subtract from Sample tool.
4. Adjust the tolerance by dragging the Fuzziness slider to the right to increase the degree to which related colors are included in the selection.
5. Choose a replacement color by dragging the Hue, Saturation, and Lightness sliders. You can see a live preview of the color change in the preview window.
6. Click OK to apply the color replacement.

Why Replace Color?

The Color Replace command and the Color Replacement tool are very powerful features of Photoshop. However, many photographers often assume that color replacement is used only when creative and subjective edits are desired. While these features are useful for those types of applications, they are also helpful for printing images in which the color is out of gamut (the range of colors an output device is capable of producing). In these cases, you can use Replace Color or Color Replacement to replace an out-of-gamut color with a color that is in gamut. This gives you full control of the final output.

#72 Adjusting Shadows and Highlights

A broad range of brightness and shadows while photographing a scene can make it difficult to get the exposure correct. For example, in **Figure 72a**, the background is properly exposed, but the boy is too dark.

Figure 72a Here just the subject is underexposed.

To remedy such problems, you can use the Shadow/Highlight command (**Figure 72b**).

Figure 72b Using the Shadow/Highlight command improved the exposure and brightened the previously underexposed subject in this image.

The Shadow/Highlight command works well for correcting photos that contain silhouetted images that are the result of strong backlighting or for correcting subjects that have been slightly washed out because they were too close to the camera flash.

To use the Shadow/Highlight command:

1. Choose Image > Adjustments > Shadow/Highlight to open the Shadows/Highlights dialog box (**Figure 72c**).

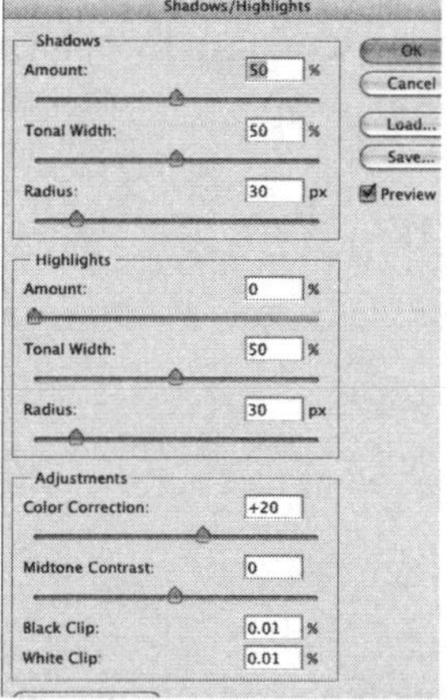

Figure 72c The Shadows/Highlights dialog box.

2. Select the Show More Options check box to reveal more controls.
3. Adjust the Shadows sliders to brighten shadow details. Then adjust the Highlights sliders to darken highlight details.

   For both the Shadows and Highlights areas:

   - Use the Amount slider to control the intensity of the adjustment.
   - Use the Tonal Width slider to control how much of the tonal range of the image will be affected.
   - Use the Radius slider to control the pixel width of the corrected area.
4. Use the Color Correction and Midtone Contrast sliders to compensate for any undesirable color or contrast changes you notice as you're making your adjustments.

Why Does Shadow/ Highlight Work?

Unlike other controls in Photoshop CS3, the Shadow/Highlight command does not simply lighten or darken an image. Rather, it lightens or darkens a part of the image based on the surrounding pixels. And this is why Shadow/Highlight works so well. The analysis of the surrounding pixels results in better darkening and brightening. Separate controls for the shadows and the highlights, as well as a Midtone Contrast slider, Black Clip option, and White Clip option for adjusting the overall contrast of the image only add to the rich functionality of the Shadow/Highlight command.

A Versatile Tool

Don't be fooled into thinking that the Shadow/Highlight command is useful only for "problem" images. On the contrary, this command is incredibly useful for brightening areas of shadow in an otherwise well lit image. If you find that your shadows are "blocked up," try the Shadow/Highlight command. The results may surprise you!

#73 Using Brightness and Contrast

In previous versions of Photoshop, the Brightness/Contrast command was not very effective, unless it was used for special effects. However, the Brightness/Contrast command in CS3 works incredibly well. It lets you make simple adjustments to the tonal range of an image. And because you can control both brightness and contrast separately, you can rectify the dark areas of an image that result from increasing the contrast by increasing the brightness, too.

To correct brightness and contrast:

1. Choose Image > Adjustments > Brightness/Contrast to open the Brightness/Contrast dialog box (**Figure 73a**).

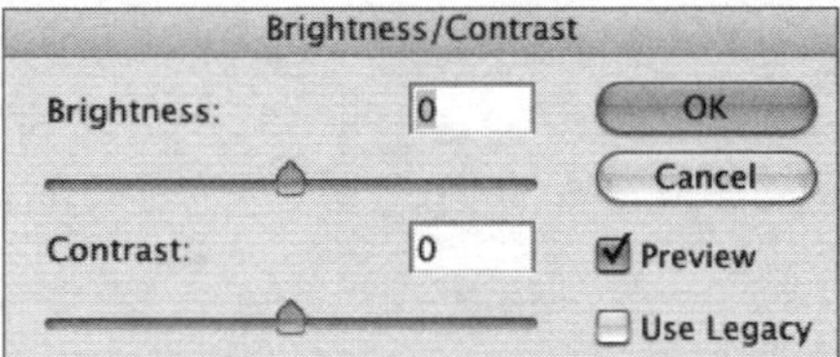

Figure 73a The Brightness/Contrast dialog box.

2. Move the sliders to the right to increase brightness or contrast, and to the left to decrease brightness or contrast.

The most important setting in Brightness/Contrast is the Use Legacy option (which causes the command to work the way it did in earlier versions of Photoshop).

In default mode, the option is not selected, so brightness and contrast adjustments are proportionate (nonlinear) to the image pixels. The way these adjustments are made is similar to the way Levels and Curves adjustments are made.

In contrast, when Use Legacy is selected, adjustments to brightness simply shift all pixel values higher or lower, which can cause clipping and loss of detail. This is a problem because while this loss of detail may look good on your monitor, it will most likely have a negative appearance when the image is printed. As a result, this option is helpful when creating special effects, but it's not ideal for high-end print output.

Figures 73b, 73c and **73d** illustrate the difference between the default and Use Legacy modes. Both images were adjusted using the

Brightness/Contrast command in the same fashion: The contrast was increased to 100. However, Figure 73b was adjusted in default mode, while the Figure 73c was adjusted with Use Legacy selected.

Figure 73b The original image without any adjustments.

Figure 73c In this image, the Contrast slider was increased to 100, with the Use Legacy option deselected.

Figure 73d In this image, the Contrast slider was increased to 100, with Use Legacy selected.

#74 Applying Photo Filters

In traditional film photography, it is a common practice to put a colored filter in front of the camera lens to adjust the color balance and temperature. This gives photographers creative control over the color shift of an image. For example, for many years, a popular filter has been the 85 warming filter, which adds a yellow or warm tone and creates a nostalgic and inviting image. The Photo Filter command mimics this traditional photographic technique and gives digital photographers the same creative control.

To apply a photo filter:

1. Choose Image > Adjustments > Photo Filter to open the Photo Filter dialog box (**Figure 74**).

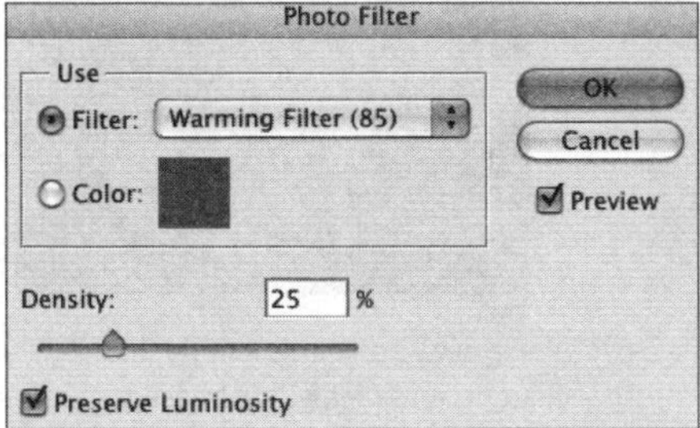

Figure 74 Choose a preset filter to warm or cool the image. Or select a custom color to correct a color cast or for special color effects.

2. Do one of the following:
   - Select the Filter radio button and choose a preset filter from the Filter menu.
   - For a custom color filter, select the Color radio button, click the color square to the right, and use the Adobe Color Picker to specify a color.
3. Adjust the amount of color applied using the Density slider. A higher number results in a stronger color adjustment.
4. To prevent the image from being darkened by the color filter, select the Preserve Luminosity option.
5. Click OK to apply the filter to the image.

Preset Photo Filters

The Warming Filter presets make the image warmer (more yellow), and the Cooling Filter presets make the image cooler (bluer). Which filter is best? It depends upon the desired intensity of the color effect:

- Warming Filter (81) and Cooling Filter (82) are best for minor adjustments.
- Warming Filter (85 and LBA) and Cooling Filter (80 and LBB) are best for making strong adjustments.

Another option is to select the Color radio button to apply a global hue adjustment to the image. A custom color can be used to neutralize a color cast or to apply colors for special color effects or enhancements. While it is possible to use the Color option for correcting color casts, I find it most helpful for special effects.

#75 Converting to Black and White

There is something powerful about a good black-and-white image. Fortunately, creating a compelling one is much easier than it used to be. The Black & White command in Photoshop CS3 allows you to convert a color image to grayscale while maintaining full control over how individual colors are converted. You can even tint the grayscale image with a color to create sepia or other tone effects.

It's also possible to use the Hue/Saturation command for black-and-white conversions, but it's less precise and thus works much less effectively than the Black & White command. For example, **Figure 75a** was converted to grayscale using the Hue/Saturation command, whereas **Figure 75b** was converted using the Black & White command.

Figure 75a A grayscale conversion using the Hue/Saturation command.

Figure 75b The same image, converted to grayscale using the Black & White Command.

A Black-and-White Speed Tip

You can use the cursor to make more precise black-and-white adjustments.

1. Open a Color Image.
2. Choose Image > Adjustments > Black & White.
3. With the Black and White dialog box open, hover the cursor over the image until it changes to an eyedropper.
4. Click an area in the image, and the corresponding color will be selected in the dialog box. Without releasing the mouse button, drag to adjust the color slider for that color.

This technique is incredibly helpful because you don't have to guess which slider affects a particular area in the image. Instead, you simply hover over a color in the image and then drag to make changes. Not only does this speed tip make your conversion execute much faster, but it also helps you create more intriguing images.

Black and White Video Tutorial

For a free training video on converting color images to black and white, see www.adobe.com/go/vid0017.

To use the Black & White command:

1. Choose Image > Adjustments > Black & White to open the Black and White dialog box. Photoshop performs a default grayscale conversion based on the colors in the image.
2. If you do not like the default conversion, click the Auto button. I have found that this creates a much more desirable starting point.
3. Manually adjust the conversion using the color sliders, or choose a preset or previously saved custom mix from the Preset menu (**Figure 75c**).

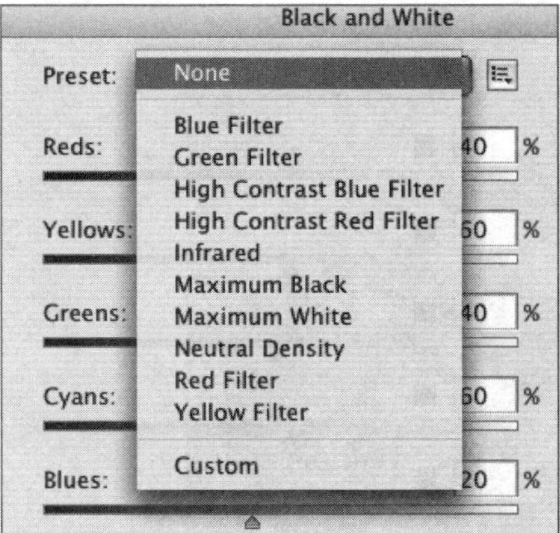

Figure 75c Choose one of the default black-and-white presets or choose a previously saved custom mix.

4. For any of the colors in the original image, drag the corresponding slider to the left to darken or to the right to lighten the gray tones of that color. For example, to darken the sky, drag the blue and cyan sliders to the left.
5. To enhance your black-and-white image by adding a color tone, select the Tint option and adjust the Hue (color) and Saturation (color intensity) sliders. Or click on the related color chip to the right of each slider to select a color from the Adobe Color Picker.

CHAPTER TEN

Masking

My older brother and I used to love running around wearing our favorite Spiderman, Batman, or Zorro masks when we were little. Masks are fun for kids because they hide a portion or all of your face. Photoshop layer masks work in a similar way in that they can be used to partially or entirely hide something, particularly the contents of a layer.

And here's the *really* good news. While masking isn't easy, it definitely isn't rocket science. Once you master the basics of masking, the efficiency of your Photoshop workflow will grow by leaps and bounds.

This chapter presents the fundamental concepts that will help you better understand and work with masks. As you read through it, keep in mind the following:

- Because masking is so important, slow down, absorb the information, and then make sure you practice each of the How-Tos presented here. Don't just read along.
- While this chapter presents just the essentials of masking, you can apply the techniques to a wide range of simple and advanced image edits and enhancements.
- If you feel like masking is difficult, don't give up. Your efforts will pay off when you see the results!

#76 Using a Layer Mask

Creating a Mask from a Selection

Painting a layer mask by hand can be a tedious chore. You can also use a selection as the source of a mask:

1. In the Layers palette, select a layer or group.
2. Use one of the selection tools or commands to make a selection in the image.
3. Create a mask using one of the following techniques:
   - Click the Add Layer Mask button in the Layers palette to create a mask that reveals the selection.
   - Alt-click (Windows) or Option-click (Mac) the Add Layer Mask button to create a mask that hides the selection.
   - Choose Layer> Layer Mask > Reveal Selection or Hide Selection.

One way to use a mask is to attach it to a specific layer. Masks can be added to any type of layer: image layers, adjustments layers, type layers, shape layers, layer groups, and so on. The advantage of using a layer mask is that when you add a mask to a layer and hide a portion of it, you are not actually deleting pixels; instead you are simply hiding them. So if you make a mistake or change your mind, you can always go back and modify the mask.

To add a mask to a layer, select the layer and do one of the following:

- Click the Add Layer Mask button in the Layers palette (**Figure 76a**).

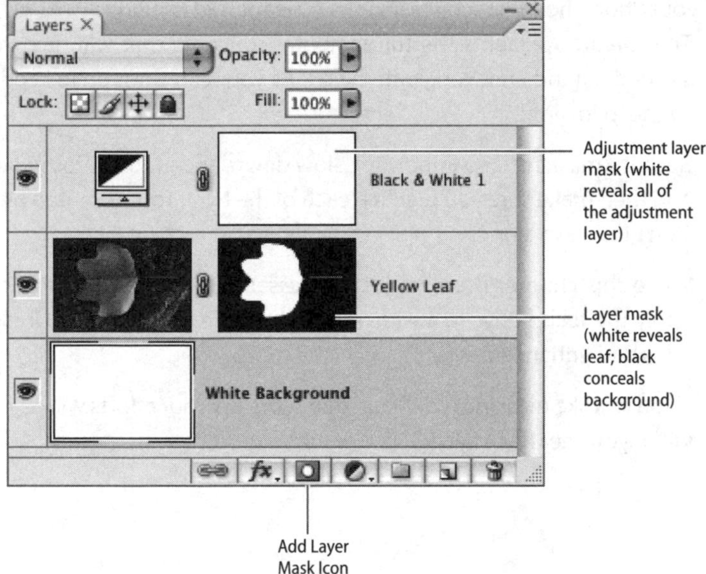

Figure 76a The quickest way to add a layer mask is to select the layer and click the Add Layer Mask button in the Layers palette. The mask will appear to the right of the Layer thumbnail.

- Choose Layer > Layer Mask > Reveal All or Hide All.

The key to understanding masks is that white reveals and black conceals. You can click on a mask to select it, then paint on it using white or black to show or hide the contents of the layer.

For example, in **Figure 76b**, I want to select the leaf to remove it from its background. I used the selection tools to select everything but the leaf (in other words, the background) and then painted the selection black. The result is the leaf by itself (**Figure 76c**).

Figure 76b The original image.

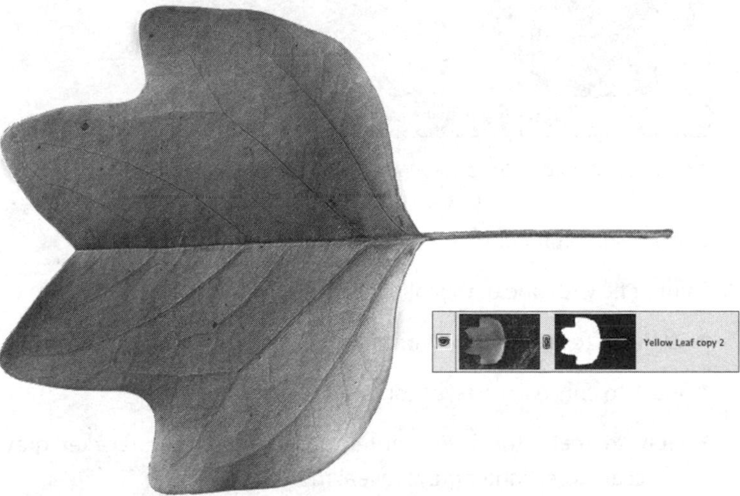

Figure 76c The background was removed using a layer mask.

Keep in mind that no pixels were harmed using this technique. I can also return and modify or remove the mask at anytime by painting with black or white (see the next How-To for more information).

Use the Same Layer Mask on Multiple Layers

There are a number of circumstances in which you may need to apply identical or similar masks to multiple layers. The quickest way to apply a layer mask from one layer to another is to duplicate the mask by holding Alt (Windows) or Option (Mac) while dragging the mask to each of the other layers.

On the other hand, if you simply need to move a mask to one other layer, just drag the mask to that layer.

#77 Modifying a Layer Mask

Modifying layer masks is easy and rewarding. If you know how to choose a color in the Toolbox and paint with the Brush tool, you know how to modify a layer mask—that's all it takes!

To modify a layer mask:

1. In the Layers palette, click the layer mask thumbnail (located to the right of the layer icon). Once you have clicked it, a border appears around the mask thumbnail, indicating it is active (**Figure 77a**).

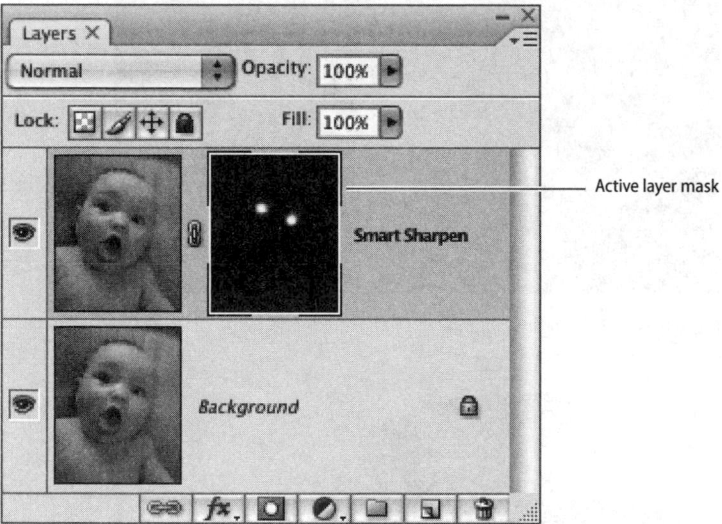

Figure 77a A border appears around an active layer mask.

2. Choose an editing or painting tool.
3. Paint or fill with one of the following:
   - White to reveal the layer contents.
   - Black to conceal the layer contents.
   - Gray to make the layer contents partially visible. Darker grays conceal more; lighter grays reveal more.

Figure 77b, a photograph of my youngest (and very cute) daughter, is a good example of an image in which modifying a layer mask is the best way to improve it.

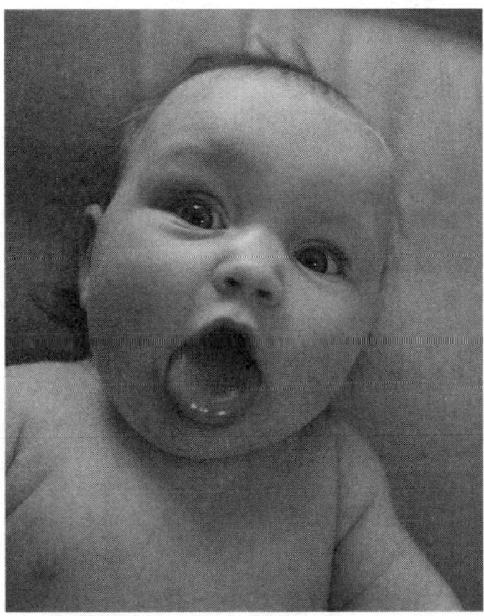

Figure 77b This image would benefit from an enhancement that involves sharpening and masking to sharpen just the eyes.

To sharpen the eyes in the image, I first copied the Background layer and then applied the Smart Sharpening filter (see Chapter 13, "Sharpening"), which sharpens the entire image. Then I created a mask filled with black to conceal the sharpening (Alt-click/Option-click the Add Layer Mask icon). I chose the Brush tool, and then chose white as the foreground color (click the Foreground Color box in the Toolbox and choose white from the

Link and Unlink a Layer Mask

By default a layer is linked to its layer mask. The link is identified in the Layers palette by a small link icon that appears between the thumbnails in the Layers palette. Typically, when you create a layer mask, it is best to leave the layer and the layer mask linked. This way, if you move either one using the Move tool, the layer and its mask move together.

However, if you need to be able to move the layer and its mask independently, click the link icon to unlink them. To re-establish the link, click in the space between the layer and its mask.

Layer Masking Shortcuts

To become more efficient at masking, try the following shortcuts:

- Shift-click on the layer mask thumbnail to toggle the mask on and off.
- Alt-click (Windows) or Option-click (Mac) the layer mask thumbnail to toggle between displaying the image and displaying the mask in the main document window.
- Shift + Alt-click (Windows) or Shift + Option-click (Mac) the layer mask thumbnail to toggle between showing the mask in red superimposed on the image and the image itself.

Color Picker). I painted on the eyes with the Brush tool, adding white to the layer mask and revealing the sharpened layer beneath (**Figure 77c**).

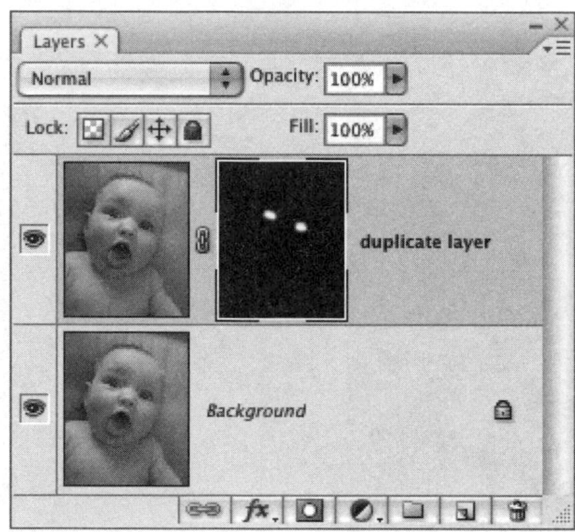

Figure 77c I painted around her eyes with white.

The eyes ended up being much sharper, making the overall image much more compelling.

#78 Removing Color Using a Mask

Sometimes you need to remove color from an image to enhance it. Using a layer mask to accomplish this gives you increased control and flexibility.

Although this How-To is very specific, keep in mind that the process and techniques described here are actually more important than the project itself. In other words, what you learn in this How-To can be applied to a wide variety of image-enhancement scenarios.

This particular masking technique is very easy to understand, and, as a result, it often helps people learn how masks actually work. Many of my photography students finally experience the "masking a-ha moment" when they practice removing color in this way.

For your first try at removing color using a layer mask, choose an image from which it's simple to remove color. In my case, I'm using an image of an orange California poppy against an out-of-focus purple and green background of wildflowers. We'll focus on removing all of the color in our image, except for the main object. In my case, it's the poppy color that will remain.

To remove color using a layer mask:

1. Click the Adjustment Layer icon at the bottom of the Layers palette and choose Hue/Saturation from the menu (**Figure 78a**). A Hue/Saturation adjustment layer is added to the image.

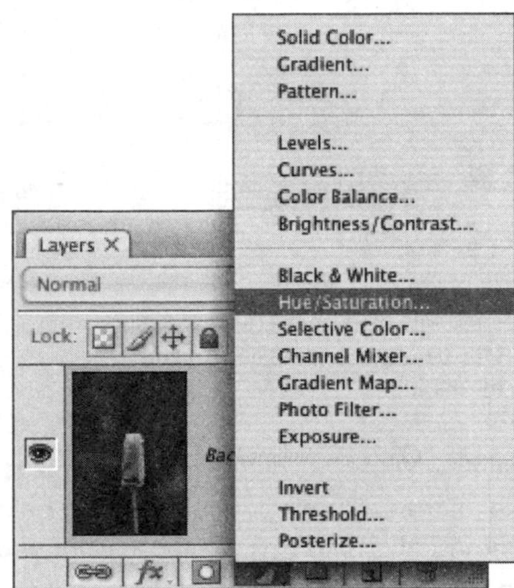

Figure 78a Create an adjustment layer above the image layer.

(continued on next page)

Adding Color Using a Mask

Sometimes an effect that's even more interesting than removing color is to add color using a mask. For example, in a portrait in which the model has blue eyes, you might want to enhance the blue eye color. To do this, you would execute the same steps as you would to remove color, except that you'd substitute the following:

1. In the Hue/Saturation dialog box, increase the saturation by 5 to 10 points and click OK.
2. Fill the mask with black to conceal the color saturation.
3. Using the Brush tool, paint with white on the eyes to reveal the more saturated layer.

2. In the Hue/Saturation dialog box, decrease the saturation by 100 points to remove all the color. Click OK. The image is now in grayscale.

   As a side note, by default, when you create an adjustment layer, a layer mask filled with white is automatically created along with it. Thus, the entirety of the adjustment is revealed.

3. Click the mask thumbnail to activate the mask. With the Brush tool, paint with black on the area that you want to restore to full color (**Figure 78b**).

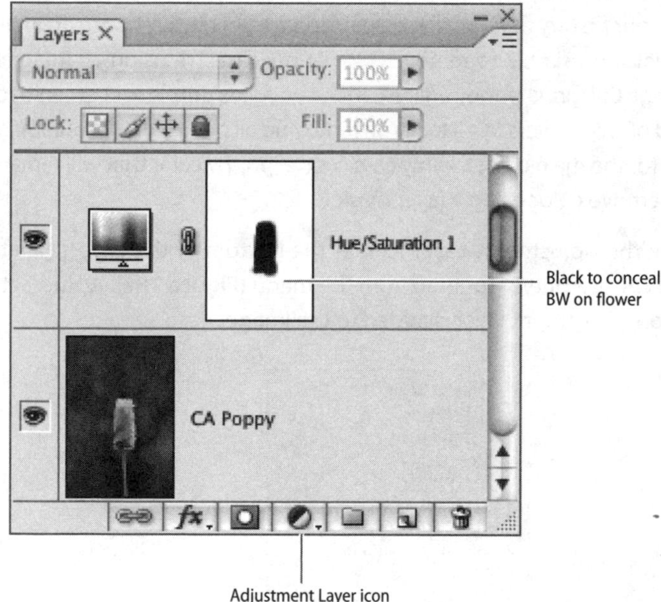

Figure 78b The area that is painted with black on the Hue/Saturation adjustment layer mask conceals the desaturation, thus allowing the original color to show through the mask.

Once you have finished painting with black on the mask, the image is complete. In my case, the color of the California poppy stands out boldly from the gray background. Because this book isn't printed in color, you'll need to use your imagination to fully visualize the effect.

#79 Blending Images Using a Mask

One of the more common uses of masking is to blend multiple images together to create a photographic collage. The advantage of using masking for this purpose is that you can blend without actually deleting pixels.

To blend images using a mask:

1. Open multiple images in Photoshop.
2. Choose the Move tool.
3. Drag the images into one document. Each image will occupy a separate layer. In my case, I'm using four images of a very happy child (**Figure 79a**).

Figure 79a Multiple images dragged into one Photoshop document.

4. Use the Move tool to position the images.
5. Select an image layer and click the Add Layer Mask icon in the Layers palette.
6. Repeat Step 5 for each image layer.
7. Choose the Brush tool, then in the options bar, and choose a brush with soft edges.

(continued on next page)

8. Paint around the edges of each of the images to soften their sharp edges. This helps to blend the layers into a unified image (**Figure 79b**).

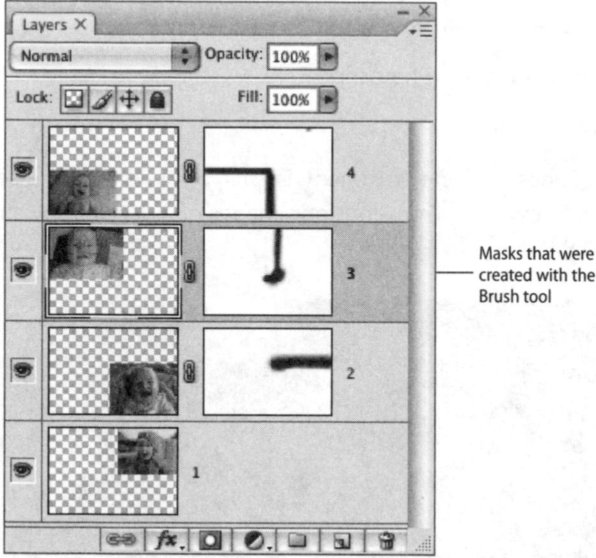

Figure 79b By creating a mask on each image, you can soften the edges and blend the images together.

When you are finished, the final image should be a more compelling and cohesive collage as a result of the masking (**Figure 79c**).

Figure 79c In my case, the final photographic collage of my daughter has softer edges, so it's more compelling.

#80 Using Quick Mask

If you enjoy being able to make "selections" by painting on a layer mask, you will really like using Quick Mask mode. As the name implies, this mode gives you the ability to make a mask quickly. Think of Quick Mask as a temporary way to make a painted or mask-based selection. The advantage of using Quick Mask is speed.

Here's how to use Quick Mask mode:

1. Do one of the following:
   - Select part of the image that you want to change—you will then refine the selection in Quick Mask mode.
   - If you want to wait until you're in Quick Mask mode before creating the selection, do nothing.
2. Click the Quick Mask Mode button in the Toolbox (**Figure 80a**) or press the Q key. If you have an active selection, a red color overlays the unselected (protected) parts of the image, signifying that Quick Mask mode is enabled. The red color represents the mask.

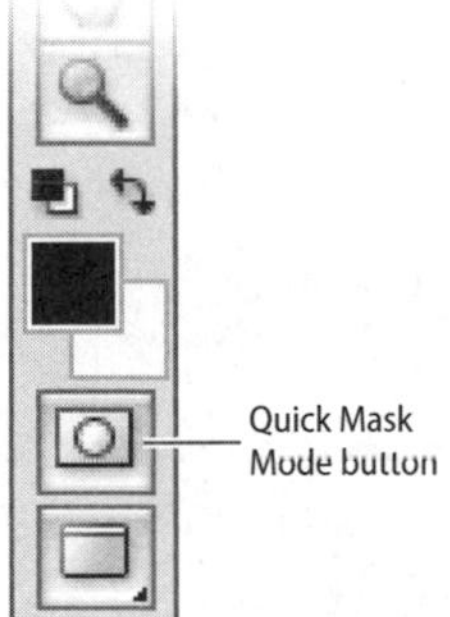

Figure 80a Click the Quick Mask icon to enter Quick Mask mode.

3. To edit the mask, paint with the Brush tool. Paint with white to select more of an image (the color overlay is removed from areas painted with white). To deselect areas, paint over them using black.
4. When you are finished painting, exit Quick Mask mode by clicking the Quick Mask Mode button in the Toolbox or by pressing the Q key. Upon exiting Quick Mask mode, the clear (non-red) area will turn into a selection.

Creating a Permanent Layer Mask

Most of the time you'll want to convert the temporary selection you created using Quick Mask mode into a permanent layer mask. Otherwise you will lose the Quick Mask mode selection. To create a permanent mask, exit Quick Mask mode, then click the Add Layer Mask button on the Layers palette.

For more Quick Mask options, double-click the Quick Mask icon in the Toolbox to open the Quick Mask Options dialog box (**Figure 80b**).

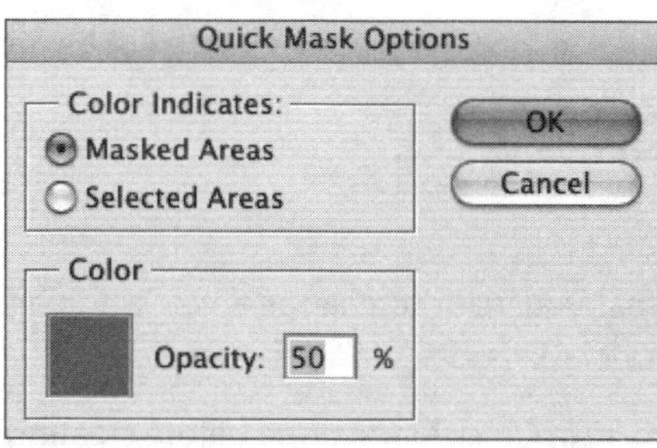

Figure 80b Double-click the Quick Mask icon to open the Quick Mask Options dialog box.

Tip
While in Quick Mask mode, painting with gray creates a semitransparent area, which can be helpful when you need to soften or feather a selection edge.

CHAPTER ELEVEN

Retouching Portraits

I recently had the opportunity to photograph one of the top-ranked triathletes in the world. My assignment was to create a telling portrait for a major publication. When I started planning the shot, my first thought was, "How do I capture the essence of this athlete and make him look good?"

When you stop to think about it, much of a photographer's work with portrait photography is to use the specific environments, lighting, perspectives, and Photoshop techniques that help make a subject look good. The important thing to keep in mind is that different genres of photography require different types of retouching. We do not simply retouch an image because we can. Rather, we retouch to fit the parameters of the genre and the goal of the image. For example, the level of skin smoothing we might do varies, depending on whether the subject is a high-end fashion model or a rural farmer.

This chapter presents a few basic and essential retouching skills that you can apply to many of your images. Before we begin, it is important to note that this chapter was intentionally placed near the end of the book because it utilizes many of the skills you learned in previous chapters. For example, some of the retouching techniques require a basic understanding of blending modes and masking. If you haven't flipped through these chapters yet, be sure to do so before you begin. This will help you make higher quality improvements to your images.

#81 Reducing Red Eye

Red eye, which is a result of the camera flash reflecting off the subject's retina, can ruin an image. Not to worry, Photoshop has a tool dedicated to quickly and easily fixing this problem.

To remove red eye using Photoshop:

1. Choose the Red Eye tool from the Toolbox (**Figure 81a**).

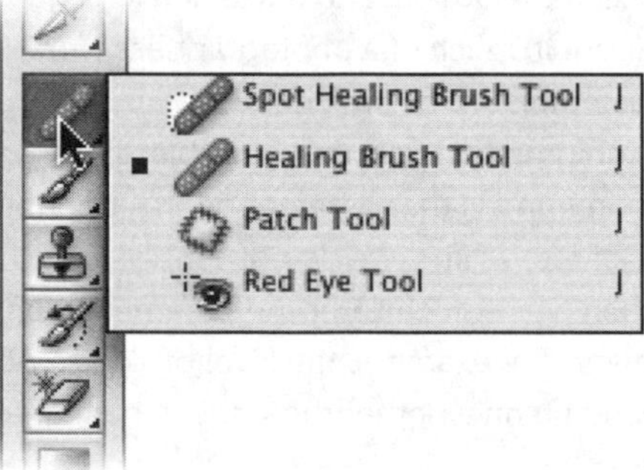

Figure 81a By default, the Red Eye tool is hidden behind the Spot Healing Brush tool.

2. Select the eye using one of the following techniques:
   - Click the center of the eye to select it.
   - Drag a rectangle around the eye to select it. It is best to create a rectangle that is slightly bigger than the iris (**Figure 81b**).

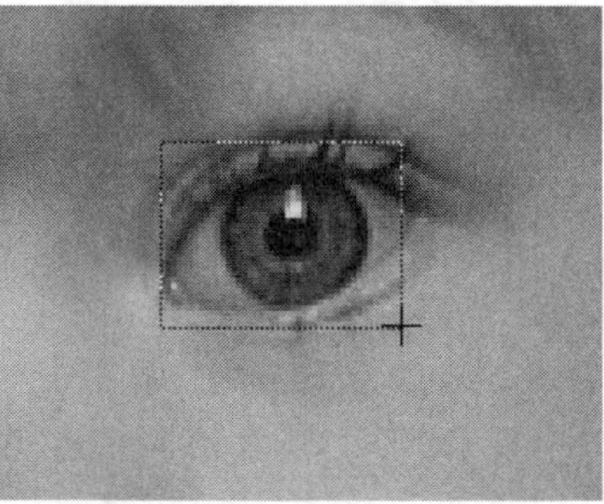

Figure 81b The eye, selected with the Red Eye tool.

3. Release the mouse button, and the red is removed automatically.

4. In the options bar, adjust the Pupil and Darken values to fine-tune the correction (**Figure 81c**). Pupil Size increases or decreases the area affected by the Red Eye tool. Darken Amount sets the darkness of the correction.

5. Repeat these steps for the other eye(s) in the image that need corrected.

Figure 81c Adjust the values for Pupil Size and Darken Amount in the options bar to fine-tune the red eye removal.

Note

To reduce red eye using Adobe Camera Raw, see How-To #35.

What Causes Red Eye?

Red eye is caused by a reflection of the camera flash in the subject's retina. Red eye occurs most frequently (yet is not limited to) the increased size of the subject's retina because of darkened conditions. Most cameras today come equipped with a red-eye reduction flash setting. However, this feature doesn't always do the trick, especially when using point-and-shoot cameras that have short distances between their lenses and their flash bulbs.

#82 Retouching Blemishes

When you clean your house, it makes more sense to dust the furniture and bookcase before you vacuum the floor than it does to do it the other way around—vacuuming before you dust. The same is true with digital retouching. It makes more sense to remove blemishes and distractions and then work on other enhancements like wrinkle reduction.

Removing blemishes

Let's begin by learning how to reduce blemishes and distracting elements in an image. One of the tools we'll use is the Healing Brush tool. The Healing Brush tool works much like the Retouching tool in the Camera Raw plug-in that we discussed back in How-To #34. It lets you sample pixels from a relatively un-blemished part of the image (known as the sample point), and blend those pixels over the part of the image you're trying to repair.

Most professional retouchers create a retouching "road map" before they begin (**Figure 82a**). This involves creating a new layer and then circling any distracting elements. A road map such as this will help you determine what needs to be retouched.

Figure 82a Before you begin retouching, create a new layer and circle the distracting elements.

Once you have your road map, you can begin to remove the rough patches:

1. Create a new layer for each type of blemish. In the example image, the created layers include Back Drop, Nose, and Zipper (**Figure 82b**).

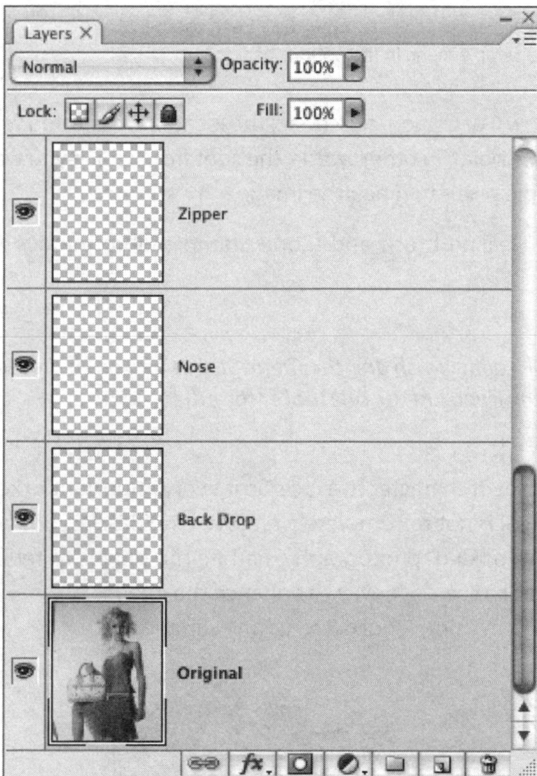

Figure 82b Create a separate layer for each type of blemish.

2. Select the layer where you want to begin your corrections.

(continued on next page)

3. Choose the Healing Brush tool. Then in the options bar, choose All Layers from the Sample menu (**Figure 82c**).

Figure 82c When healing to separate layers, be sure to choose All Layers from the Sample menu in the options bar.

4. Alt-click (Windows) or Option-click (Mac) the location where you want to set the sample point; in other words, the spot from which you want to borrow sample pixels to repair the image.

5. Paint with the Healing brush and Clone Stamp tool to remove the blemishes.

Tip

Using both the Healing brush and the Clone Stamp tool often produces better results than if you just use one tool or the other.

Reducing wrinkles

Wrinkles can add a lot of character to a face. So it's very important to keep in mind that the goal is not to completely remove wrinkles, lest you end up practicing "fake-looking" photography. Rather, the goal is to reduce the intensity of the shadows as a way to enhance the image.

For this exercise, I'm using **Figure 82d** as an example.

Figure 82d This image would benefit from a little massaging around the corners of the eyes.

1. Create a new layer for each area that you want to touch up, such as the left or right corners of the eyes or the forehead (**Figure 82e**).

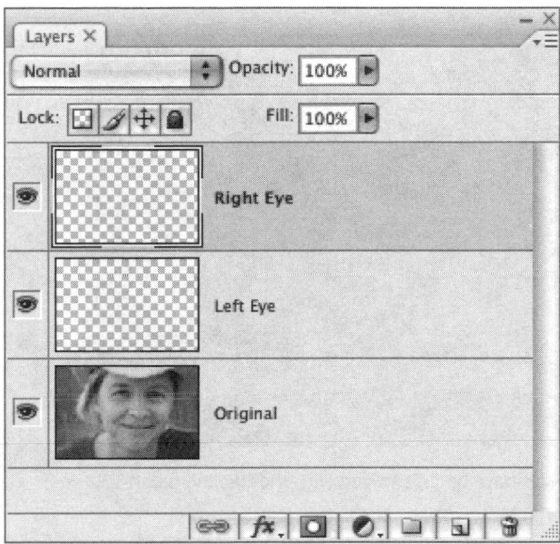

Figure 82e Create new layers for each area to be retouched.

2. Set the sample area that you want to copy pixels from by choosing the Healing Brush, and Alt-clicking (Windows) or Option-clicking (Mac) the area just below the wrinkles. You want a sample source that is "clean" and free of blemishes (**Figure 82f**).

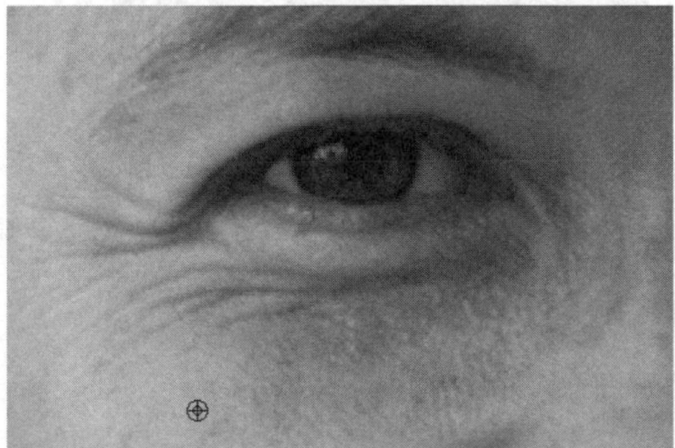

Figure 82f Alt-click (Windows) or Option-click (Mac) to set the sample area on a patch of skin that does not have wrinkles.

(continued on next page)

Advanced Retouching

Here is a professional portrait-retouching secret that is worth its weight in gold: Most professional retouching is actually done using the Clone Stamp tool and different blending modes. This technique can be a bit trickier than using the Healing Brush, but the potential for much more rewarding results is worth it.

1. Choose the Clone Stamp tool.
2. Choose these options from the options bar:
   - To remove dark blemishes, choose the Lighten blending mode. This way, the cloning affects only the darker pixels. Then choose a low opacity.
   - To remove light blemishes, select the Multiply or Darken blending mode. This way, the cloning affects only the lighter pixels. Then choose a low opacity.
3. Create a new layer for each type of blemish, such as freckles, skin blemishes, and so on.
4. Paint over the blemish using the Clone Stamp tool.

3. Paint the wrinkled area with the Healing Brush (**Figure 82g**). Be careful to not paint over high contrast or dark areas like eyelashes, eyebrows, and hair.

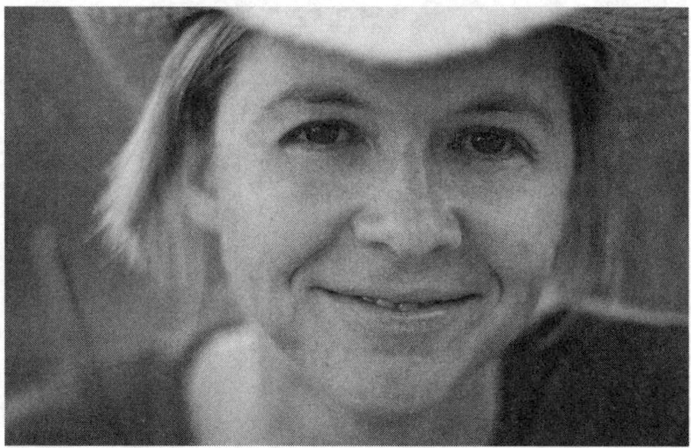

Figure 82g Wrinkles have been removed with the Healing brush.

4. To keep the image from looking unnatural, lower the opacity of the layer on which you painted to bring back some of the wrinkles and character (**Figure 82h**).

Figure 82h The final Image with Left and Right Eye layers set to a lower opacity. The final result is not a complete wrinkle removal, but rather a smoothing of the wrinkles.

#83 Smoothing Skin

If you look closely at skin, it is anything but smooth and consistent. Instead, the tone, structure, and texture in even just a small area of skin can be very complex.

To create a more flattering portrait, try practicing the comprehensive set of skin-smoothing instructions in this How-To. It involves four processes:

- Setting up the image
- Creating a mask and applying a blur
- Copying the mask to a Texture layer
- Adding some texture

This is an advanced technique, so put on your thinking cap, fasten your seat belts, and get ready to for a wild ride!

Setting up the image

To begin the process of smoothing skin in a photograph, add two layers to your original image by clicking the Background and pressing Ctrl + J (Windows) or Command + J (Mac) twice. Double-click the Background to open the New Layer dialog box and name it Original (this converts it into a real layer). Then rename the other layers from top to bottom: Texture and Gaussian (**Figure 83a**).

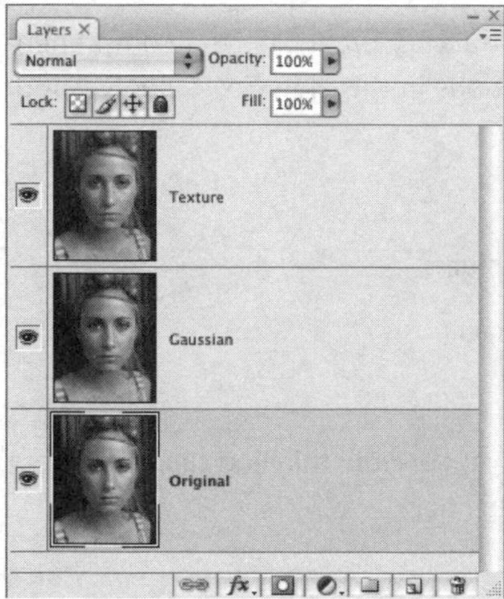

Figure 83a The layer stack for our skin-smoothing project.

Next, click the Eye icon to hide the Texture layer.

Applying the blur

To apply a blur to smooth the skin:

1. Select the Gaussian layer and choose Filter > Blur > Gaussian Blur.
2. In the Gaussian Blur dialog box that appears, drag the Radius slider to set the amount of Gaussian Blur so that the image appears to be

behind a piece of slightly frosted glass. The actual amount will vary depending upon the image resolution. Click OK (**Figure 83b**).

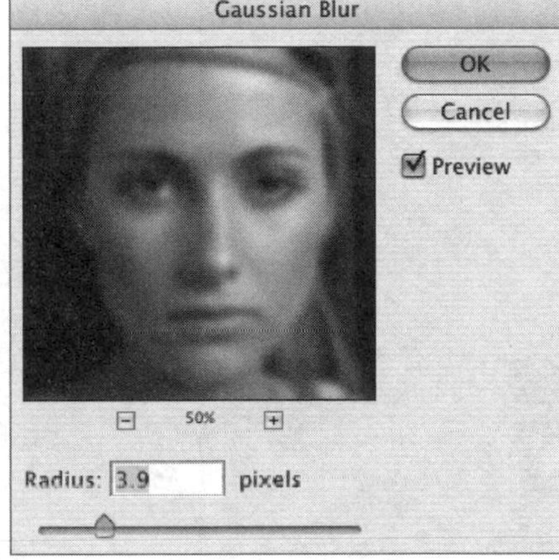

Figure 83b Apply the Gaussian Blur filter until the image is blurred but still recognizable.

3. Alt-click (Windows) or Option-click (Mac) the Add Layer Mask button in the Layers palette. This creates a mask filled with black, which conceals the Gaussian Blur effect.
4. Choose the Brush tool, and then paint with white on the areas of skin that need softening. Be careful not to paint on the lips, eyes, eyebrows,

(continued on next page)

hair, and so on. Painting on the layer mask with white reveals the blurred image (**Figure 83c**).

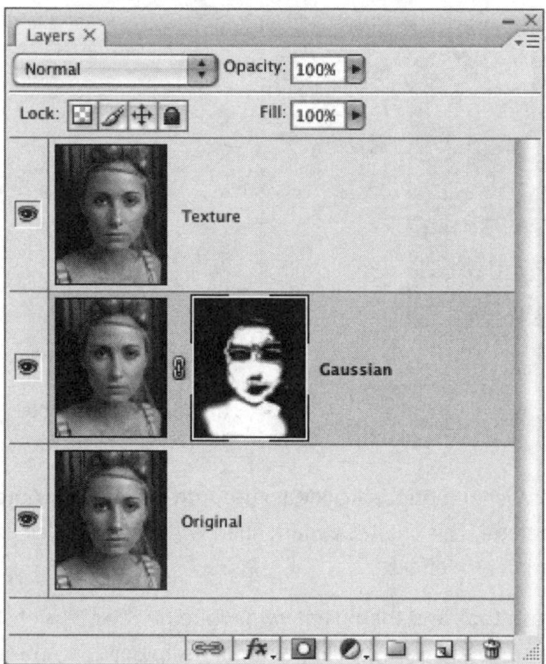

Figure 83c A layer mask hides the Gaussian layer except where skin is exposed.

5. Make the Original and Gaussian layers visible by clicking their eye icons. In the options bar, lower the opacity of the Gaussian layer to approximately 50%, or whatever percentage that looks best.

Copying the mask

Now it's time to copy this mask to the Texture layer. Alt-drag (Windows) or Option-drag (Mac) the mask from the Gaussian layer to the Texture layer. This applies a copy of the mask you just created to the Texture layer (**Figure 83d**).

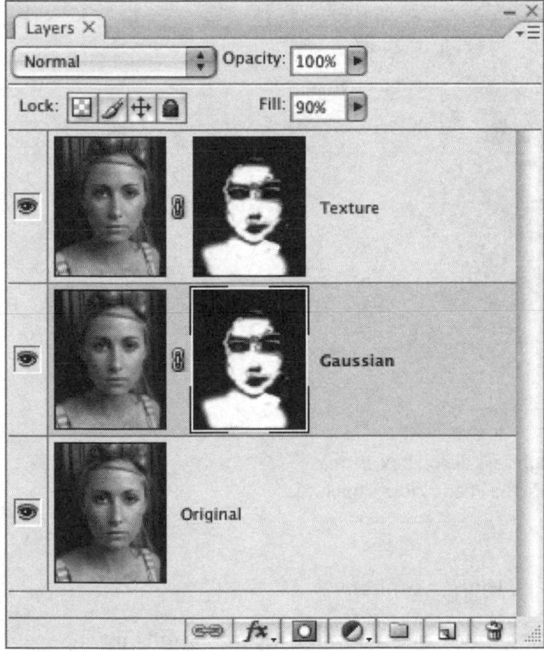

Figure 83d The mask from the Gaussian layer is duplicated and added to the Texture layer.

Adding texture

Without some added texture, the blurred image you just created will look too soft. Even the smoothest skin has some texture, so we'll add some using the High Pass filter.

1. Click the Eye icon to make the Texture layer visible.
2. Select the Texture layer and remove the color by choosing Image > Adjustments > Desaturate.
3. Select Filter > Other > High Pass.

(continued on next page)

Smooth Skin Guidelines

Smoothing skin in Photoshop can really enhance a portrait, as long as you follow a few guidelines:

- Remove blemishes and clean up image first, and then smooth the skin.
- Make sure the smoothing amount is appropriate for the subject—a higher amount for fashion, a lower amount for character portraits.
- Resist the temptation to over-smooth the skin as this can actually detract from the impact of the image.
- Keep in mind that the intensity of the smoothing will be contingent upon the subject and the lighting. If the subject has clear skin and is lit with very soft lighting, apply less skin softening.

4. In the High Pass dialog box, increase the Radius setting until you see what looks like a white and gray drawing in the High Pass filter preview. While the Radius amount you specify is largely based on the image's resolution, you should still be able to see the shape of the image in the preview window (**Figure 83e**).

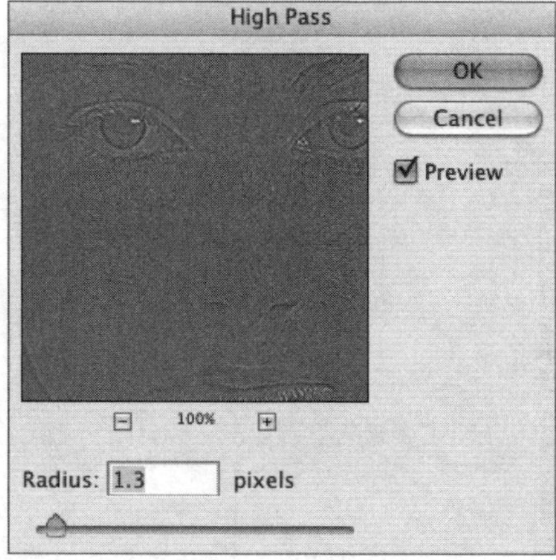

Figure 83e In the High Pass dialog box, increase the Radius setting until the image looks similar to the image here.

5. Click OK to apply the High Pass filter.
6. Change the blending mode of the Texture layer to Soft Light.
7. Decrease the Layer Opacity to approximately 40% (again, the actual amount is contingent upon image resolution).

Tip

If at the end of these steps you find that the skin smoothing isn't ideal, don't worry. I typically find that it is necessary to go back to make some minor adjustments to the Masks and Layer opacities, once I am able to see the cumulative effect.

#84 Improving Eyes

In a portrait, the first aspect of the image that draws our attention is the human eye. Some even go so far to say that the eyes are the most important aspect of an image. Therefore, it's definitely worthwhile to learn how to help the viewer focus in on the eyes. This How-To shows you three eye-enhancing techniques that use curves and the Smart Sharpen filter.

Brightening using curves

1. Make a selection of the eyes using the Lasso or Elliptical Marquee tool. Later we'll turn this selection into a mask on an adjustment layer (**Figure 84a**).

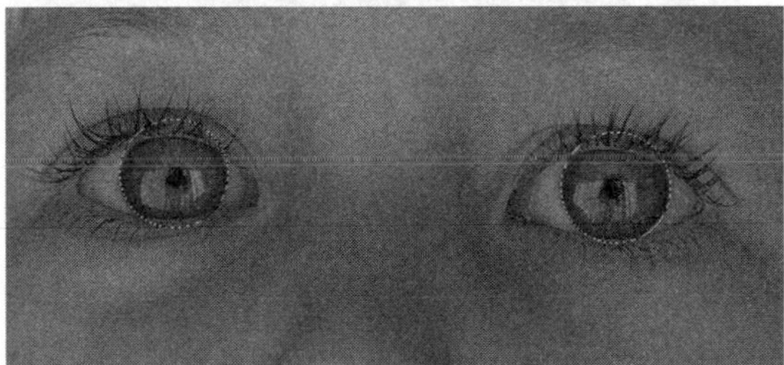

Figure 84a Create a rough selection of the eyes using one of the selection tools.

2. In the Layers palette, click the Add Adjustment Layer icon and choose Curves.
3. In the Curves dialog box that appears, click the middle of the curve and drag up to brighten the eyes (**Figure 84b**).

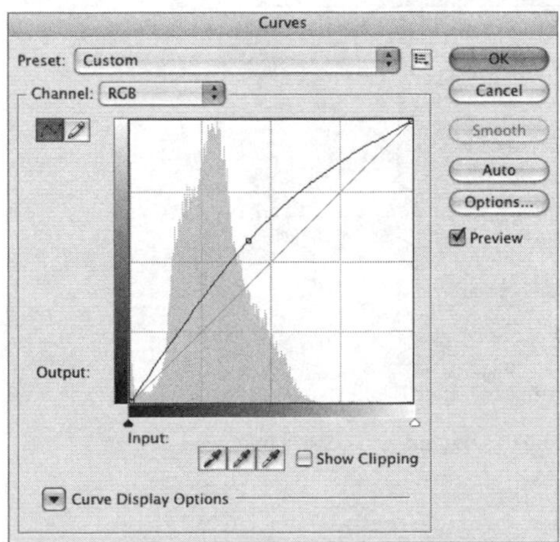

Figure 84b Use a Curves adjustment layer to brighten the eyes.

(continued on next page)

4. Paint on the Curves layer mask so that the brightening is limited to the irises.

Enjoy the final results (**Figure 84c**).

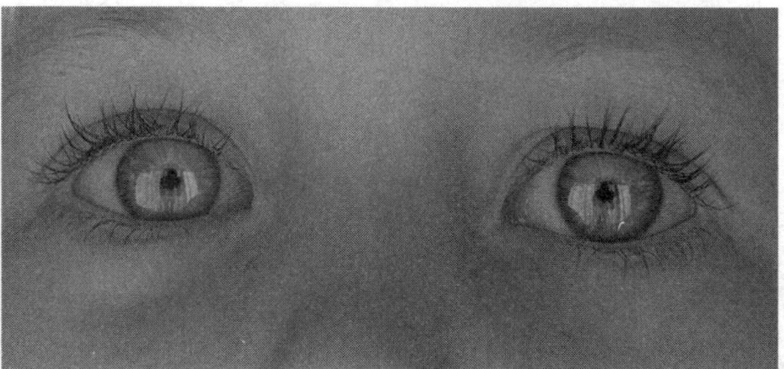

Figure 84c The eyes have been brightened.

Adding sparkle using the Smart Sharpen filter

1. Select the iris of the eye using the Lasso or Elliptical Marquee tool.
2. Press Ctrl + J (Windows) or Command + J (Mac) to copy the selection to a new layer.
3. Rename the layer Smart Sharpen (**Figure 84d**).

Figure 84d The eyes have been selected and copied to a new layer.

4. Select Filter > Sharpen > Smart Sharpen.

5. In the Smart Sharpen dialog box, increase the sharpening. The Amount and Radius settings you choose will depend upon the image resolution; however, try an Amount setting of somewhere near 100% and a Radius setting of between 1 and 3 (**Figure 84e**).

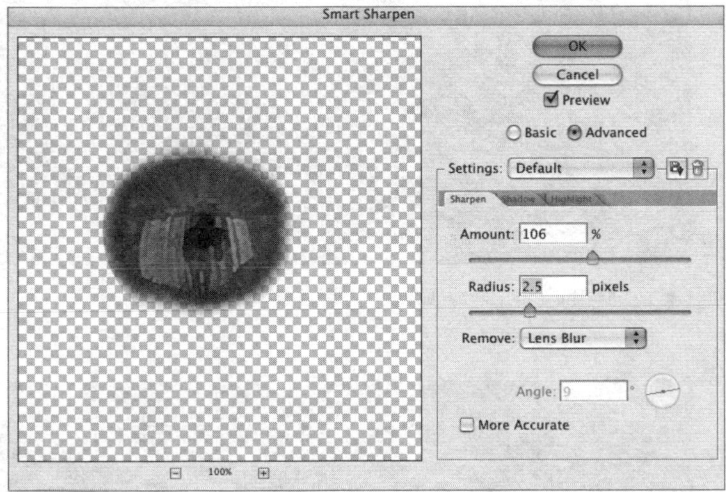

Figure 84e Increase the Amount and Radius settings until you see the desired amount of sharpening.

6. Click OK to apply the Smart Sharpen filter.

(continued on next page)

7. Lower the opacity of the Smart Sharpen layer and preview the final results (**Figures 84f** and **84g**).

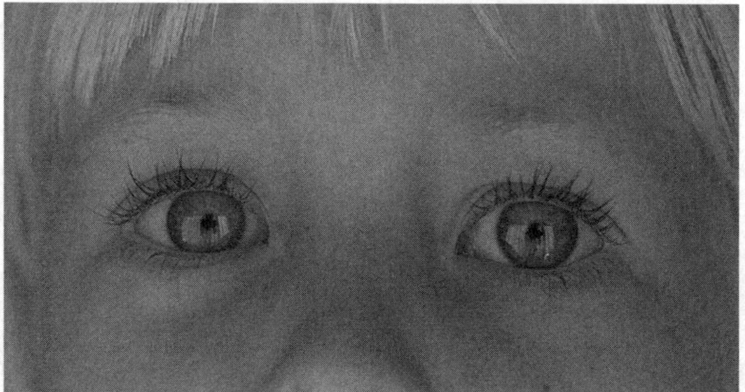

Figure 84f The original image.

Figure 84g The image with eyes sharpened.

#85 Changing Eye Color

Changing eye color can add a creative twist to an otherwise ordinary image. By making just a small color adjustment to the eyes, the same subject can take on a completely new personality. This How-to presents three techniques for changing eye color.

Using the Color Replacement tool

The advantage of using the Color Replacement tool to enhance eye color is speed—it is the fastest way to change eye color. The disadvantage of using this technique is that it is not as flexible as the other techniques.

1. Select the iris of the eye with the Lasso or Elliptical Marquee tool.
2. Choose Select > Modify > Feather and add a 1-pixel feather to soften the selection edge.
3. Press Ctrl + J (Windows) or Command + J (Mac) to copy the selection to a new layer.
4. Rename the layer New Eye Color (**Figure 85a**).

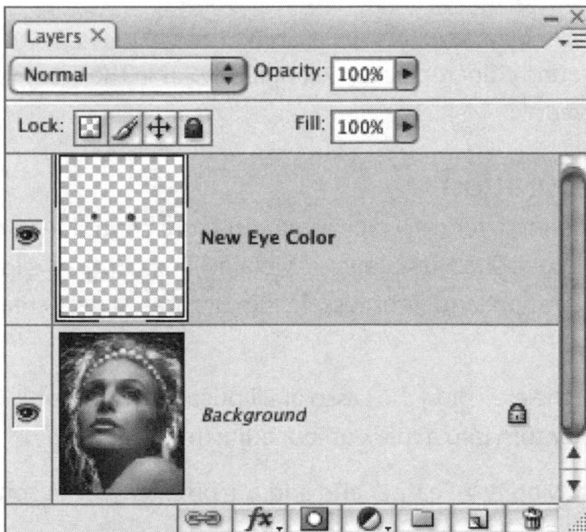

Figure 85a Select eyes and copy them to a new layer for added flexibility.

(continued on next page)

Color Replacement

For more information about the Color Replacement tool, see How-To #71.

5. Choose the Color Replacement tool from the Toolbox (**Figure 85b**).

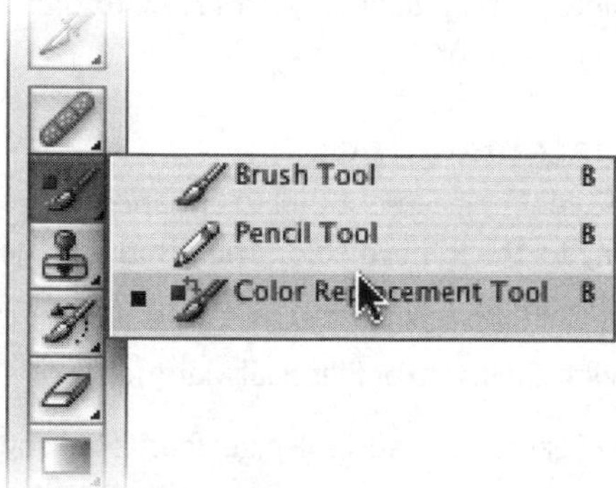

Figure 85b The Color Replacement tool is hidden behind the Brush tool.

6. Click the Foreground Color box on the Toolbox to open the Color Picker, and choose a foreground color.
7. Select the New Eye Color layer and paint using the Color Replacement tool. The foreground color replaces the original color in the areas your brush passes over.

Using Hue/Saturation

Using Hue/Saturation to alter eye color gives you more control than the Color Replacement tool. The Hue/Saturation dialog box contains sliders to control hue, saturation, and lightness. Using all three sliders creates the best color.

1. Select the iris of the eye using the Lasso or Elliptical Marquee tool. This selection will later turn into a mask on our adjustment layer.
2. Choose Select > Modify > Feather and add a 1-pixel feather to soften the selection edge.
3. In the Layers palette, click the Add Adjustment Layer icon and choose Hue/Saturation from the menu.

4. In the Hue/Saturation dialog, drag the Hue slider to change the eye color (**Figure 85c**).

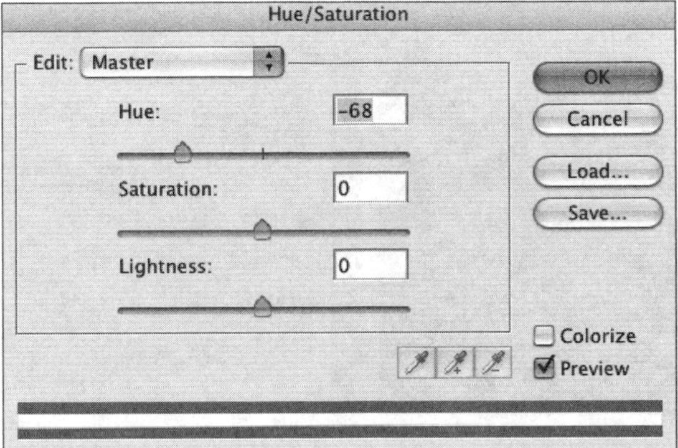

Figure 85c Drag the Hue slider in the Hue/Saturation dialog box to change color.

5. Click OK to apply the color adjustment.

6. Change the opacity of the Hue/Saturation layer to fine-tune the color change.

Applying solid color

The advantage of applying solid color to change the look of the eyes is that it's quick and easy.

1. Select the iris of the eye using the Lasso or Elliptical Marquee tool. This selection will later turn into a mask on the adjustment layer.

2. Choose Select > Modify > Feather and add a 1-pixel feather to soften the selection edge.

3. In the Layers palette, click the Add Adjustment/Fill Layer icon and choose Solid Color.

(continued on next page)

4. Choose a color from the Color Picker (**Figure 85d**).

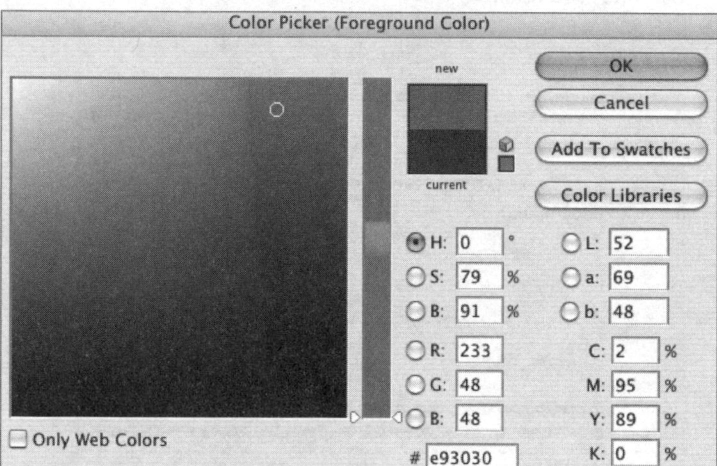

Figure 85d Choose a color that you think will look good.

5. Click OK.

Note

Don't evaluate the results of the color you've chosen until you execute the next step.

6. In the Layers palette, change the blending mode of the Color Fill adjustment layer to Color (**Figure 85e**).

Figure 85e Be sure to change the blending mode to Color.

7. Evaluate the results. If you are unhappy with the color you've chosen, it's easy to change. In the Layers palette, double-click the Color Fill adjustment layer icon to reopen the Color Picker. Choose a new color and click OK.

#86 Whitening Teeth

Yesterday, I was standing in the line at the grocery store, and someone standing near me pointed to the cover of a magazine and said to me, "Whoa, those teeth are white!" The teeth were so white that they overpowered the photograph. In reality, the problem with natural teeth isn't that they aren't pure white, it is that they are a bit yellow. Thus, our goal is to brighten and whiten teeth by removing some, but not all, of the yellow.

1. Select the teeth using one of the selection tools, such as the Magnetic Lasso, Lasso, or Quick Select tool. This selection will later turn into a mask on our adjustment layer.
2. Choose Select > Modify > Feather and add a 1-pixel feather to soften the selection edge (**Figure 86a**).

Figure 86a The teeth are selected.

3. In the Layers palette, click the Add Adjustment Layer button and choose Hue/Saturation from the menu.
4. In the Hue/Saturation dialog box, choose Yellows from the Edit menu.
5. Use the Saturation slider to reduce the saturation of the yellows until the yellow is diminished. Don't go too far or the teeth with look gray (**Figure 86b**).

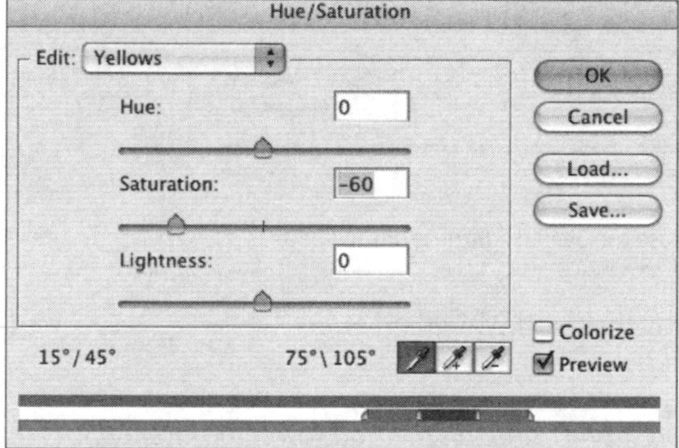

Figure 86b Reduce the saturation of the yellow tones in the image.

6. From the Edit menu, choose Master.

(continued on next page)

7. Increase the Lightness approximately 20 points (**Figure 86c**).

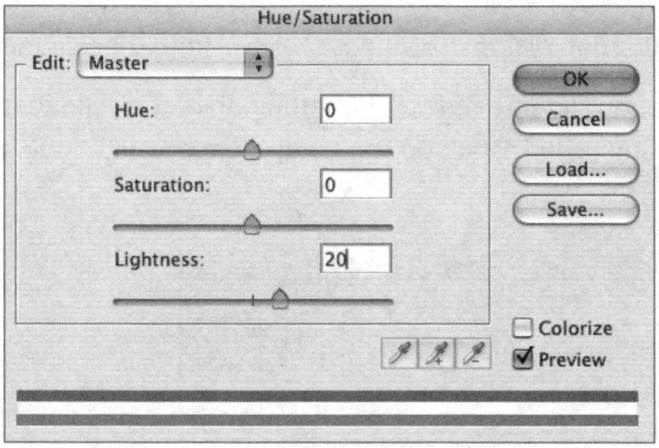

Figure 86c Increase the overall lightness of the image.

8. Click OK to apply the teeth-whitening effect.

Note

If the effect is too strong using this method, lower the layer opacity in the Layers palette.

CHAPTER TWELVE

Working with Type

Learning how to effectively work with type can set you apart from the typical Photoshop user. People often concentrate on learning how to utilize Photoshop's core strengths for image editing and then overlook the many powerful and creative Photoshop type tools and tricks. Those who take time to learn about type are well rewarded, as they will have the ability to combine image, design, and type with unparalleled possibilities. This chapter will get you up to speed on type essentials and further your progress on becoming a Photoshop expert.

Before we begin, it's worth pointing out that type in Photoshop is vector-based. In other words, Photoshop type consists of vector-based outlines—mathematically defined shapes that describe the letters, numbers, and symbols of a typeface. In contrast, the bulk of our work in Photoshop comprises pixel-based bitmap images.

What's the big deal about type being vector-based? Vector-based type can be scaled without any degradation of quality. How does this actually work? Photoshop preserves vector-based type outlines and uses them when you scale or resize type, output a PDF or EPS file, print the image to a PostScript printer, or save for the Web or for other devices. All of this empowers us to produce printed or Web-based type with crisp, resolution-independent edges.

#87 Adding Type

Commit or Cancel

Working with type can be a bit cumbersome at first. So learning how to quickly add or cancel type is important. Immediately after you have finished entering text, you have the option to commit to or cancel the newly added type. To cancel it, press Esc (or as I like to think or it—the "Great Escape" key). To commit to the type, press Enter (Windows) or Return (Mac).

Adding type to your document is easy:

1. Choose one of the Type tools in the Toolbox (**Figure 87a**).

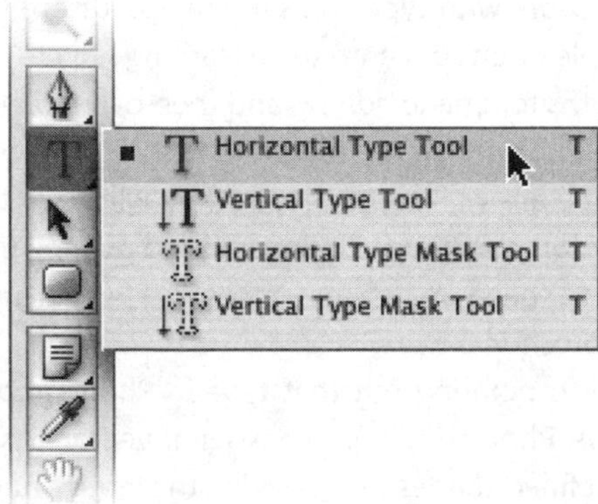

Figure 87a The various Type tools all live on the same tile in the Toolbox.

2. In the options bar, choose the font, font size, and type of anti-aliasing you want (**Figure 87b**).

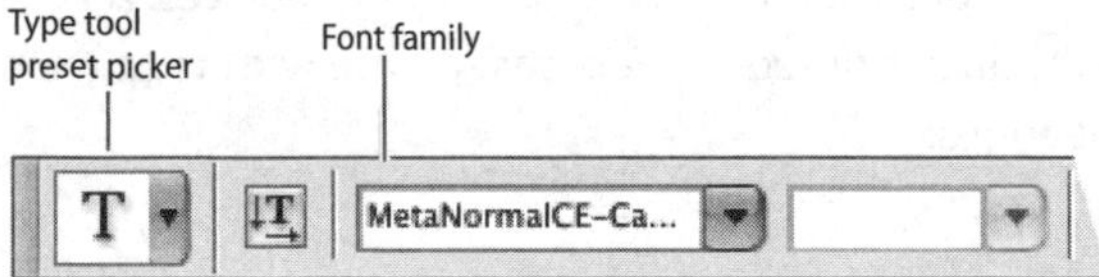

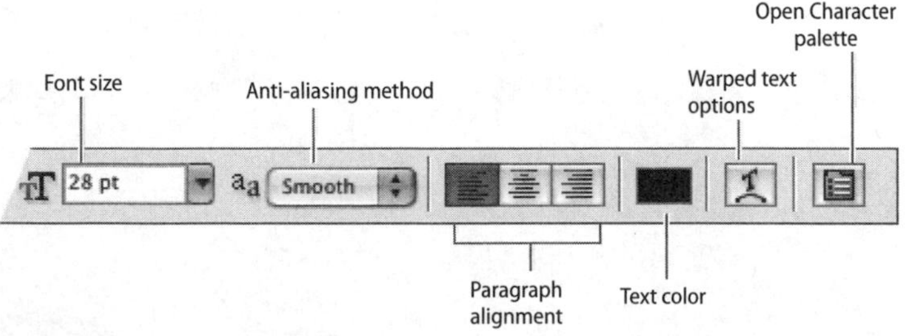

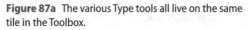

Figure 87b Choose the appropriate Type tool settings in the options bar.

3. Move the cursor over the document window and click to add type. By default, this will create a new type layer, (**Figure 87c**). The cursor will change to a blinking horizontal line to signify that you can begin typing.

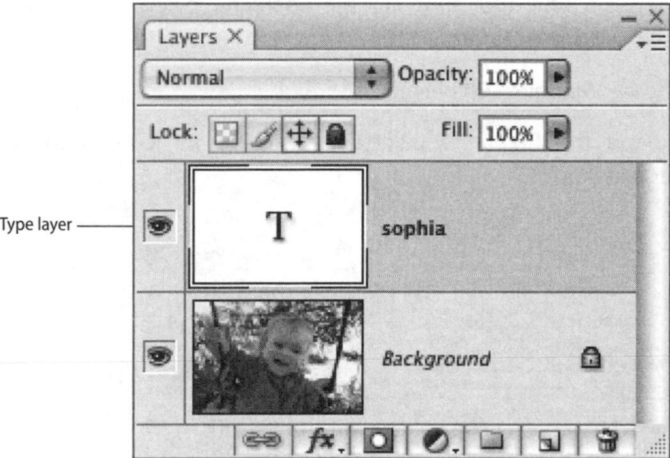

Figure 87c When you use a Type tool, by default it creates a new type layer.

4. Enter the text you want.
5. Press Enter (Windows) or Return (Mac) or select another tool in the Toolbox to commit the changes.

   Once you have created a type layer, it can be edited at any time:

1. Select the type layer in the Layers palette.
2. Select a Type tool from the Toolbox.
3. Position the cursor over the text field, where it will change its appearance from the default cursor to the insertion point cursor, signifying that you can click and select or edit the text.
4. Click to place the insertion point in the text.
5. Select one or more characters you want to edit.
6. Enter text or change the font, font size, and so on.
7. Press Enter to commit the changes.

Not All Text Is Editable

In most typical color modes like RGB, type is completely editable. However, this is not the case in Multichannel, Bitmap, or Indexed Color mode. Because these modes don't support layers, type layers aren't created. As a result, in these modes, type appears in the background as rasterized and uneditable text.

Modifying and Rasterizing Type

Certain type modifications require that you rasterize the type layer. For example, you must first rasterize a type layer before you can apply the Distort filter. When you rasterize type, you turn the type layer into bitmapped artwork, rendering the text uneditable. To rasterize type, choose Layer > Rasterize > Type.

#88 Customizing Type

Type Layer Shortcut

To quickly select an entire type layer, double-click the Type thumbnail for that layer in the Layers palette.

The Character palette is a powerful type-customization engine. Once you have added type to your document, you can use this palette to give it that extra boost.

You can open the Character palette in a number of ways:

- Choose a Type tool and click the Character palette button in the options bar (see Figure 87b).
- Choose Window > Character.
- Expand the Character palette by clicking its icon in the dock (**Figure 88a**).

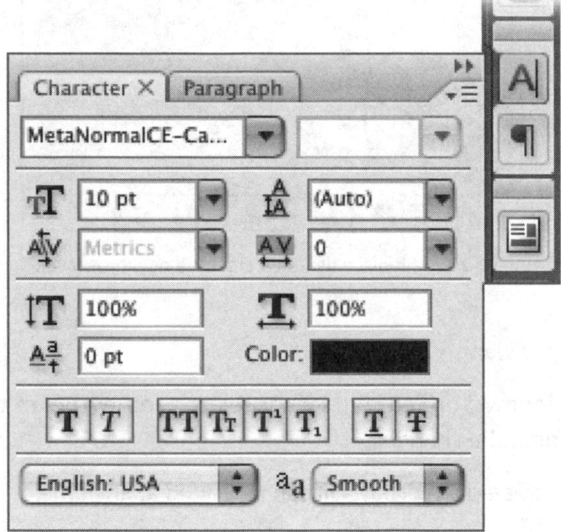

Figure 88a The Character palette, expanded from the dock.

Once the palette is open, you can customize your text. First, select the text you want to modify as described in the previous How-To (#87). Then in the Character palette, choose options for the type (**Figure 88b**). For example, you might alter any of the following:

- **Font.** Choose a different font from the Font menu.
- **Color.** Click the color swatch to open the Color Picker.
- **Leading** or **Tracking.** For either property, choose a value from the menu or, use the up and down arrows to set the value, or edit the value directly in the text box. Press Enter (Windows) or Return (Mac) to apply a value.

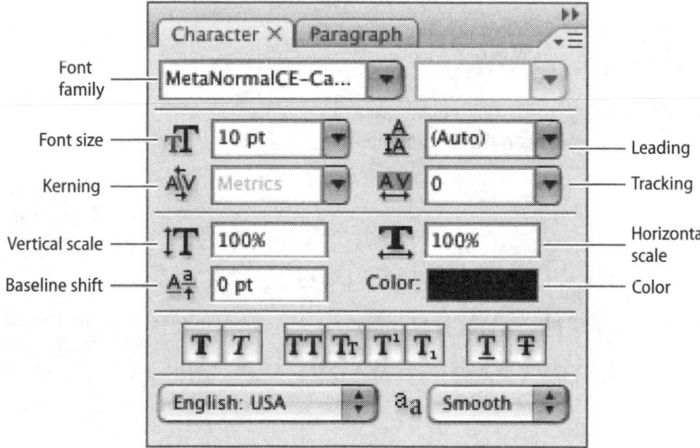

Figure 88b A guide to the Character palette.

Paragraph Formatting

To change the formatting of a paragraph, use the Paragraph palette.

Simply select the paragraph you want to format, and then open the Paragraph palette. There you can alter the alignment, justification, left or right indentation, spacing before and after the paragraph, and hyphenation.

Type Preferences

Choosing the correct font for a project is tricky. However, you can configure your Photoshop preferences to make it easier by increasing the font preview size. The following setting lets you choose the size at which typefaces are displayed in the various Font menus in Photoshop.

First choose Tools > Preferences > Type (Windows) or Photoshop > Preferences > Type (Mac). Then select Font Preview Size and choose a preview size from the menu. The choices are Small, Medium, Large, Extra Large or Huge. Using Medium or Large gives you a larger preview of the font, which will speed your font selection.

If you are new to typography, the most common (and essential) type modifications are for leading and tracking. Leading (rhymes with wedding) refers to the vertical space between lines of type (**Figure 88c**). Tracking is the loosening or tightening the spacing between the characters in selected text or an entire block of text (**Figure 88d**).

CREATIVITY IS SEEING
THE ORDINARY
AS EXTRAORDINARY

Leading = 24PT

CREATIVITY IS SEEING
THE ORDINARY
AS EXTRAORDINARY

Leading = 9PT

Figure 88c Change the leading to increase or decrease the vertical space between the lines of type.

CREATIVITY IS SEEING
THE ORDINARY
AS EXTRAORDINARY

Tracking = 0

C R E A T I V I T Y   I S   S E E I N G
T H E   O R D I N A R Y
A S   E X T R A O R D I N A R Y

Tracking = 270

Figure 88d Change the tracking to increase or decrease the space between the characters.

#89 Adding Creative Type Effects

This How-To focuses on three creative type effects that can increase your type skills and hopefully inspire you to be more creative with type in Photoshop.

Warp effects

Warp type effects are really fun as they give you the ability to change the shape, orientation, or perspective of the type. For example, you can make the type warp to fit inside the shape of a flag or arc the type up or down. These effects are most useful when you are interested in adding creative type to your document.

1. Choose a Type tool from the Toolbox.
2. Add type to your document (**Figure 89a**).

ANNIKA KAI ORWIG

Figure 89a Default type without warp effects.

3. Select a type layer in the Layers palette.
4. Click the Create Warped Text button in the options bar. The Warp Text dialog box opens.
5. Choose a warp style from the Style menu (**Figure 89b**).

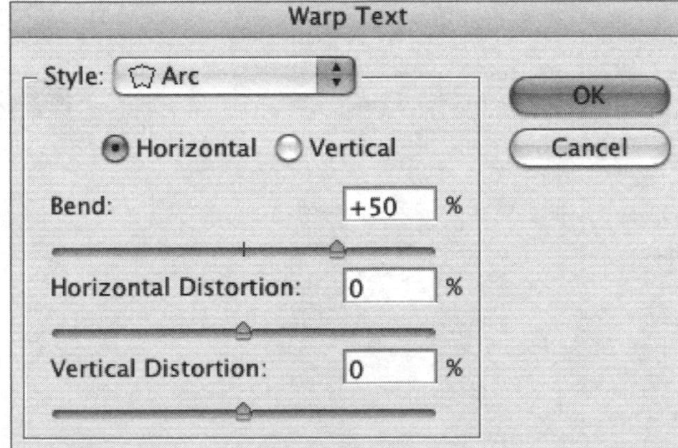

Figure 89b In this case, I have chosen the Arc style.

6. In the Warp Text dialog box, drag the sliders to change the Bend and Horizontal and/or Vertical Distortion settings.

(continued on next page)

Undoing a Warp Effect

To undo a warp effect, follow Steps 1 through 3, and then choose None from the menu. This will completely remove the warp effect.

7. Click OK to apply the warp effect (**Figure 89c**).

Figure 89c The final results of the Arc warp style.

Drop shadow

A drop shadow is a shadow that appears behind the text. Adding a drop shadow to type can potentially add dimension and visual interest to the type.

1. With any tool chosen, select a type layer in the Layers palette.
2. Choose Layer > Layer Style > Drop Shadow.
3. In the Layer Style dialog box, modify the controls in the Structure and Quality areas (**Figure 89d**).

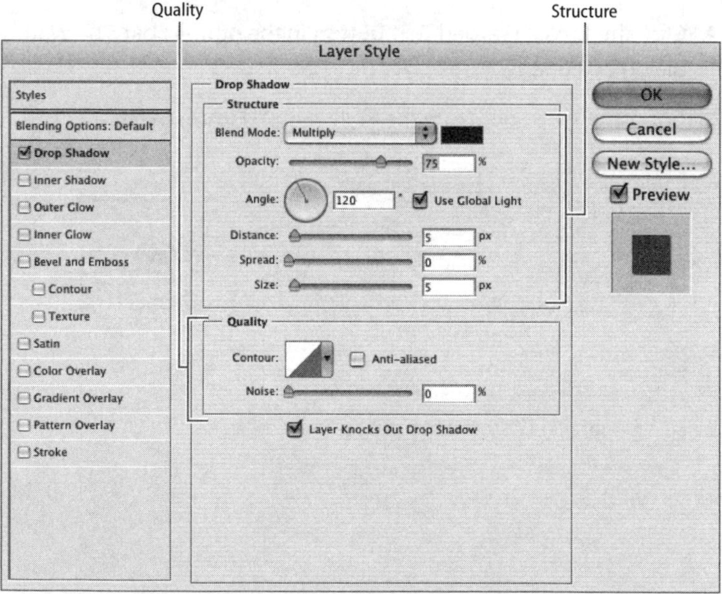

Figure 89d Use these controls to fine-tune the Drop Shadow effect.

4. Click OK to apply the effect.

5. The Drop Shadow effect will appear in the Layers palette below the type layer (**Figure 89e**). Click the eye icon to hide or show the effect. Double-click the word *Drop Shadow* to reopen the Layer Style dialog box to change the drop shadow controls.

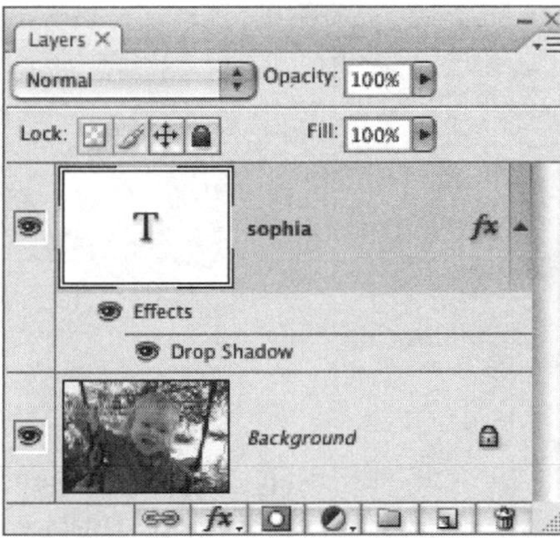

Figure 89e The Layers palette, showing the Drop Shadow effect listed underneath the type layer to which it is applied.

Fill type with an image

Type usually is filled with a solid color or gradient. However, there are times when you need to go beyond the typical. Here I show you how to fill type with an image by applying a clipping mask:

1. Create a document with a type layer and an Image layer (**Figure 89f**).

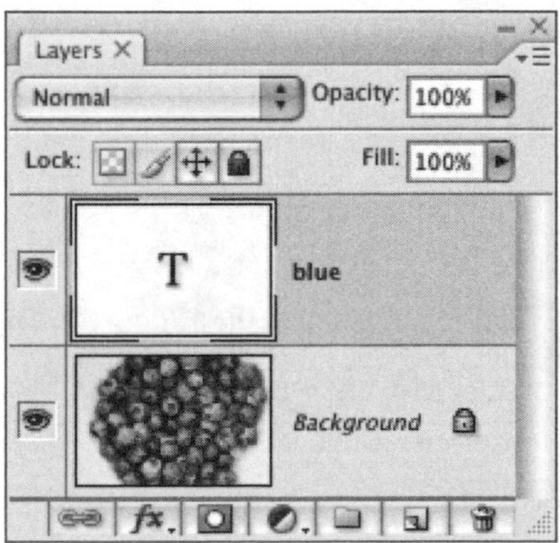

Figure 89f A document with an image of blueberries and a type layer.

(continued on next page)

Creative Type Effects Resource

This How-To only scratches the surface of applying creative type effects. For more inspiration, check out the free Photoshop Creative Type tutorials at: www.planetphotoshop.com/category/text/

2. If the image is the Background, double-click it to convert it to a regular layer and give it a name.
3. Reposition the layers by dragging so that the image layer is on top of the type layer (**Figure 89g**).

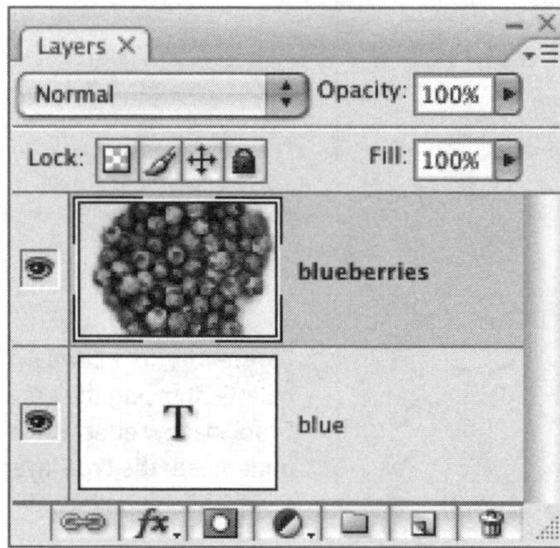

Figure 89g The image layer has been restacked above the type layer.

4. Select the top layer. Choose Layer > Create Clipping Mask. The clipping mask is displayed in the Layers palette (**Figure 89h**).

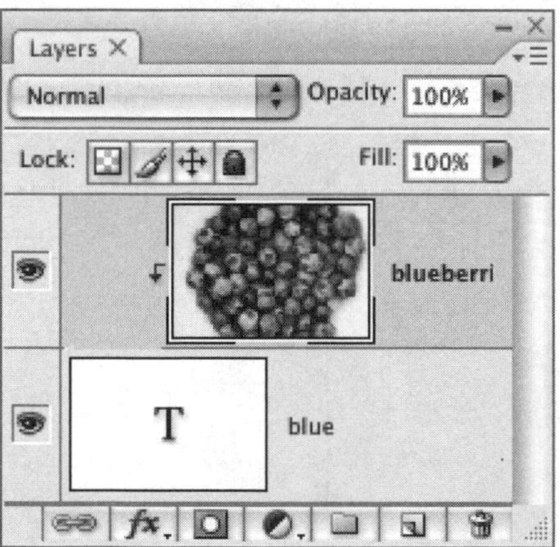

Figure 89h The Clipping Mask as displayed in the Layers palette.

The result of applying a clipping mask is that the text is filled with the image (**Figure 89i**).

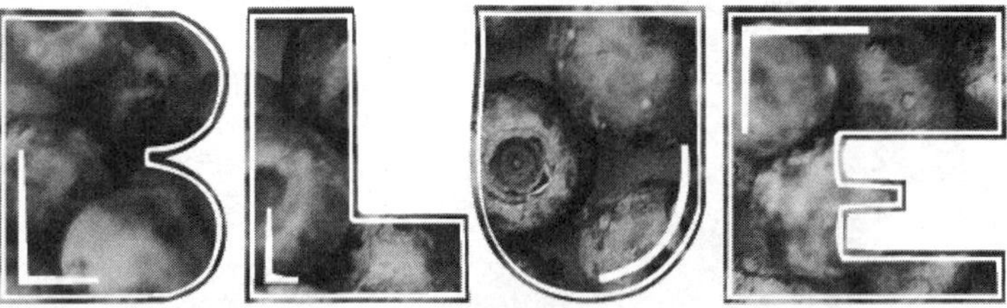

Figure 89i The final result: The type is filled with the image of the blueberries.

Tip

Once you have filled text with an image, experiment with the text and image layers. Click the image layer and drag it around so that different parts of the image fill the text. Then click the type layer and change the font, font size, and so on.

CHAPTER THIRTEEN

Sharpening Images

There is something incredibly compelling about photographs that are vivid and sharp. It's as if the sharpness draws us in, making us want to look closer. As we strive to create sharp images, we stand on the shoulders of many great photographers, including Ansel Adams, who pioneered and evangelized the idea that precision and sharp focus are fundamental to good photography.

While Adams' pursuit to capture sharp images was focused on the camera and printing, we now have an even bigger advantage—Photoshop, which provides a number of sharpening filters. This chapter focuses on the most useful of these.

Keep in mind that no one sharpening filter is best, and no one sharpening technique works for every image. It's important for you to be familiar with and practice using all of them so that you have a broad base of sharpening skills that you can apply, as appropriate, when fine-tuning your images.

It's also important to remember that it's best to incorporate sharpening as the last step in your imaging workflow. Completing all other enhancements, such as retouching, color and tone adjustments, image enhancements, and resizing, *before* you sharpen is critical. This approach delivers the best sharpening results for that particular image size and resolution.

Of course, Adams was interested in more than just the fundamentals of precision and sharpness. His goal was to create strong and compelling photographs. As he once said, "There's nothing worse than a sharp photograph of a fuzzy concept."

As you learn how to sharpen images in Photoshop, remember not to lose sight of this ultimate goal: to create images that have impact. If you do lose sight and end up oversharpening your images (a predicament common to those who are new to digital imaging), you run the risk of calling attention to the sharpness, rather than the images themselves.

#90 Using the Unsharp Mask Filter

One of the most useful sharpening tools Photoshop provides is the Unsharp Mask filter. (Yes, the name sounds like it does the opposite of sharpening—it's derived from an old darkroom technique where the name does make sense.) This filter scans the image for areas where pixels whose tonal values differ by a certain quantity (the "threshold," chosen by you) are right next to each other. These areas tend to be edges, and the filter lets you sharpen these edges by increasing the contrast of pixels within those areas. In other words, you lighten the light pixels, and darken the dark pixels, and the boundaries between them become more pronounced.

Sharpening an image involves a bit of "give and take." While you want to increase the overall sharpness of the image, you do not want to increase or exaggerate noise or artifacting. Fortunately, the Unsharp Mask filter has controls that help you specify an ideal amount of sharpening without degrading the overall image quality. Use this filter, as opposed to the others, when you're interested in making precise sharpening improvements to your image.

To use the Unsharp Mask filter:

1. Select the layer you want to sharpen.
2. Choose Filter > Sharpen > Unsharp Mask. The Unsharp Mask dialog box appears (**Figure 90a**).

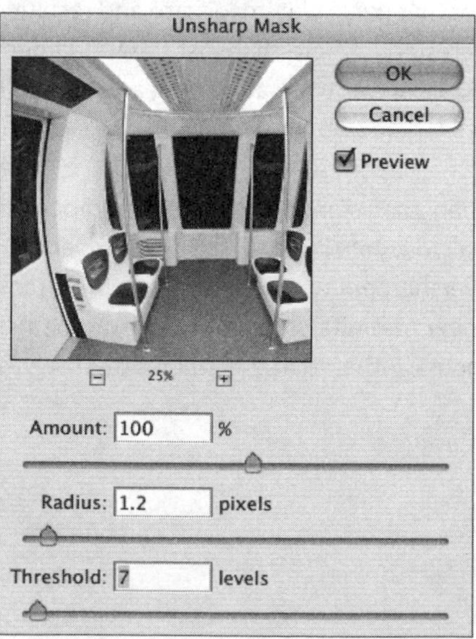

Figure 90a The Unsharp Mask dialog box.

3. Select the Preview option, and adjust the Amount using the slider or enter a percentage.

   The Amount setting controls the overall intensity of the sharpening. The value you specify determines how much to increase the contrast of pixels. The actual amount will depend on your image's size and resolution. For medium to high-resolution images, try an amount of 100%. For higher resolution images, try a higher percentage.

4. Now adjust the Radius setting, which controls the "reach" of the sharpening. If you are sharpening any edge, for instance, the Radius setting defines how far the sharpening will extend on either side of this line. In more specific terms, the setting determines the number of pixels surrounding the edge pixels that will be affected.

   The greater the radius value, the wider the edge effects will be, and the more obvious the sharpening. So your radius amount will typically be low. For example, for images destined for Web pages, try a radius between .1 and .3. For high-resolution print images, try a radius between 1 and 3.

5. Finally, adjust the Threshold setting. This setting "saves the day" by limiting the extent of your sharpening. When the filter evaluates a pixel for sharpening, it compares its tonal value with that of its neighbors. If the difference is less than the Threshold setting, nothing happens. If the difference is greater, the contrast between the pixel and the ones around it is increased.

   When the Threshold value is set to 0 (the default setting), if there's any difference at all between tonal values, sharpening is applied. This means that even tiny fluctuations in tone, such as image noise and film grain, will be exaggerated. Raising the value above 0 means that only more defined features, such as edges with contrast, will be sharpened, whereas broad areas of near-uniform texture, like skin and sky, will be protected from sharpening.

   The appropriate setting will vary, depending on the nature of the image. The more detail there is, the lower the setting. For starters, try a value between 2 and 20. Images with a lot of detail usually require a low setting; use higher settings for images with less detail (like portraits).

(continued on next page)

Best Practices

When using the Unsharp Mask filter, it is often difficult to see the results in the image. Follow these steps to improve your sharpening:

- The Unsharp Mask dialog box often obscures important parts of the image in the document window. Therefore, it's important to reposition the dialog box so that you can effectively preview the sharpening. This may seem obvious, but it's easy to forget.
- Clicking the preview image in the dialog box and holding down the mouse shows you the preview without the sharpening. Releasing the mouse button lets you see the preview with the sharpening applied. Toggling back and forth lets you more easily notice the effects of the sharpening.
- In the dialog box, click and drag the preview to see different parts of the image. You can also click the plus (+) or minus (-) buttons under the preview image to zoom in or out.

6. When your sharpening appears to look its best, click OK to apply the sharpening.

Figure 90b shows the Before and After versions of a sharpening project.

Figure 90b The image on the right is stronger because it has been sharpened with the Unsharp Mask filter.

Tips

To accurately evaluate and dial in the appropriate amount of sharpening, always make sure you're looking at the image in the document window at 100%.

If after applying the Unsharp Mask filter, you notice that noise has become exaggerated or that bright colors appear overly saturated, choose Edit > Fade Unsharp Mask, and then choose Luminosity from the Mode menu. This reduces potential color problems caused by the Unsharp Mask filter.

The Halo Effect

Oversharpening can produce a halo effect around the edges of a subject that has been sharpened (**Figure 90c**). Look closely at your image, and if you see the halo effect, reduce sharpening.

Figure 90c The right half of the image has been over sharpened and the result is an overexaggerated amount of edge contrast and brightness. It is as if the edges glow or have a halo.

The Monitor vs. Print

It is much easier to see the effects of the Unsharp Mask filter on your monitor than it is in a print. However, if your final destination is print, be sure to experiment to determine what settings work best for your image. Keep in mind that a certain level of sharpening will look good on matte paper, but that same level may not look good on glossy paper.

#91 Using the Smart Sharpen Filter

The Smart Sharpen filter, as its name implies, seems almost as if it is truly smart. It is more powerful than the Unsharp Mask filter (Tip #90), with sharpening controls that Unsharp Mask doesn't share, and can provide better results. So why not always use Smart Sharpen instead of Unsharp Mask? The process of sharpening an image with Smart Sharpen is slightly slower than with Unsharp Mask. Yet, some things, like the high-quality results of Smart Sharpen, are worth the wait

To use the Smart Sharpen filter:

1. Select the layer you want to sharpen.
2. Choose Filter > Sharpen > Smart Sharpen to open the Smart Sharpen dialog box (**Figure 91a**).

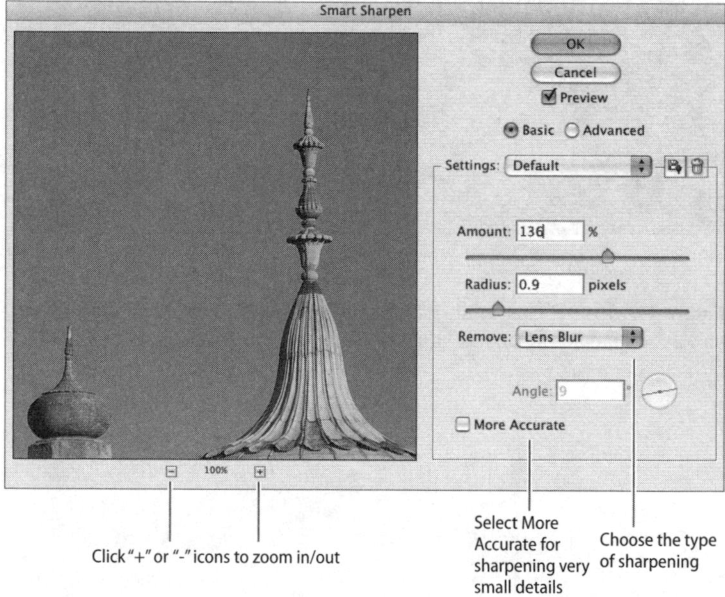

Figure 91a The Smart Sharpen dialog.

3. From the Remove menu, choose the mode of sharpening you want:

- **Gaussian Blur** sharpens identically to the Unsharp Mask filter.
- **Lens Blur** is the best choice of the group as it allows you to sharpen typical optical lens blurring. It provides finer sharpening of detail and does a better job of reducing sharpening halos than the Gaussian Blur setting.
- **Motion Blur** works best when you want to remove small amounts of motion blur that resulted from camera movement. Click the wheel to the right of the Angle field to set the direction of the motion that needs to be removed.

4. Adjust the Amount and Radius controls, which work just like their counterparts in the Unsharp Mask dialog box (see the previous How-To), so that the sharpening looks best.
5. Click OK to apply the sharpening.

Tip
Choose the More Accurate option when sharpening images with very small details.

Figure 91b shows the result of using the Smart Sharpen filter. Edges are crisper, especially boundaries between contrasting areas.

Figure 91b On the left before sharpening. On the right after using Smart Sharpening.

Where's the Threshold Slider?

The Threshold slider plays an integral role in the Unsharpen Mask filter, but as you may have noticed, Smart Sharpen does not have a Threshold setting. Does this make Smart Sharpen inferior to the Unsharp Mask filter? Definitely not! The threshold algorithm is built into Smart Sharpen and automatically applied—that's one of the reasons it's so smart!

Advanced sharpening

If you notice strong, dark or light sharpening halos (Figure 90c) after you have doctored your image, you can reduce them for optimal sharpening using the more advanced controls in the Smart Sharpen dialog box. Select the Advanced radio button in the Smart Sharpen dialog to gain access to the Shadow and Highlight tabs (**Figure 91c**). On these tabs, you can adjust the following:

- The **Fade Amount** slider controls the overall amount of sharpening in the highlights or shadows. Choose a higher value to reduce the overall sharpening in the shadows or highlights.
- The **Tonal Width** slider, as the name implies, limits the sharpening to specific tonal regions of the image. For example, if you choose a lower Tonal Width in the Shadow or Highlight tabs, the sharpening will be limited to the respective tones. On the Shadow tab, it limits sharpening of the darker tones. On the Highlights tab, it limits sharpening to the brighter tones. A higher value set on either tab expands sharpening to a wider ranges of tones.
- The **Radius** slider works like its equivalent in the Unsharp Mask dialog box and controls the size of the area around each pixel taken into account by the filter. Moving the slider to the left specifies a smaller area, and moving it to the right specifies a larger area.

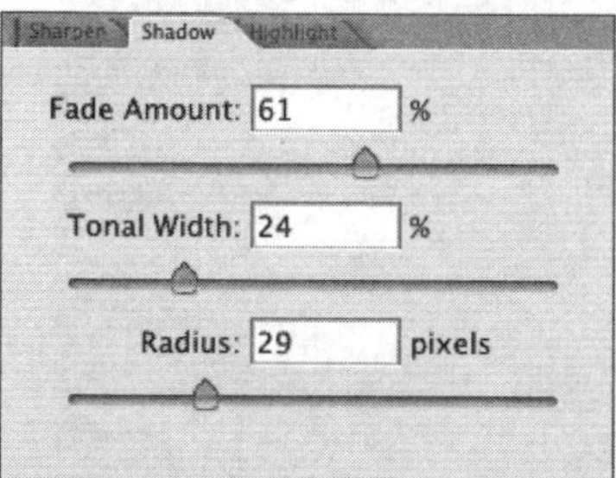

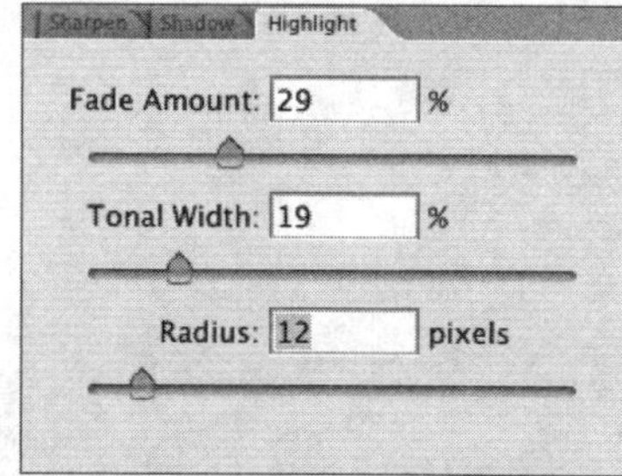

Figure 91c Fine-tune the sharpening of the dark and light areas using the Shadow and Highlight tabs. These tabs are especially effective at removing the halo effect.

Tip

The Fade Amount slider often is the only slider you will need to effectively remove halos. Try that slider first. After you have adjusted the Fade Amount slider, experiment with the Tonal Width and Radius sliders to fine-tune your adjustment.

#92 Using High Pass Sharpening

High pass sharpening is an advanced sharpening technique that is easy to learn and apply. I have found this technique to be especially helpful for visual learners who like to see how the sharpening is being applied in a step-by-step fashion.

By way of introduction, this technique uses the High Pass filter, which was originally created for extracting line art and large black-and-white areas from scanned images. However, we are going to be creative and use this filter to generate a grayscale image, which retains edge details and removes low-frequency detail. This grayscale image is exactly what we'll use to sharpen images. You will find this sharpening technique helpful when you have an image with strong edges that need to be sharpened.

To apply high pass sharpening:

1. Copy the Background layer by choosing Layer > Duplicate Layer. Name the duplicate layer High Pass (**Figure 92a**).

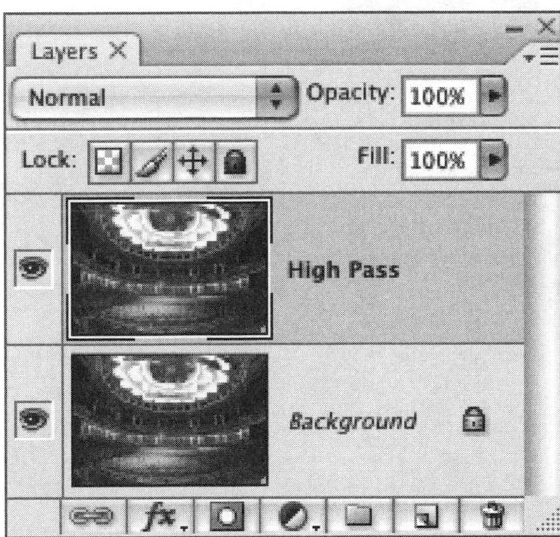

Figure 92a To apply High pass sharpening, you need to duplicate the Background layer.

2. Choose Filter > Other > High Pass.

(continued on next page)

3. In the High Pass dialog box, set the Radius to a low value (**Figure 92b**). The exact amount will vary based on the image size and resolution. Try a low filter setting of 1.0. The level of grayscale in your image should look something like the one in the preview window of Figure 92b.

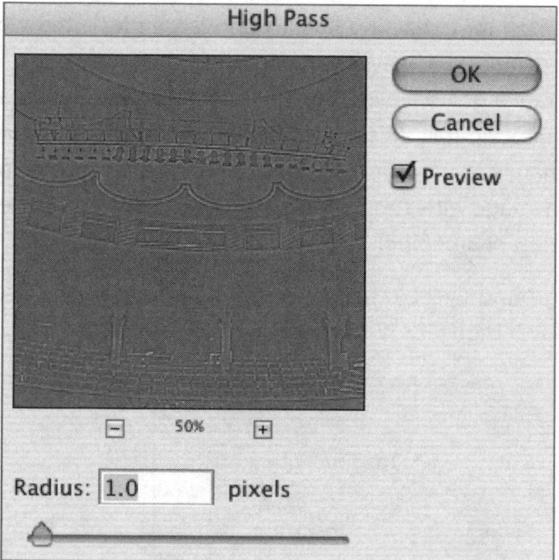

Figure 92b When applying the High Pass filter, modify the Radius slider so that you can see a grayscale image with edge detail, as shown here.

4. Click OK to apply the filter.

5. Change the blending mode of the High Pass layer to Soft Light (or Hard Light for a stronger sharpening effect). Lower the Opacity to fine-tune the amount of sharpening. Typically, the Opacity amount will be below 50% (**Figure 92c**).

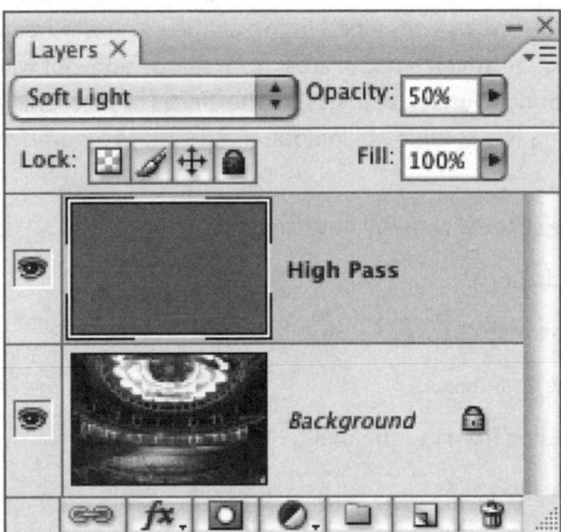

Figure 92c To apply the sharpening, be sure to change the blending mode to Soft Light. To fine-tune sharpening, lower the Opacity setting.

#93 Applying Edge Sharpening

Edge Sharpening Advice

As you can tell by the length of this How-To, edge sharpening is involves quite a number of steps. Therefore, when you sit down to try it for yourself, be sure to take your time and follow each step. It might also help to buckle your seat belt and put on your thinking cap!

One of the goals of sharpening in Photoshop is to sharpen the content that needs the most help. In many cases, the content that needs the most amount of sharpening are edges. Edge sharpening is a technique that creates a mask to apply sharpening selectively. In other words, it is a technique that limits the sharpening to the edges to a greater degree than the other sharpening techniques described in this chapter. You will create a mask which protects relatively smooth areas from sharpening, but which exposes lines of strong contrast (or edges) to the effects of sharpening.

Edge sharpening is a complex technique that involves a number of phases:

1. Duplicating the channel with the best contrast
2. Preparing the channel
3. Applying filters to the channel
4. Cleaning up the channel
5. Creating a selection from the channel
6. Applying sharpening

To successfully execute this technique, you must work successively through each of these phases.

Duplicate the channel with the best contrast

1. Choose Window > Channels to open the Channels palette.
2. Examine the channels to find the one that displays the greatest contrast. The channel with the strongest contrast has the most distinct

edges, making it a good source for our edge mask. In many cases, this is the green or the red channel (**Figure 93a**).

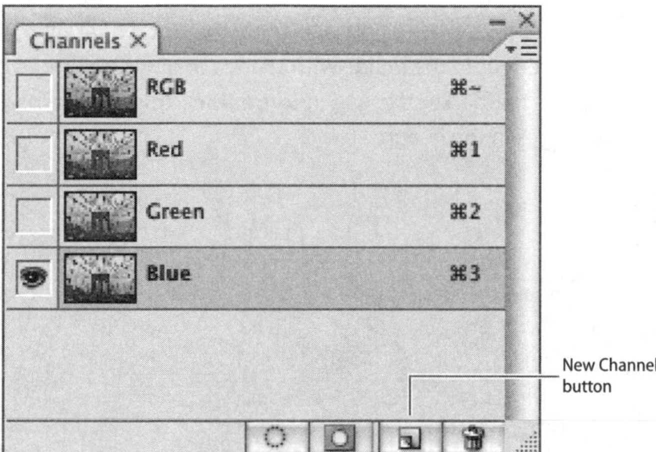

Figure 93a In this case, I have selected the blue channel because it contains the highest level of contrast.

3. Now duplicate the channel by dragging it to the New Channel button in the Channels palette.
4. Name the duplicate channel Edges (**Figure 93b**).

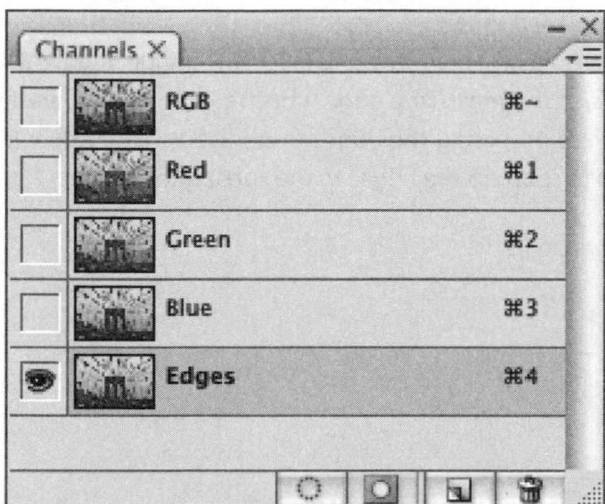

Figure 93b The duplicate channel will appear at the bottom of the Channels palette.

Prepare the channel

1. Select the Edges channel.
2. Choose Filter > Stylize > Find Edges to apply the Find Edges filter. This highlights the edges in the image with shades of gray—the more distinct the edge, the darker the gray (**Figure 93c**). This step helps you define the edges in the image.

Figure 93c The result of the Find Edges filter.

3. Choose Image > Adjustments > Invert to invert the image (**Figure 93d**). The black areas of the mask (the edges) become white. By inverting the image you are preparing the edges to be used as a mask, which will enable you to sharpen the edges in the subsequent steps.

Figure 93d The result of inverting the Edges channel.

The basic mask is now ready: Strong edges have been outlined with white, areas of low contrast are black, and areas of intermediate contrast are shades of gray. When the sharpening filter is applied, it will only affect the edges (the unprotected parts of the image).

The rest of the procedure is devoted to refining the mask.

Refine the mask

1. Choose Filter > Other > Maximum to thicken the lines along the edges. Be careful to set the radius to a low number to minimize the thickening.

(continued on next page)

2. Click OK to apply the Maximum filter (**Figure 93e**).

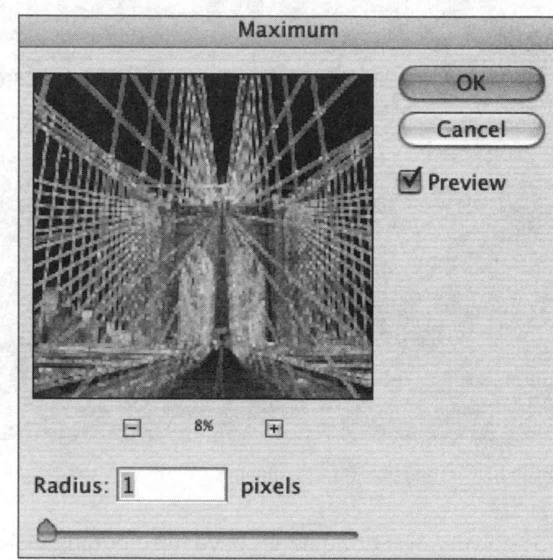

Figure 93e Use the Maximum filter to thicken the edges.

3. Choose Filter > Noise > Median. Set the radius to a low number to average neighboring pixels and smooth edges (**Figure 93f**).

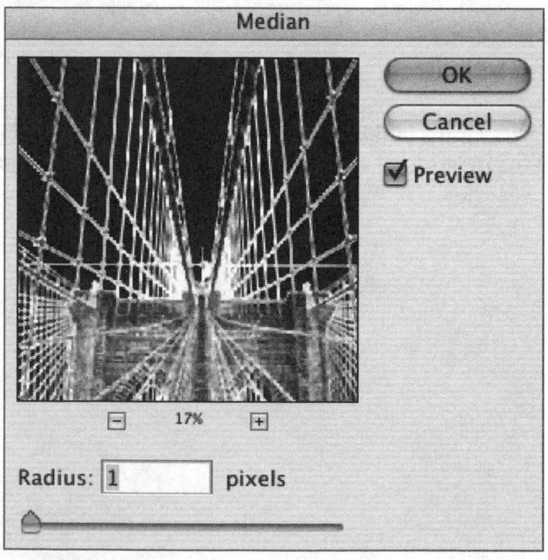

Figure 93f Use the Median filter to smooth edges.

4. Click OK to apply the Median filter.

Clean up the channel

1. Choose the Brush tool.
2. Select Black as the foreground color.
3. Find areas that should be black, but are marked by image noise, and paint them solid black to eliminate random pixels.
4. Choose Filter > Blur > Gaussian Blur to feather the edges (**Figure 93g**).

Figure 93g Use the Gaussian Blur filter to feather the edges.

Load the Edges channel as a selection

1. Ctrl-click (Windows) or Command-click (Mac) the Edges channel to load the Edges channel as a selection (**Figure 93h**).

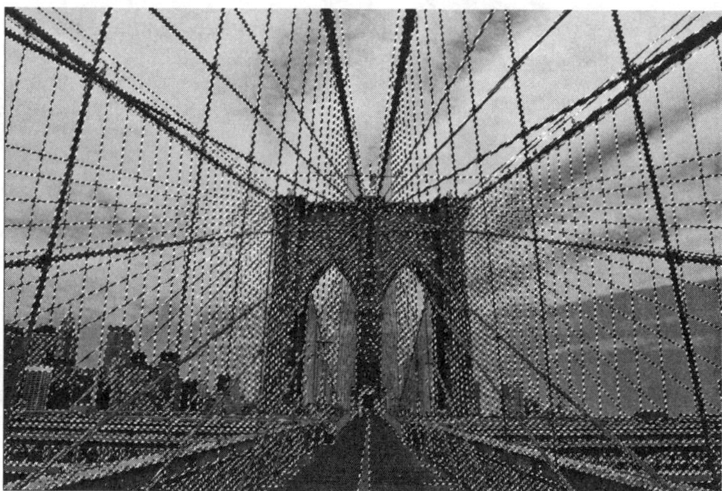

Figure 93h The selection created from the Edges channel.

2. In the Layers palette, select the image layer.

Apply sharpening

1. Make sure the selection is active. You should see the Photoshop "marching ants" around the edges of your image.

2. Choose Filter > Sharpen > Unsharp Mask. Set the desired options (see How-To #90). This limits the sharpening to only the edges.

   To illustrate what is being sharpened, I have copied the edge selection to a new layer (**Figure 93i**). You do not *have* to take this step, but it is useful if you need a visual illustration of what is being sharpened.

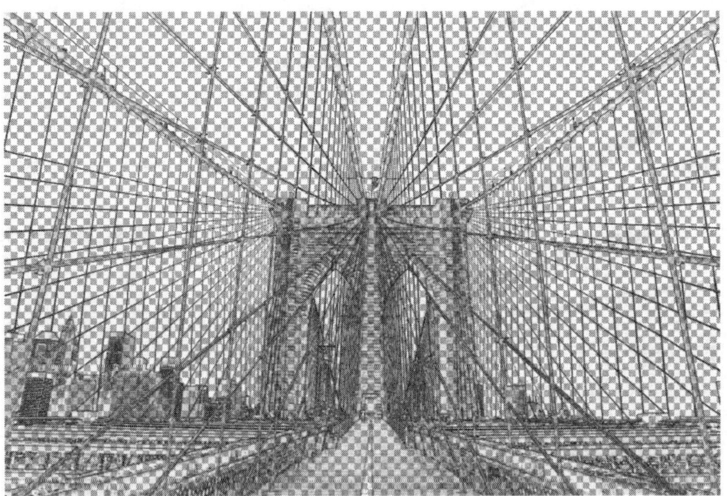

Figure 93i A visual illustration of the part of the image that will be sharpened.

3. Click OK to apply the sharpening.
4. To view the results, choose Select > Deselect.

Tip
If you find this technique useful, you may also find it useful to record an action to conveniently apply all the steps in the procedure.

#94 Sharpening Selectively

In my opinion, learning how to selectively sharpen an image is one of the most essential skills for any Photoshop user, regardless of his or her experience. Why? Because this technique is based on a core photographic truth: Viewers are attracted to sharpness in an image. Therefore, it is not always best to sharpen everything; sharpening just the key aspects of an image will have more impact. And that's exactly what we'll learn how to do in this How To. Selective sharpening is a technique that is easy to apply and master.

To apply selective sharpening:

1. Duplicate the Background layer by selecting it, and then choosing Layer > Duplicate.
2. Name the duplicate layer Sharpening (**Figure 94a**).

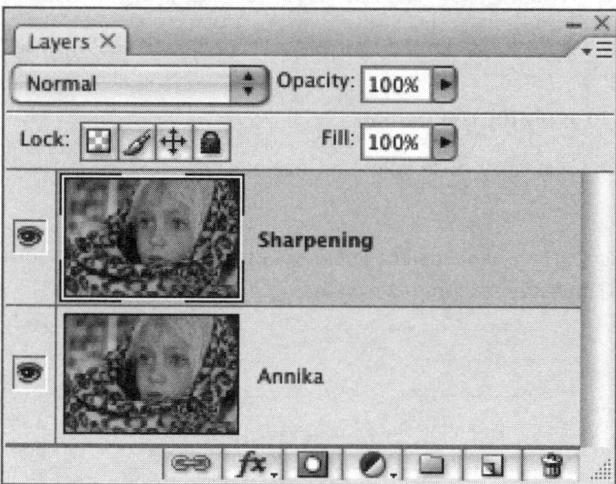

Figure 94a To apply selective sharpening, you first need to duplicate the Background layer. In this case, I have named the duplicate layer Sharpening.

3. Apply sharpening using the one of the techniques presented in this chapter.

4. Alt-click (Windows) or Option-click (Mac) the Add Layer Mask button to add a layer mask filled with black to the Sharpening layer. The layer mask thus created will hide all of the sharpening (**Figure 94b**). (For more on masking, see Chapter 10.)

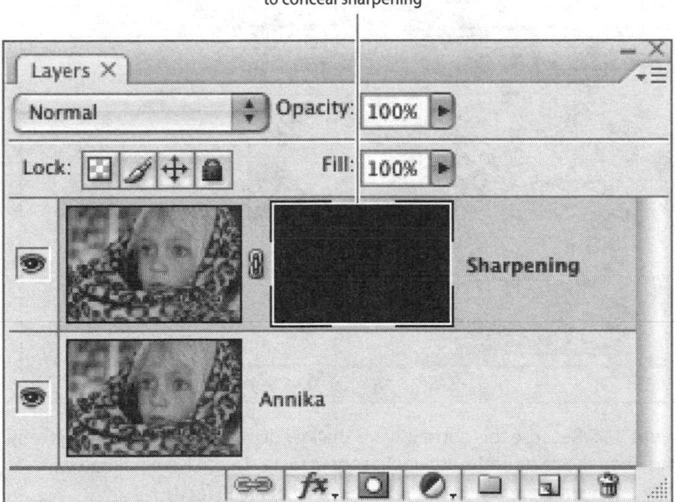

Figure 94b Create a layer mask that is filled with black to conceal the sharpening.

5. Choose the Brush tool.

6. Choose white as the foreground color.

(continued on next page)

More on Photography and Selective Sharpening

Photographers know the truth that viewers are attracted to sharpness. Thus, they create images that direct the viewer's eye to what is important.

For example, a common portrait technique is to create an image so that the person's eyes and face are in focus, while the background is out of focus. As a result, the viewer knows where to look, and the image is flattering. In contrast, if everything was in focus, the viewer wouldn't know what to look at, and the background would become distracting.

Therefore, it is helpful to learn how to sharpen key elements of an image so that you direct the viewer's eye away from distraction and toward what is most important in an image.

7. Paint on the parts of the image you want to sharpen. White will be added to the layer mask, revealing the Sharpening layer below (**Figure 94c**).

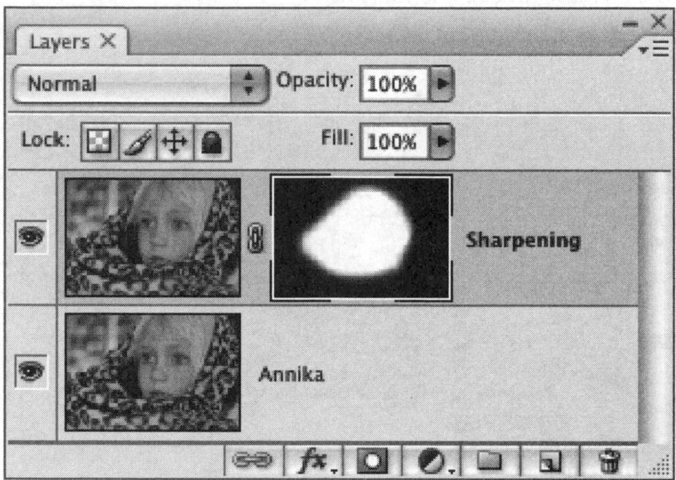

Figure 94c Because this portrait has a shallow depth of field, I have selectively sharpened the parts of the image that are in focus. Thus, I have painted with white on the face and the surrounding areas that are in focus.

8. If needed, change the layer opacity setting to decrease the sharpening amount.

9. Click the Eye icon on the Sharpening layer to show or hide the sharpening to determine the quality of the sharpening.

CHAPTER FOURTEEN

Output

I recently came across a weathered wood box in my parent's attic. The old box caught my eye, so I opened it up and discovered hundreds of well-preserved glass plate negatives that were taken in China in 1906. As I carefully looked through these old images, I thought that I absolutely had to make some prints so that others could see these powerful images.

The same can be said about all our images stored on our boxy computers: Viewing them on a computer is wonderful, but there is something more powerful about seeing them in print.

This chapter focuses on the essential skills needed for outputting images from Photoshop to the Web, devices, PDFs, and prints. I like to think of this chapter as the moment we shift focus from creation to completion. It is in this final stage of outputting our images from Photoshop, where we get to enjoy the fruits of our labor!

#95 Optimizing Images for the Web

The Web is an incredibly powerful medium for displaying and distributing images. However, high-quality digital image files can be so large that they take too long to download. The solution is to *optimize (or* decrease the file size and dimensions) for Web delivery—to compress them so that they download more quickly, but still maintain the highest quality possible. However, optimizing images for the Web can be problematic. If the proper techniques aren't used, most images end up looking drab. This How-To remedies that problem—it shows you the essential techniques for optimizing your images so that they look their best.

Optimizing an image for the Web is complex process that involves several phases:

1. Resizing
2. Preparing image color and contrast
3. Sharpening
4. Saving for the Web

Resizing the image

Resizing an image correctly can make the difference between a having a tack-sharp or less-than-ideal soft Web image.

Before you resize the image, take a moment to consider that you will need to change the pixel dimensions to the appropriate size for the intended output. For example, a typical monitor resolution is 1024 x 768, so the image dimensions will need to be sized down to something less than that. The final size of the image will vary; an appropriate sample image size is 700 x 500.

1. Open the image in Photoshop.
2. Choose Image > Image Size to display the Image Size dialog (**Figure 95a**).

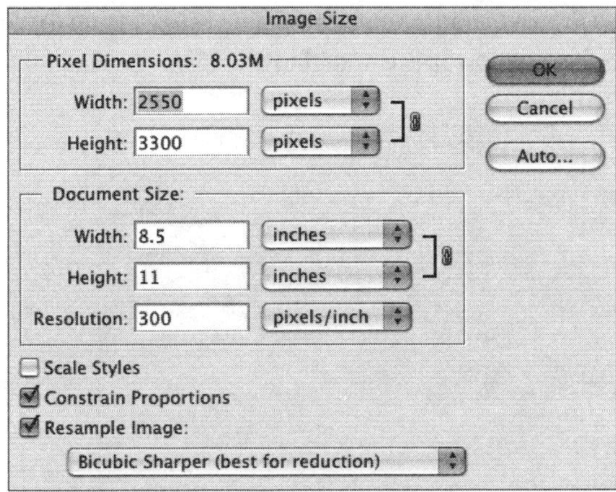

Figure 95a The Image Size dialog box.

3. Select the appropriate interpolation method from the Resample Image menu at the bottom of the dialog. If you need to decrease the image dimensions, choose Bicubic Sharper. If you need to increase the image dimensions, choose Bicubic Smoother.
4. Change the settings in the Pixel Dimensions area to the desired height and width, such as 700 x 500.
5. Click OK to commit to the image resizing.

Preparing image color and contrast

For an image to look its best on the Web, it's important to assign the proper color profile to it, and to boost its contrast and color saturation.

1. Choose Edit > Convert to Profile.

(continued on next page)

2. In the Convert to Profile dialog, choose sRGB IEC1966-2.1 from the Profile menu in the Destination Space area (**Figure 95b**).

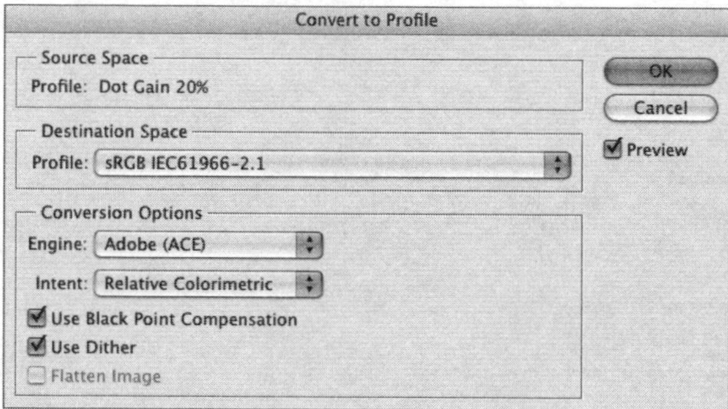

Figure 95b For images to look their best on the Web, they need to be converted to the sRGB profile.

3. Choose Image > Adjustments > Curves.
4. In the Curves dialog, choose Medium Contrast (RGB) from the Preset menu. This will add contrast and a bit of color saturation.
5. Choose Image > Adjustments > Hue/Saturation.
6. In the Hue/Saturation dialog, drag the Saturation slider to the right 5 to 10 points to increase the overall color saturation of the image.

Sharpening

The sharpening that you apply to Web images is unique because the images are relatively small and have a low resolution. As a result, you will want to apply a high amount of sharpening that is very evenly distributed across the image.

To sharpen images effectively:

1. Select the layer to be sharpened.
2. Choose Filter > Sharpen > Smart Sharpen to open the Smart Sharpen dialog.
3. From the Remove menu, choose what you would like sharpened, such as Lens Blur (see Chapter 13 for a discussion of the options in this dialog box).

4. Set the sharpening controls: The Amount typically needs to be high. Try somewhere between 100% and 150%. The Radius needs to be low; try somewhere between .1 and .3 (**Figure 95c**).

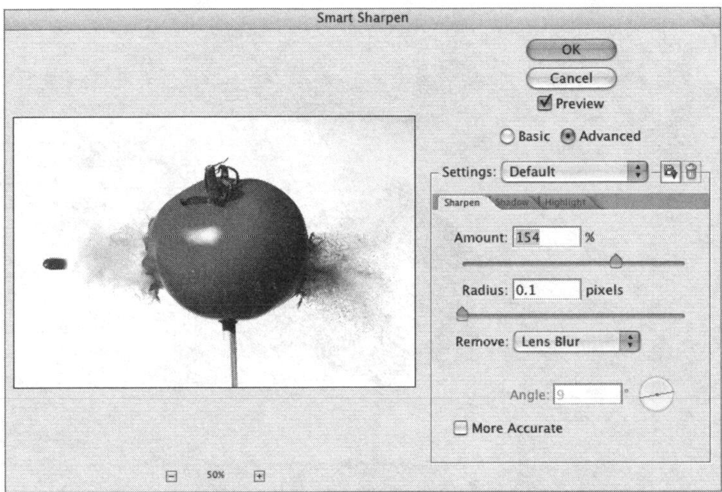

Figure 95c Sharpening for the Web involves setting a high amount of sharpening with a low radius.

5. Click OK to apply the sharpening.

Note

For more details on sharpening, see Chapter 13.

Web Image Optimizing Considerations

Before you begin the process of Web image optimization, it is worth taking a moment to realize that preparing images for the Web involves compromise. Specifically, you will need to compromise between image display quality and the file size of the image.

It is also critical to realize that the optimization involves decreasing the amount of pixels in an image so that the image size is smaller. The process of reducing pixels can cause image degradation. Thus, it is critical to take certain steps so that the smaller and more optimized image can look its best.

Saving for the Web

1. Choose File > Save for Web & Devices. This will open the Save for Web & Devices dialog (**Figure 95d**).

Figure 95d Use the Save For Web & Devices dialog box to achieve the best compromise between file size and image quality for your Web images.

2. Click the Optimized tab to see a full view of the image with the applied optimization settings.
3. On the right side of the dialog box, choose JPG from the first menu on the left (which lists available optimized file formats), and then choose the image compression quality from the second menu on the left. I recommend Medium or High for best results.
4. Press OK to save the optimized JPG file.

   Congratulations, the image is now ready for the Web!

#96 Creating a Web Gallery

Photoshop's Web Photo Gallery command allows you to easily get your images online. What exactly is a Web photo gallery? It is a freestanding Web site that includes a navigation system, thumbnail images, and full-size images. The best part of the deal is that you can use Photoshop to automatically generate a Web gallery from a set of images.

To make your own Web photo gallery:

1. Open Adobe Bridge.
2. Select the files or folder you want to use in your gallery.
3. Choose Tools > Photoshop > Web Photo Gallery to display the Web Photo Gallery dialog (**Figure 96a**).

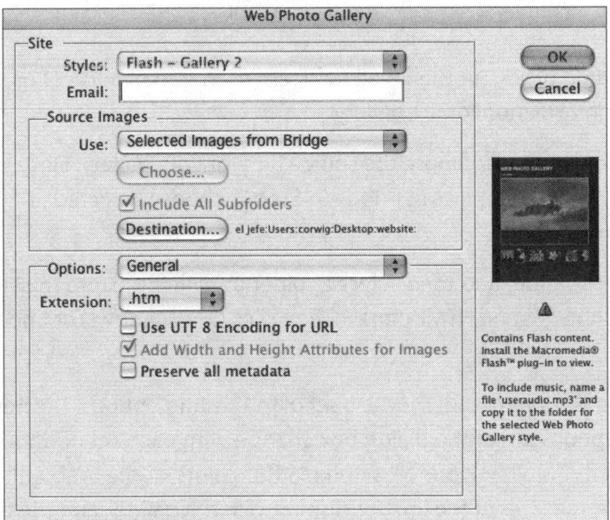

Figure 96a In the Web Photo Gallery dialog, you can choose options for your gallery.

4. From the Styles menu, choose a style for the gallery (**Figure 96b**). After you have selected a style, a preview of the style will appear in the Web Photo Gallery dialog.

(continued on next page)

The Web Gallery Files

After you have created a Web Gallery, you may want to investigate exactly what Photoshop created for you. Open the destination folder where the files are saved. Inside this folder, you will discover subfolders for the HTML, thumbnail JPGs, and gallery JPGs. More importantly, you will find that the first page (or home page) for the gallery is named index.htm. Double-click this file to open it in any Web browser to preview your gallery.

Web Gallery Image Order

When Photoshop creates a Web Photo Gallery, the images are presented in the order in which they're displayed in Bridge. Therefore, it is best to create a custom image order before you create the gallery. From within Bridge, choose View > Sort > Manually. Then drag and reposition the thumbnails in the Content panel to create a manual or custom image order. Once you have finished ordering the images, proceed to create the Web photo gallery.

Customizing the Web Galleries

Photoshop provides a variety of pre-built styles for your gallery. These can be selected using the Web Photo Gallery command. However, if you have HTML knowledge, you can create a new style or customize a style by editing a set of HTML template files in another program like Adobe Dreamweaver.

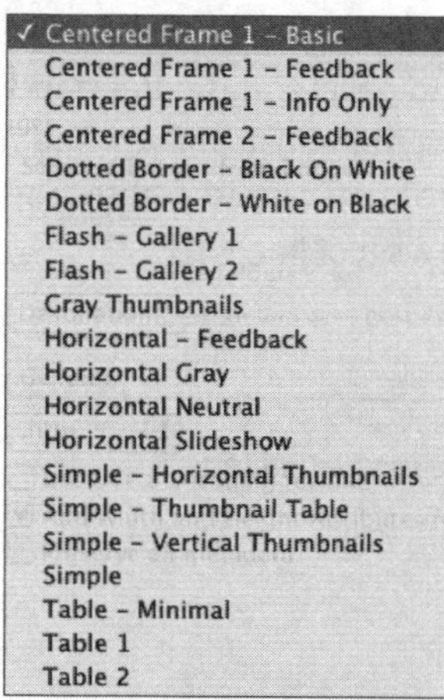

Figure 96b Choose one of the twenty Web Gallery styles.

5. In the same dialog, in the Email field, enter an e-mail address as the contact information for the gallery.

6. From the Use menu, choose the source files for your gallery. Since you already selected the files in Bridge in Step 2, choose Selected Images from Adobe Bridge.

7. Click Destination, and then select a folder in which to store the Web site files (images and HTML pages). Then click OK (Windows) or Choose (Mac).

8. From the Options menu, choose a set of formatting options. The items in the Options are of the dialog box change with each set of options. These options allow you to customize the colors of the Web gallery interface, the sizes of the images displayed in the gallery, and the text of the Web pages (**Figure 96c**).

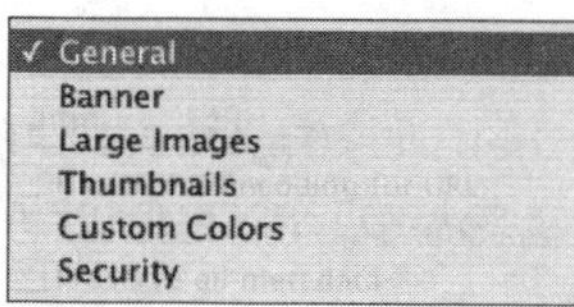

Figure 96c Select each of the formatting options in turn to customize the gallery.

9. Click OK to create the Web gallery. Photoshop optimizes the images, creates the HTML, and places them in the destination folder.

The Web Gallery is now complete and ready to be uploaded to your Web server.

#97 Introducing Device Central

In today's culture, mobile devices are ubiquitous, and the demand for visual content for these devices is growing rapidly. That's where Device Central comes into play. This application provides an easy way to create visual content for mobile devices.

Device Central acts as a staging ground for viewing how pages and graphics will look on different mobile devices that have different screen resolutions, color depths, and so on. It is designed to simplify the mobile authoring workflow by providing an opportunity to preview designs and test content on the desktop before loading it on the mobile devices for final testing.

More specifically, Device Central allows you to rescale graphics, simulate a mobile phone's backlight dimming, add artificial screen reflections, and change the color balance. In sum, this allows creative amateurs and professional to test and fine-tune graphics in different conditions with ease. Imagine if you had to actually load the graphics onto all the different types of devices—it would be unbearable and impossible. Ultimately, Device Central takes the complexity out of creating visual content for mobile devices and thus enables you to be more creative.

To begin using Device Central:

1. Choose File > Device Central to open the application (**Figure 97a**).

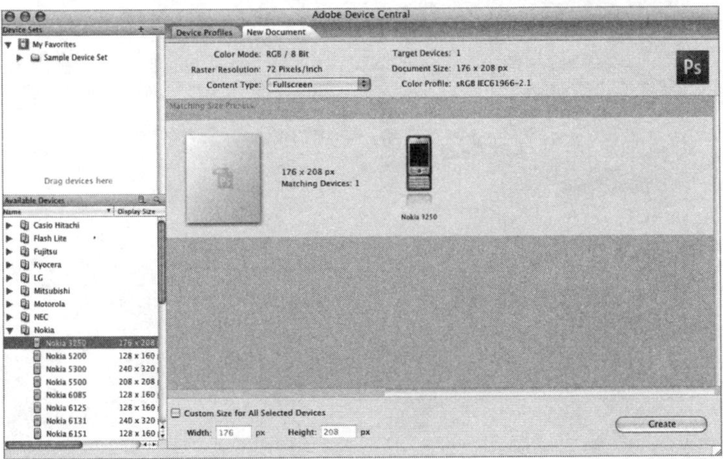

Figure 97a The Device Central interface, with the New Document tab active.

(continued on next page)

2. Click the New Document tab.
3. Select a device from the devices list on the left.
4. Click Create. A new document opens in Photoshop that includes the following default settings:
    - **Color Mode:** RGB/8bit
    - **Resolution:** 72 ppi
    - **Color Profile:** sRGB IEC61966 2.1
    - **Pixel dimensions:** Based on the screen size of the selected device
5. Add text, images, graphics, and so on to the new Photoshop document.
6. To compress and optimize the document, select File > Save For Web & Devices.
7. In the Save For Web & Devices dialog box, choose JPG, as that is the most widely supported format, and change the Quality setting to a high number like 80 (**Figure 97b**).

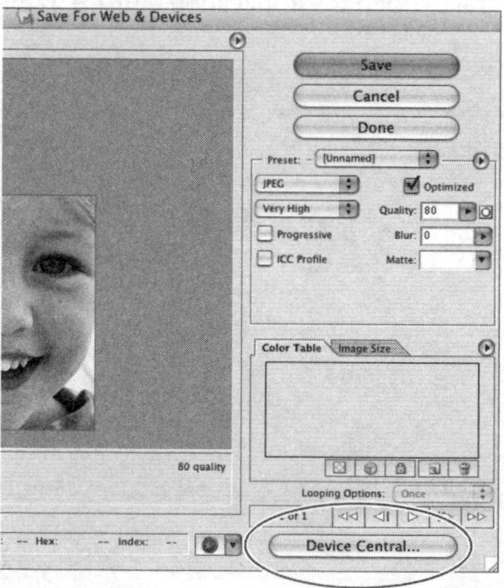

Figure 97b In the Save for Web & Devices dialog, choose a file format and image optimization options.

8. Click the Device Central button to test and preview the content as it would appear displayed on the screens of different devices.
9. After previewing (**Figure 97c**), close Device Central.

Figure 97c Preview of the content inside Device Central.

10. In the Photoshop Save For Web & Devices dialog box, click Save. Navigate to the folder where you want to store the file, and click Save again.

Device Central Tutorial

To learn more about Device Central, watch this free tutorial about creating content using Photoshop and Device Central: www.adobe.com/go/vid0185

#98 Saving a PDF

Portable Document Format (PDF) is a flexible, cross-platform, cross-application file format. Created originally by Adobe, PDF is now used by many developers for a variety of different applications. Files saved in PDF format can be shared among various applications on different platforms, while retaining their appearance, and often their editability.

To save a file in Photoshop PDF format:

1. Create a document in Photoshop.
2. Choose File > Save As, choose Photoshop PDF from the Format menu, and click Save. If an alert appears, click OK. The Save Adobe PDF dialog box opens (**Figure 98**).

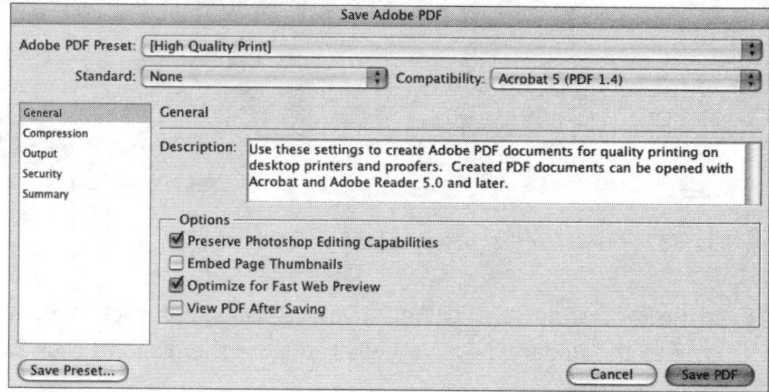

Figure 98 The Save Adobe PDF dialog lets you choose settings for the appropriate destination for the PDF, such as printing, Web, email, and so on.

3. Choose a setting from the Adobe PDF Preset menu. The different options in the menu allow you to select whether the Photoshop PDF file will be printed on a desktop printer, sent to a commercial printer, distributed by e-mail, displayed on the Web, and so on.
4. Click Save PDF to generate your Photoshop PDF file.

Photoshop and Generic PDFs

In Photoshop, you can open and work with two types of PDF files: Photoshop PDF files and generic PDF files. The main difference between Photoshop and generic PDF files is that Photoshop PDF files can contain only a single image, while generic PDF files can contain multiple pages and images. When you save PDF files, Photoshop saves them as Photoshop PDF files by default. To save them as generic PDF, in the Save Adobe PDF dialog, deselect the Preserve Photoshop Editing Capabilities option.

PDF Presets

Photoshop is equipped with powerful default PDF presets. However, there may be times when your workflow requires customized PDF settings. In these situations, it is advantageous to create and save your own custom presets for reuse in Photoshop or any product in the Adobe Creative Suite.

To create a PDF preset, in the Save Adobe PDF dialog, set the PDF options you desire and click the Save Preset button.

#99 Soft-Proofing Images

The final step before you print is to view your image as a soft proof. This technique lets you simulate how your image will appear when printed on a particular printer with a particular type of paper. Think of a soft proof as a way to preview the print before the print is actually created.

Soft-proofing may not seem all that important, but in reality, it is an essential step toward getting your image to print the way you envision it. This is because color and tone are created differently on a monitor vs. on a printer, which, of course, affects the final print. Color and tone are created via light on a monitor, whereas on a printer they are created via ink that is laid down on a specific type of paper.

The end result of soft-proofing is an increase in color fidelity between the monitor and printer. This extra bit of color accuracy ultimately leads to the creation of a more "color-correct" and compelling image.

To create a soft proof:

1. Make any final modifications to your image.
2. Choose View > Proof Setup > Custom. The Customize Proof Condition dialog opens.
3. Choose options that correspond to the output condition you want to simulate (**Figure 99**).

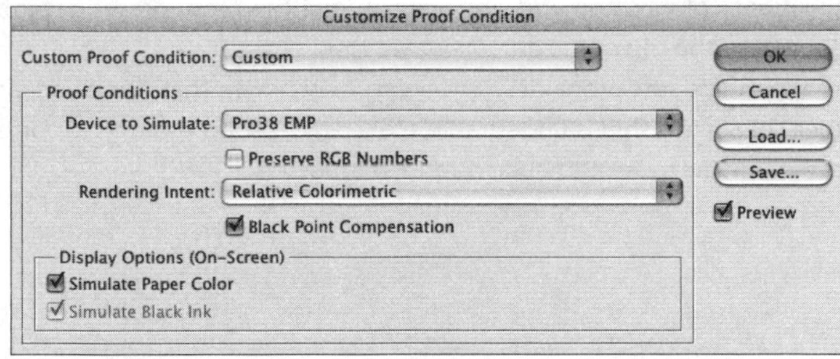

Figure 99 Choose the appropriate Proof Setup options to allow Photoshop to simulate onscreen how the image will appear when it has been printed.

4. From the Device To Simulate menu, choose the color profile of the device on which you intend to print the proof, and which you wish to simulate onscreen.

(continued on next page)

Soft-Proof Comparison

The best way to evaluate a soft proof and to make any needed changes to the image is to first duplicate the original file. Select Image> Duplicate. This gives you two versions of the same image open in Photoshop. Target the original and choose View > Proof Colors. By comparison, you will see a distinct difference between the original and duplicate documents. Once you can see the differences, make any needed changes so that the original (with the soft-proof view on) appears similar to the duplicate (without the soft proof).

5. Deselect Preserve RGB Numbers (or Preserve CMYK Numbers if your image is CMYK).

6. From the Rendering Intent menu, choose a rendering intent for converting colors to the device you are trying to simulate. Typically, Relative Colorimetric works best for photographs.

7. Select the Black Point Compensation option in order to preserve important shadow detail when the image is printed. Select this option if you plan to use black point compensation when printing (which is recommended in most situations).

8. If the profile for the device you have chosen to simulate supports the Simulate Paper Color option, you should select it. This option ensures that your soft proof simulates the actual white of the paper.

9. If your profile supports this option, select Simulate Black Ink to simulate the way in which many printers create black, which is using dark gray tones.

10. Click OK to view a soft-proof review.

You may want to turn soft-proofing on or off. To do this, choose View > Proof Colors. When soft-proofing is on, a check mark appears next to the Proof Colors command, and the name of the proof preset or profile appears at the top of the document window.

When the soft-proof view is on, you may notice that the colors and tone shift. If this shift is undesirable, make any needed changes to correct the image for those particular output settings.

#100 Printing Images

There is something magical about creating a print. It is as if printing has the ability to bring one's photographic vision to a sense of completion. Creating stunning prints of your images is a complex process, one that's best broken down into four phases:

1. Completing your Photoshop workflow
2. Configuring your print setup options
3. Choosing output and color settings
4. Configuring the Printer dialog

Completing your Photoshop workflow

Make sure that you create a soft proof to simulate how the image will print (see the previous How-To). Make any final color and tone adjustments based on the soft-proof view.

Configuring your print setup

1. Choose File > Print to open the Print dialog (**Figure 100a**).

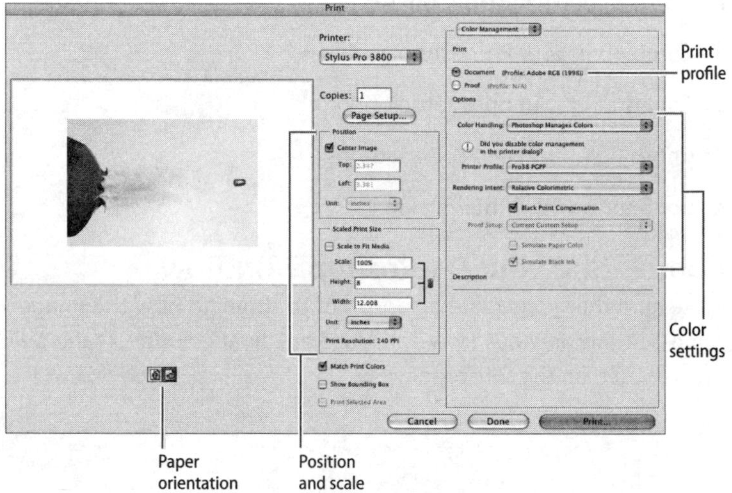

Figure 100a Utilize the Print dialog to choose the printer, and modify page setup and color settings.

2. Set the paper orientation to portrait or landscape by clicking on the icons below the image preview.
3. Choose the printer from the Printer menu.
4. Enter the number of copies to print.
5. Click the Page Setup button. In Windows, the Properties dialog box for your specific printer opens; on the Mac, the Page Setup dialog box opens. Choose the size and other characteristics of the paper you intend to print on. The available options depend on your printer, printer drivers, and operating system.

6. The Position and Scaled Print Size areas of the dialog enable you choose how the image is placed on the paper. Typically, it is better to configure these settings in Photoshop. However, you may find you want to fine-tune or adjust the position and scale of the image in relation to the selected paper size and orientation.

7. Select the Match Print Colors check box if you want the preview inside the Print dialog to display a soft-proof color simulation.

8. Select the Show Bounding Box option to view the edges of the image in the preview area. This lets you reposition or scale the image on the print media by dragging.

Choosing output and color settings

1. In the Print dialog, choose Color Management from the menu on the upper right.

2. Select the Document button to print the image using the color characteristics of the selected printer. (Select Proof to print a simulation of how the image would look if printed on another device.)

3. From the Color Handling menu, choose Photoshop Manages Color.

4. From the Printer Profile menu, choose the profile for your printer and paper. In this case, I have chosen Pro38 PGPP, which is the profile for Epson 3800 Premium Glossy Photo Paper.

5. From the Rendering Intent menu, choose one of the four options. Relative Colorimetric works best for most photographs.

6. Select Black Point Compensation. This is useful to ensure that the blacks in the image are reproduced accurately to your printer.

7. Click Print. This opens your printer's dialog box.

Configuring the Printer dialog box

In the Print dialog, you will need to make a few settings changes. The actual setting options will vary depending on your printer. To demonstrate sample settings, I'm using an Epson 3800 on a Macintosh. (If you're using Windows, you generally access similar controls by clicking the Preferences button in the Print dialog.)

Printing on Different Types of Paper

There are a wide array of quality printers and types of paper. In my own professional photographic workflow, I have had great success with Epson printers and papers. Whatever type of printer you choose, be sure to experiment with various types of papers. It is typically best to begin experimenting with paper that was created by your brand of printer. I have found some images look great with the extra shine and color saturation that comes with printing on glossy papers. On the other hand, certain images look more natural on a textured velvet fine art paper.

1. Choose Printer Color Management from the third menu in the Print dialog and select Off (**Figure 100b**). It is critical that you turn off the printer's color management because we have previously determined that Photoshop will manage the color.

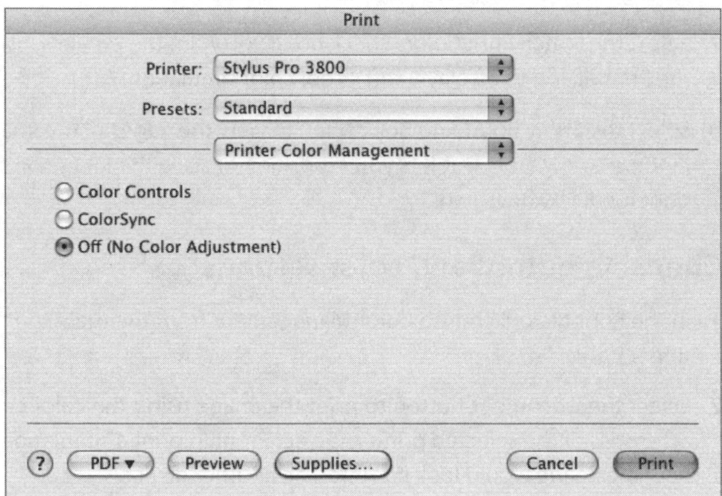

Figure 100b Turning color management off is perhaps the most important of these final steps.

2. From the third menu in the dialog (the same one you used to choose Color Management), now choose Print Settings, and then choose the appropriate paper type and other settings (**Figure 100c**).

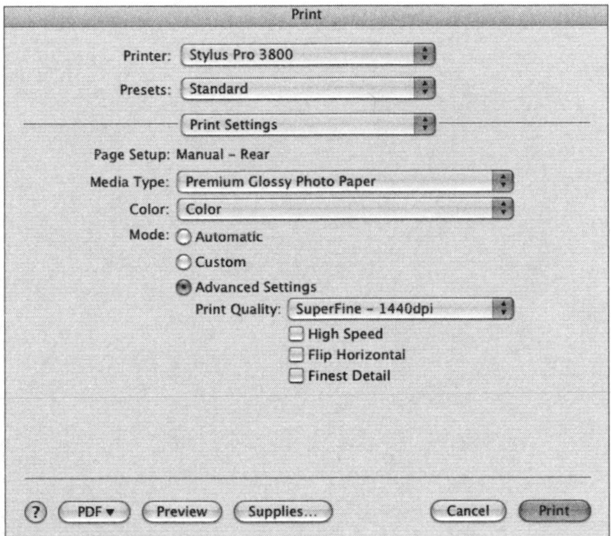

Figure 100c Don't overlook this critical step of selecting the paper type; otherwise, the print quality will not be accurate.

3. Click Print.

   Enjoy your final results!

Printing Video Tutorial

Printing photographs is viewed by many as an art. In fact, in photographic circles, there are those who are defined as "print masters."

To gain more mastery over printing, be sure to watch this free video tutorial that I have authored: www.adobe.com/go/vid0015.

Index

C

G

H

P

Q

R

S

T

U

V

W

X

Z